CONTEMPORARY ECONOMIC ISSUES
Volume 2: Labour, Food and Poverty

This is IEA conference volume no. 122

CONTEMPORARY ECONOMIC ISSUES

Congress Editor: Michael Bruno

Volume 1 REGIONAL EXPERIENCES AND SYSTEM REFORM
Justin Yifu Lin (*editor*)

Volume 2 LABOUR, FOOD AND POVERTY
Yair Mundlak (*editor*)

Volume 3 TRADE, PAYMENTS AND DEBT
Daniel Cohen (*editor*)

Volume 4 ECONOMIC BEHAVIOUR AND DESIGN
Murat Sertel (*editor*)

Volume 5 MACROECONOMICS AND FINANCE
Holger C. Wolf (*editor*)

International Economic Association
Series Standing Order ISBN 0–333–71242–0
(*outside North America only*)

You can receive future titles in this series as they are published by placing a standing order. Please contact your bookseller or, in case of difficulty, write to us at the address below with your name and address, the title of the series and the ISBN quoted above.

Customer Services Department, Macmillan Distribution Ltd
Houndmills, Basingstoke, Hampshire RG21 6XS, England

Contemporary Economic Issues

Proceedings of the Eleventh World Congress of the International Economic Association, Tunis

Congress Editor: Michael Bruno

Volume 2 LABOUR, FOOD AND POVERTY

Edited by

Yair Mundlak

in association with the
INTERNATIONAL ECONOMIC ASSOCIATION

First published in Great Britain 1998 by
MACMILLAN PRESS LTD
Houndmills, Basingstoke, Hampshire RG21 6XS and London
Companies and representatives throughout the world

A catalogue record for this book is available from the British Library.

ISBN 0–333–69806–1

First published in the United States of America 1998 by
ST. MARTIN'S PRESS, INC.,
Scholarly and Reference Division,
175 Fifth Avenue, New York, N.Y. 10010

ISBN 0–312–17744–5

Library of Congress Cataloging-in-Publication Data
International Economic Association. World Congress (11th : 1995 : Tunis, Tunisia)
Contemporary economic issues / congress editor Michael Bruno.
p. cm. — (IEA conference volume ; 122, 123, 125)
Includes bibliographical references and index.
Contents: — v. 2. Labour, food and poverty / edited by Yair Mundlak — v. 3. Trade, payments and debt / edited by Daniel Cohen — v. 5. Macroeconomics and finance / edited by Holger Wolf.
ISBN 0–312–17744–5 (cloth : v. 2). — ISBN 0–312–17760–7 (cloth : v. 3). — ISBN 0–312–17759–3 (cloth : v. 5)
1. Economics—Congresses. 2. Economic policy—Congresses. 3. Finance—Congresses. I. Bruno, Michael. II. Mundlak, Yair, 1927– . III. Cohen, Daniel, 1953– . IV. Wolf, Holger C. V. Title. VI. Series: I.E.A. conference volume ; no. 122, etc.
HB21.I65 1995
330—dc21 95–4526
CIP

UNESCO Subvention 1994–95/SHS/IDS/41

This book is printed on paper suitable for recycling and made from fully managed and sustained forest sources.

10 9 8 7 6 5 4 3 2 1
07 06 05 04 03 02 01 00 99 98

Printed and bound in Great Britain by
Antony Rowe Ltd, Chippenham, Wiltshire

Contents

The International Economic Association

A non-profit organization with purely scientific aims, the International Economic Association (IEA) was founded in 1950. It is a federation of some sixty national economic associations in all parts of the world. Its basic purpose is the development of economics as an intellectual discipline, recognizing a diversity of problems, systems and values in the world and taking note of methodological diversities.

The IEA has, since its creation, sought to fulfil that purpose by promoting mutual understanding among economists through the organization of scientific meetings and common research programmes, and by means of publications on problems of fundamental as well as of current importance. Deriving from its long concern to assure professional contacts between East and West and North and South, the IEA pays special attention to issues of economies in systemic transition and in the course of development. During its nearly fifty years of existence, it has organized more than a hundred round-table conferences for specialists on topics ranging from fundamental theories to methods and tools of analysis and major problems of the present-day world. Participation in round tables is at the invitation of a specialist programme committee, but eleven triennial World Congresses have regularly attracted the participation of individual economists from all over the world.

The Association is governed by a Council, composed of representatives of all member associations, and by a fifteen-member Executive Committee which is elected by the Council. The Executive Committee (1995–98) at the time of the Tunis Congress was:

President:	Professor Jacques Drèze, Belgium
Vice-President:	Professor Anne Krueger, USA
Treasurer:	Professor Erich Streissler, Austria
Past President:	Professor Michael Bruno, Israel (deceased 25 December 1996)
Other members:	Professor Anthony B. Atkinson, UK
	Professor Vittorio Corbo, Chile
	Professor Karel Dyba, Czech Republic
	Professor Jean-Michael Grandmont, France

Sir Austin Robinson was an active Adviser on the publication of IEA Conference proceedings from 1954 until his final short illness in 1993.

The Association has also been fortunate in having secured many outstanding economists to serve as President:

Gottfried Haberler (1950–53), Howard S. Ellis (1953–56), Erik Lindahl (1956–59), E. A. G. Robinson (1959–62), Ugo Papi (1962–65), Paul A. Samuelson (1965–68). Erik Lundberg (1968–71), Fritz Machlup (1971–74), Edmund Malinvaud (1974–77), Shigeto Tsuru (1977–80), Victor L. Urquidi (1980–83), Kenneth J. Arrow (1983–86), Amartya Sen (1986–89), Anthony B. Atkinson (1989–1992) and Michael Bruno (1992–95).

The activities of the Association are mainly funded from the subscriptions of members and grants from a number of organizations, including continuing support from UNESCO, through the International Social Science Council.

Preface

Michael Bruno

The World Congress of the International Economic Association held in Tunis in December 1995 was the eleventh in a series that started in Rome in 1956, with the most recent one being held in Moscow in 1992. This Congress was marked by being the first to take place in Africa and the Middle East. This was reflected in having special sessions devoted to the Economic Development of Sub-Saharan Africa, Maghreb Economies and the Economics of the Middle East Peace Process, besides a wide array of topics in contemporary economics of development, trade, economic growth and general economic theory. Quoting from the opening speech by the President of Tunis, His Excellency Zine El Abidine Ben Ali:

> Tunisia is very proud that your Association is holding its eleventh congress – the first such event to take place in Africa and the Middle East – on our soil. This will give you a good opportunity to concentrate your attention on the most recent developments in economics and their role in strengthening development, as can be seen from the items on your agenda. The situation now prevailing in many countries, particularly those on our African continent, more than confirms the necessity of giving such issues an essential place in contemporary economic thinking.

Tunisia's impressive recent development effort, marking both a vigorous growth rate, low inflation, marked improvement in its social indicators, greater openness to international trade, as well as its ample cultural and historical treasures, made it a particularly interesting host country for our Association. It was a very lively Congress, with many high quality sessions, interspersed with several cultural and other events which introduced the broadly international group of attendees to the host country's institutions and culture.

The Congress programme consisted of four plenary sessions (those by Professor Edmond Malinvaud, Professor Robert Putnam, the Austin Robinson Memorial lecture delivered by Professor Assar Lindbeck, as well as the Presidential Address). It had three panel sessions (chaired by Professors U. Reinhardt, A. Tornell and S. Fischer), and 41 regular sessions. In these there were 43 invited papers and 278 contributed papers. The Congress was attended by abut 700 participants coming from 68 different countries.

The full list of the Programme Committee is as follows:

Bina Agarwal, University of Delhi, India
Kenneth Arrow, Stanford University, USA
Anthony Atkinson, Oxford University, UK
David Audretsch, Wissenschaftszentrum Berlin, Germany
Richard Baldwin, University of Wisconsin, USA
Kaushik Basu, Delhi School of Economics, India
David Begg, Birkbeck College, London, UK
François Bourguinon, DELTA, Paris, France
Daniel Cohen, CEPREMAP, Paris, France
Vittorio Corbo, Catholic University of Chile, Santiago, Chile
Partha Dasgupta, University of Cambridge, UK
Peter Diamond, MIT, Cambridge, Mass, USA
Juan Dolado, CEMFI, Madrid, Spain
Bernard Dumas, Groupe Hautes Etudes Commerciales, Jouy-en-Josas, France
Ibrahim Elbadawi, African Economic Research Consortium, Nairobi, Kenya
Riccardo Faini, University of Brescia, Italy
Stanley Fischer, The World Bank, Washington, USA
Nancy Folbre, University of Massachusetts, USA
Alberto Giovannini, Department of the Treasury, Rome, Italy
Vittorio Grilli, Department of the Treasury, Rome, Italy
Oliver Hart, Harvard University, USA
Sergiu Hart, Hebrew University of Jerusalem, Israel
Elhanan Helpman, Tel Aviv University, Israel
Wontack Hong, Seoul National University, Korea
Susan Horton, University of Toronto, Canada
Peter Howitt, Université des Sciences Sociales, Toulouse, France
Ponciano Intal, Philippine Institute for Development Studies, Manila, Philippines
Takatoshi Ito, NBER, Cambridge, Mass, USA
Ravi Kanbur, The World Bank, Washington, USA
Heinz Kurz, University of Graz, Austria
Jean-Jacques Laffont, Université des Sciences Sociales, Toulouse, France
Donald Lessard, MIT, Cambridge, Mass, USA
Justin Yifu Lin, China Centre for Economic Research, Beijing, China

Millard Long, The World Bank, Budapest, Hungary
Karl-Göran Mäler, Stockholm School of Economics, Sweden
John Moore, London School of Economics, UK
Yair Mundlak, University of Chicago, USA
Mustapha Kamel Nabli, University of Tunis, Tunisia
Benno Ndulu, African Economic Research Consortium, Nairobi, Kenya
Takashi Negishi, Aoyama Gakuin University, Tokyo, Japan
Siddiq Osmani, University of Ulster, Coleraine, UK
Kirit Parikh, Indira Gandhi Institute of Development Research, Bombay, India
Richard Portes, CEPR, London, UK
Martin Ravaillon, The World Bank, Washington, USA
Sergio Rebelo, University of Rochester, USA
Uwe Reinhardt, Princeton University, USA
Dani Rodrik, Columbia University, New York, USA
Agnar Sandmo, Norwegian School of Economics, Bergen, Norway
Murat Sertel, Boğaziçi University, Istanbul, Turkey
Dennis Snower, Birkbeck College, London, UK
Jan Svejnar, CERGE, Charles University, Prague, Czech Republic
Peter Swan, University of New South Wales, Kensington NSW, Australia
Peter Temin, MIT, Cambridge, Mass, USA
Jacques Thisse, Ecole Nationale des Ponts et Chaussées, Paris, France
Aaron Tornell, Harvard University, Cambridge, Mass., USA
Hirofumi Uzawa, Japan Development Bank, Tokyo, Japan
Oliver Williamson, University of California at Berkeley, Cal., USA
Charles Wyplosz, INSEAD, Fontainebleau, France
Shahid Yusuf, The World Bank, Washington, USA
Stefano Zamagni, University of Bologna, Italy
Klaus Zimmerman, University of Munich, Germany

The proceedings of the Congress are being published in five volumes under the general title *Contemporary Economic Issues*:

Vol. 1: *Regional Experiences and System Reform* edited by Justin Yifu Lin
Vol. 2: *Labour, Food and Poverty* edited by Yair Mundlak
Vol. 3: *Trade, Payments and Debt* edited by Daniel Cohen
Vol. 4: *Economic Behaviour and Design* edited by Murat Sertel
Vol. 5: *Macroeconomics and Finance* edited by Holger C. Wolf

I would like to record our gratitude to our Tunisian hosts who made this a highly successful conference. Besides thanking our illustrious host, His

Excellency President Zine El Abidine Ben Ali, I would like to thank the local Organizing Committee, and first and foremost its Chairman, Mustapha Kamel Nabli, who bore the brunt of the responsibility for the logistics and successful implementation of the Congress. He was helped by Mongi Safra (Vice-Chairman), Mongi Azabou (Executive Secretary), Salah Maoui (Minister of Tourism), Salah Baccari (Minister of Culture) and the able Tunisian staff assisting them in their task.

I would like to thank Francis Ghilès (Volume 1), Michael Kaser (Volume 2), John Butler (Volume 3), Maureen Hadfield (Volume 4) and Lesley Cook (Volume 5) for taking charge of the editorial preparation of these volumes. I am as always grateful to Michael Kaser, the General Editor of these series. Finally, I would like to record my thanks to Jean-Paul Fitoussi, the Secretary General of the International Economic Association, not only for initiating the Congress in Tunis, but for his constant support with the preparations along the way.

List of Contributors

Rupert Baber, Department of Agricultural Economics, University of Natal, Pietermaritzburg, South Africa

Al Crego, The World Bank, Washington, DC, USA

Israel Finkelshtain, Department of Agricultural Economics and Management, The Hebrew University of Jerusalem, Rehovot, Israel

Robert W. Fogel, Center for Population Economics, Graduate School of Business, University of Chicago, USA

Peter Gottschalk, Department of Economics, Boston College, Chestnut Hill, Massachusetts, USA

Susan Horton, Department of Economics, University of Toronto, Canada

Ravi Kanbur, The World Bank, Washington, DC, USA

Yoav Kislev, Department of Agricultural Economics and Management, The Hebrew University of Jerusalem, Rehovot, Israel

Donald Larson, The World Bank, Washington, DC, USA

Denis Lawrence, Business Infrastructure Branch, Bureau of Industry Economics, Canberra, ACT, Australia

Zvi Lerman, Department of Agricultural Economics and Management, Hebrew University of Jerusalem, Rehovot, Israel

Assar Lindbeck, Institute for International Economic Studies, Stockholm University, Sweden

Dipak Mazumdar, Department of Economics, University of Toronto, Canada

Graham Moor, Department of Agricultural Economics, University of Natal, Pietermaritzburg, South Africa

Yair Mundlak, Department of Economics, University of Chicago, USA

W. Lieb Nieuwoudt, Department of Agricultural Economics, University of Natal, Pietermaritzburg, South Africa

Thomas Piketty, Economics Department, Massachusetts Institute of Technology, Cambridge, Massachusetts, USA, and CNRS–CEPREMAP, Paris, France

Marianne Røed, Department of Economics, University of Oslo, Norway

Oded Stark, Department of Economics, University of Oslo, Norway

John Strauss, Department of Economics, Michigan State University, East Lansing, Michigan, USA

Peter L. Swan, Department of Finance, University of Sydney, NSW, Australia

Timothy M. Smeeding, Center for Policy Research, Maxwell School of Citizenship and Public Affairs, Syracuse University, Syracuse, New York, USA

Duncan Thomas, RAND, Santa Monica, California, and University of California, Los Angeles, USA

Gianni Toniolo, Dipartimento di Scienze Economiche, Università di Roma Tor Vergata, Italy, and Duke University, Durham, North Carolina, USA

John Zeitsch, Swan Consultants (Canberra) Pty Ltd, Lyneham, Canberra, ACT, Australia

List of Abbreviations

AEASA	Agricultural Economics Association of Southern Africa
ADL	Activity(ies) of daily living
BCE	Before the Common Era
BIE	Bureau of Industry Economics (Australia)
BMI	body mass index
BMR	basic metabolic rate
CA	communal area
CEE	Central and Eastern Europe
CEPREMAP	Centre d'Etudes Prospectives d'Economie Mathématique Appliquées à la Planification (France)
CILSS	Côte d'Ivoire Living Standards Study
CNRS	Centre National de la Recherche Scientifique (France)
COSI	cost of service incentive
CPI	consumer price index
DEA	date envelopment analysis
DPI	disposable personal income
EAAE	European Association of Agricultural Economists
ECE	East-Central Europe
EITC	earned income tax credit
ENDEF	*Estudo Nacional da Depesa Familiar* (Brazil)
EWG	Exempt Wholesale Generators
FAO	Food and Agriculture Organization
FAWOB	FAO, WHO and World Bank
FE	fixed effects
FSS	former socialist states
FSU	Former Soviet Union
GDP	gross domestic product
GNP	gross national product
ICRISAT	International Crops Research Institute for the Semi-Arid Tropics
IFLS	Indonesian Family Life Survey
ILO	International Labour Office
INSEE	Institut Nationale de la Statistique et des Etudes Economiques
IPP	independent power producers
IV	instrumental variables

LAPC	Land and Agricultural Policy Centre
LIS	Luxembourg Income Study
LOWESS	locally-weighted smoothed scatterplots
MI	market income
NAIRU	non-accelerating inflation rate of unemployment
NCHS	National Center for Health Statistics (United States)
NGC	National Grid Company (United Kingdom)
NEP	New Economic Policy (Malaysia)
NHANES	National Health and Nutrition Examination Survey (United States)
NHIS	National Health Interview Survey (United States)
NSS	National Sample Survey (India)
OECD	Organisation for Economic Co-operation and Development
OLS	ordinary least squares
OPEC	Organization of Petroleum Exporting Countries
PCE	*per capita* expenditure
PEM	protein–energy malnutrition
PPC	partial productivity comparison
PPP	purchasing power parity
PSID	Panel Study of Income Dynamics
R&D	research and development
RA	resettlement area
REC	Regional Electricity Company (United Kingdom)
SSCS	small-scale commercial sector
TFP	total factor productivity
WDR	*World Development Report*
WHO	World Health Organization

Introduction

Yair Mundlak

Societies, at all levels of development, search continuously for policies that will facilitate growth and at the same time will allow all members of society to benefit from the fruits of growth. In this endeavour, the state takes on a leading role through legislation, taxation and expenditure programmes. Such programmes vary considerably across countries. The more demanding programmes have been exercised by some of the affluent countries, and their experience is valuable in evaluating the potential, limitations and costs of the welfare state for countries that have yet to embark on or expand such programmes. This is the theme of Part I, of which Chapter 1 by Assar Lindbeck reviews and summarizes the pertinent issues against the background of the experience gained in the OECD countries and lessons that can be drawn for would-be welfare states.

Redistribution of income (or consumption) takes place among individuals and for a given individual over his or her lifetime or states of nature. In part, the programmes deal with decisions that otherwise would have been taken by individuals. They change the economic environment faced by households and firms and thereby affect their behaviour. For example, augmentation of income generates an income effect of expanded leisure and as such it reduces effort by the recipient in generating his or her own income. Consequently, the net impact of the programme on the income level of the recipients is less than the amount allocated to him or her. This is an example of the disincentive aspect of government programmes. Social programmes differ across countries in the extent to which they rely on the state, firm and family. The lower is the support of the compulsory system, the stronger is the incentive for private solutions.

Lindbeck reviews the static and dynamic effects and counter-effects of the programmes. For instance, static achievements of the welfare state include income redistribution over the life-cycle of individuals, risk reduction, stimulation of consumption of social services and mitigation of poverty. The achievements involve efficiency costs associated with financing the programmes and with the distortion that the programmes, including the benefits, generate. The dynamic achievements listed include the positive impact on growth due to the investment in human capital, mitigation of 'social exclusion' by drawing minorities into the labour force, an increase in productivity and in labour-force participation which in turn increases the tax base and helps to mitigate social conflicts. However, the programmes have important counter-effects. Subsidies to human capital, such as schooling, increase income. However, a progressive income tax takes away some of the returns and the net effect may be negative. Taxes on returns from physical capital discourage savings and as such investment. At a more profound level, high taxes increase the propensity to tax evasion and break norms of society. This process takes time and its full consequences are not immediately realized.

Lindbeck indicates that the welfare state is unstable in the sense that 'the more "humane" it tries to be, the greater is the risk that it undermines its own economic foundations in the long run, and that it will not be able to live up to its promises'. In his Conclusion Lindbeck states that the most important positive lessons from the welfare state in OECD countries are the achievements in terms of economic security and mitigation of poverty. Unfortunately, a tradeoff exists between the improvement of economic security for the majority and the mitigation of poverty for a minority.

There are various reasons for income inequality. Some reflect attributes of the individual and his or her decisions, whereas others are related to the environments and the settings within which the individual operates. Thomas Piketty in Chapter 2 reviews several topics, recently developed, in the income distribution literature dealing with the impact of the environment, credit rationing, neighbourhood segregation and the role of self-fulfilling beliefs. Credit rationing occurs when the credit is positively related to wealth and as such is not available to the poor in amounts needed to finance investment projects. Consequently poor dynasties will continue to stay poor. Alternative models are developed where moral hazards limit the credit and the long-run wealth distribution depends on the interest rate environment, leading to 'low mobility'. Although interesting, as Piketty indicates, the models lack empirical support. Social segregation into spatially distinct neighbourhoods can be generated in the presence of cost-externalities of education. A decision of a family to move to a high-education neighbourhood affects the cost in a low-education neighbourhood. Under specified conditions on the education cost function, segregation is socially inefficient. Again, this model lacks empirical support. However, empirical research shows that financial support to poor neighbourhood schools had practically no meaningful effect. Thus, what is more important is the 'peer' effect.

Timothy M. Smeeding and Peter Gottschalk in Chapter 3 bring an empirical dimension on the recent experience in income distribution. They compare inequalities in market and in disposable income across countries during the 1980s and the 1990s. Admittedly, they deal with an incomplete concept of income, and as such the results do not fully reveal the inequality in welfare. With this caveat, they report a wide range of income inequality across the 25 nations under investigation. Higher inequality leads to the fact that the poor in a high-income country such as the United States have a lower real income than the poor in a middle-income country such as Finland. To the extent that the 1990s differ from the 1980s, it is largely in the direction of higher inequality. Smeeding and Gottschalk found no relationships between the change in inequality and the initial level. Nor is there a group or country story.

Chapter 3 does not deal with causes of inequality nor, knowingly, with welfare measures. Possible causes of market inequality are related to variability in personal attributes which affect factor income. However, the macro-environment is also important and it has an immediate effect on the range of technologies employed in a country. Techniques differ in their demand for various skills, and thereby the implemented technology affects the demand for skills and their returns.

Susan Horton, Ravi Kanbur and Dipak Mazumdar in Chapter 4 examine the link between openness and inequality within developing countries through a review of the literature. The point of departure is the Heckscher–Ohlin model according to which an increase in trade increases the demand for the factor which is relatively abundant and thereby its return and reduces inequality. However, this trickling down view is not supported by the evidence which is rather heterogeneous and ambiguous. In passing we note that the Heckscher–Ohlin framework assumes that the trading partners employ the same technology and full employment; both assumptions are unrealistic. This is the reason for much of the irregularity discussed in this chapter.

Part II deals with development issues, beginning with Chapter 5 by Gianni Toniolo that examines the explanations given for the fast growth in Europe in the period 1950–73, referred to as the 'golden age', when the *per capita* growth reached an average annual rate of 3.8 per cent. This performance, common to almost all European countries, was mostly a European phenomenon. During this period European unemployment reached its lowest level and *per capita* output converged to that of the United States. The common explanations offered for this performance deal with high investment rates, export development that added to scale economies, labour abundance that contributed to wage moderation and demand management that stabilized expectations. However, all these components had been there for a long time and hence cannot account for the performance. What then triggered the 'golden age'? Toniolo attributes it to a combination of economic, institutional and broad socio-economic forces and develops an explanation for their influence. All these factors generated the appropriate timing of the implementation of new technology that had previously been available, already used in the United States but not in Europe.

There is a growing interest in the role of health in economic development. Health is both a consumer and a producer good. It is a desirable attribute, and as such it has a utility of its own in addition to its positive effect on productivity and thereby on wealth. As a consumer good, the level of health acquired by individuals depends on their wealth. Wealth affects nutrition which in turn affects health. These relationships seem acceptable, but their measurements and full implications are not straightforward, as becomes clear from the discussion in Chapter 6 by Robert Fogel.

Fogel develops the idea that in evaluating the extent of malnutrition we ought to consider the effect of nutrition on the utilization of the genetic potential. He assumes that there exists a synergy between technological and physiological improvements that has produced a form of human evolution that is biological but not genetic and not necessarily stable. Fogel calls it 'technophysio evolution'. He criticizes the conventional methods of measuring malnutrition in that they underestimate the full impact of malnutrition. Human physiology is not static and the body size increases with time. Poor body builds increase vulnerability to diseases. Empirical comparisons of nutrition effect based on cross-section data underestimate the importance of nutrition. The reason is that the effect of nutrition on longevity and on the participation in the labour force is neglected.

An essential element of development is a continuous reallocation of labour to new activities. Such reallocation also takes the form of international migration. The driving force of migration is the income differential between the source and the destination. In some cases, the migrants return to their country of origin after spending some time abroad. Marianne Røed and Oded Stark in Chapter 7 present a model to explain this phenomenon where the main ingredients are the preference to stay in the country of origin on the one hand and a skill enhancement of work abroad on the other, which augments the income of the migrants after their return to the country of origin.

Agriculture has played a key role in economic development. As indicated by Fogel in Chapter 6, world food supply sustained a world population of half a billion in 1650, 4 billion in 1974 and is expected to support a population of 8 billion in 2020. Part III begins with a review of the development in world agriculture in the post-war period by Yair Mundlak,

Don Larson and Al Crego (Chapter 8). During this period, the growth of supply exceeded that of demand, and as a result the terms of trade of agriculture deteriorated. The growth was achieved in part due to a slight increase in land and labour and a more substantial increase in capital. However, the bulk of the increase is due to technical change. In most countries, the growth in average labour productivity in agriculture exceeded substantially that in non-agriculture. A distinction is made between agriculture and farmers. The welfare implications for agriculture of the changes in supply and demand are captured by the rent and reflected in land prices. It appears that in real terms land prices fluctuated, but their level today is about the same as it was at the beginning of the century. This implies that the benefits of the changes in technology have been captured by the consumer and not by agriculture. The welfare of farmers is measured by their income. The off-farm migration, which accounted for a drastic decline in the share of agriculture in the total labour force, indicates that for most people the opportunities outside agriculture dominated those in agriculture. As such, that migration has been the most important instrument in eliminating rural poverty. The empirical record is summarized in terms of empirical distributions of the various variables in question. There is a great spread in performance attributed to the variability in the economic environment. Chapter 8 outlines the approach for empirical analysis needed to account for the heterogeneity in country performance.

One aspect of the dependence of agricultural productivity on the economic environment is provided by the land tenure arrangements. In Chapter 9, W. L. Nieuwoudt, G. M. Moor and R. A. A. Baber discuss the impact of incentive distortions in South African agriculture where 13 per cent of the land is in communal ownership 'characterized by stagnation and widespread resource degradation'. The reasons are lack of state support and lack of incentives to invest. Communal ownership restricts the rights of the cultivator. Low productivity in agriculture contributes to migration to non-agriculture, and does not attract capital. Therefore no advantage is taken of available productive techniques. It is claimed that private titling will resolve the present difficulties by eliminating the negative externalities of communal grazing. Interestingly, the opposition to privatization of land comes from the tribal chiefs, whose power would be diminished by the act.

Another example of changes in tenancy is provided by Zvi Lerman in Chapter 10, who discusses land reforms in former socialist countries. The history of private ownership and of tenure arrangements differs among countries but the general tendency is to move in the direction of more liberal policies of land tenure. The change in title, however, does not necessarily imply a change in the farm structure – these are two different processes. It is the change in farm structure that affects productivity. Like the influence of chiefs in South Africa, discussed by Nieuwoudt *et al.*, the traditional managers want to maintain their power and resist structural reforms. Other factors that have a negative effect on the speed and extent of structural reforms are political and legal uncertainty, and lack of needed supportive infrastructure for private farming such as input markets, credit market and means of eliminating risks. Also, farmers are unable to transfer their land to other forms of assets that will allow them to leave agriculture and thereby facilitate the consolidation of farms. All these factors favour inertia and watered-down transition. The reluctance of farmers to move completely to private farming can be explained as risk-reduction behaviour: lack of confidence in their ability to perform in an environment without adequate markets, credit and legal conventions of business practices which require considerable input in dealing with the outside world and generate economies of scale of larger farms. This is another illustration of the argument put forth by Toniolo in Chapter 5 of the importance of socio-political influences on development.

Part IV of the volume deals with policies related to industrial organization. It is now well recognized that lack of infrastructure slows down development. However, despite the rapid growth in infrastructure in most countries, performance has been disappointing, largely due to poor competition. To fully benefit from the development of infrastructure, the providers should not be allowed to exploit monopolistic profits. Peter Swan, Denis Lawrence and John Zeitsch in Chapter 11 discuss methods of controlling the prices of products delivered by firms with monopolistic elements. In such price controls, allowance is made for improvements in productivity, but these are not easy to estimate from the data of the firms in question. Therefore, it is proposed to make use of productivity performance of other firms, domestic or abroad.

Regulation is influenced by political pressure which dilutes the economic considerations. Based on this theme, Israel Finkelshtain and Yoav Kislev in Chapter 12 compare indirect regulation by prices to direct administrative control of quantities in industries that employ factors with external effects. The role of the social planner is taken by a government where the politicians respond favourably to rent-seeking efforts. The model produces conditions for the preferred mode of control.

Part I

Income Distribution and the Welfare State

1 Incentives in the Welfare State: Lessons for Would-be Welfare States[1]

Assar Lindbeck
INSTITUTE FOR INTERNATIONAL ECONOMIC STUDIES, STOCKHOLM, SWEDEN

This chapter deals with economic incentives and welfare-state arrangements in OECD countries. It also offers some lessons for would-be welfare states. The welfare-state arrangements differ, of course, among OECD countries. In particular, there is wide variation in the extent to which countries rely on four basic institutions – the state, the firm, the family and the market. Countries also differ in their reliance on (i) a common *safety net* in the form of flat-rate benefits tied to specific contingencies; (ii) *means-tested benefits* for low income groups; and (iii) *income protection*, i.e., benefits that are positively linked to previous income. Another distinction is between *corporatist* welfare states, where benefits are tied to labour contracts, and *universal* welfare states in which benefits are conditioned on residence or citizenship. This distinction is in reality blurred, however, by recent tendencies in corporatist welfare states to extend coverage to individuals who have very weak attachment to the labour market, and in universal welfare states to tie benefits to previous or contemporary work under the slogan 'workfare' rather than 'welfare'.

The degree of *generosity* of benefits is another important distinction. Of course, the lower the benefit levels in the compulsory systems, the stronger the incentives for citizens to add voluntary (market) solutions, in the form of private saving and private (individual or collective) insurance arrangements.

This chapter emphasizes what may be called 'dynamic' incentive issues, i.e., incentive effects that evolve over time. The discussion also covers the interplay between incentives and social norms among individuals, including endogenous changes in these norms. I will also consider endogenous adjustments in political behaviour. This approach makes it necessary to move outside conventionally defined 'economic analysis'. Let me begin, however, with some more familiar 'static' aspects of welfare-state incentives.

1 STATIC ASPECTS

The most obvious *achievements* of the modern welfare state are probably (i) to redistribute income over the life-cycle of the individual, and in this context equalize the distribution of yearly income between individuals and households; (ii) to reduce income risk; (iii) to stimulate the consumption of various social services, often with strong elements of investment in human capital; and (iv) to mitigate poverty. In some countries, welfare-state arrangements may also (v) equalize the overall distribution of disposable lifetime income, i.e., wealth, among individuals, as well as the distribution of specific social services. This enumeration illustrates the common view that welfare-state arrangements may be motivated on both efficiency grounds (achievements (i)–(iii)) and distributional grounds ((iv)–(v)).

How, then, can we be sure that more or less the same efficiency gains would not have taken place *without* welfare-state arrangements, i.e., on a voluntary basis? The 'paternalistic' answer, of course, is that many individuals are myopic, and that they would therefore not have chosen equally elaborate economic security on their own. Economists, however, usually emphasize various deficiencies of voluntary market solutions to problems of economic security. The most obvious ones are perhaps difficulties in borrowing with human capital as collateral and the high administrative costs of voluntary insurance policies. Compulsory social security is, as we know, also rationalized as (i) a way to overcome tendencies towards free-riding by individuals who expect the government to help them if they encounter difficulties; (ii) a method to prevent 'cream-skimming' by insurance companies if they are able to identify high-risk individuals; and (iii) a technique to avoid adverse selection when insurance companies are not able to make such identification, or when some individuals find out that they, or their children, are low-risk cases (and therefore withdraw from voluntary insurance schemes that cover also high-risk individuals). There is also general agreement among economists that various positive externalities of investment in human capital tend to make such investment sub-optimal, and that these problems may be mitigated by government loan guarantees and subsidies to education.

But how do we know that welfare-state arrangements, in fact, also equalize the distribution of disposable income among individuals? One piece of evidence is that the dispersion of disposable income in most OECD countries is much smaller than the dispersion of factor income, and that this holds for the overall distribution as well as for its lower tail.[2] The weak point of this evidence is, of course, that it neglects the general equilibrium effects of taxes and benefits on factor income, via various behavioural adjustments – and that these effects have turned out to be difficult to calculate empirically. There is, however, some supporting evidence. For example, in most countries, the factor-income distribution among citizens in active working age did not become more uneven when today's welfare-state arrangements were being built up during the first decades after the Second World War. (Factor incomes for pensioners have, of course, fallen after the introduction of compulsory pension systems.)

It is, however, important to emphasize that these various rationales for building up welfare-state arrangements do not, by themselves, *explain* why these arrangements have actually been made. Such explanations would require an analysis of the political processes that have generated these outcomes. Moreover, the achievements referred to above do not mean that the specific forms of the welfare-state arrangements in various OECD countries have been particularly efficient; in fact, the opposite is often the case, as is discussed below.

The most widely discussed problem with welfare-state arrangements probably concerns the 'static' efficiency costs associated with the *financing* of the welfare state, and hence with various tax wedges – often measured by the 'marginal costs of public funds'.[3] My only point on this well-known issue is to emphasize the *pervasiveness* of such disincentive effects. In addition to frequently studied (substitution) effects against hours of work, and somewhat less frequently studied effects on private saving and investment in physical capital, it is also important to consider the effects on, for instance, do-it-yourself work, barter of goods and services, the intensity and quality of work, investment in human capital, the choice of job, the allocation of investment in real and human capital, tax avoidance and tax evasion. Unfortunately, our knowledge of these matters is fragmented, sometimes even anecdotal; this does not, however, mean that it is without value.

Distortions that are directly connected with welfare-state *benefits* are probably no less pervasive. Not only are means-tested benefits bound to create 'benefit wedges', i.e., *implicit* tax wedges, including poverty traps, the most severe problem inherent in various benefit systems is probably that, like private insurance, they are plagued with moral hazard because the individual is able to adjust his or her own behaviour to qualify for benefits. Outright benefit-cheating is also bound to occur. Among major welfare-state arrangements, problems of moral hazard and cheating seem to be particularly pervasive in the case of sick benefits, work-injury benefits, housing subsidies, economic support to single parents (read: mothers), subsidized early retirement (disability pensions), and unemployment benefits.

In particular, the number of beneficiaries tends to rise with the generosity of the benefits due to moral hazard and cheating. On these matters, we have plenty of fragmented empirical indications that substantial problems have emerged.[4]

2 DYNAMIC ACHIEVEMENTS

Rather than dwelling on 'static' aspects like these, I would like to concentrate on incentive effects of a more *dynamic* nature, in the sense that the effects accumulate only gradually, and that they interact strongly with other factors over time, possibly in the form of virtuous or vicious circles.

Starting with dynamic *achievements*, it is likely that government subsidies to investment in human capital result not only in a rise in the future level of GNP, but also in faster long-term GNP *growth*, as asserted by contemporary theories of 'endogenous growth'. This would be expected to be the case not only for education and general health care, but also for policies that mitigate child poverty and provide specific social services such as pre-natal care and better nutrition for mothers and children. Indeed, the effects of improvements in these fields seem to be transmitted over generations within the family; see Haveman and Wolfe (1993).

Another potentially important dynamic contribution of welfare-state arrangements is to bring various minority groups into ordinary labour-market activities, and hence to mitigate what is often called 'social exclusion', manifested in long-term open unemployment, withdrawal from the labour force, or highly unstable and uncertain job prospects. This contribution presupposes that long-term benefit dependency can be avoided, which is more likely to succeed if the policy relies on work-oriented welfare-state arrangements, so-called 'workfare', than on pure transfer payments. As an illustration, the main reason for the high and long-term dependency on income transfers among single mothers in the United States is probably not that these benefits are particularly generous, but rather that they are not consistently and effectively combined with requirements for work or education – and organized child care.

Policies that counteract 'social exclusion' may also, in a long-term perspective, mitigate the development of cultures of criminal behaviour such as street crime, burglary, physical violence and drug addiction, cf. Hagen (1994). Poor labour-force attachment is, in fact, often regarded as a key factor that embeds crimes in poor neighbourhoods, cf. Wilson (1987). Indeed, it is often argued that the more ambitious welfare-state arrangements in Western Europe than in the United States help explain the smaller incidence of such phenomena in the former part of the world; cf. Coder *et al.* (1989); Jäntti and Danziger (1994).

The emergence of long-term dynamic effects such as these was already a basic notion in Gunnar Myrdal's *An American Dilemma* (1944, Appendix 3), where he emphasized the possibilities of what he called positive (or negative) processes of 'cumulative causation' between variables such as 'employment, wages, housing, nutrition, clothing, health, education, stability in family relations, manners, cleanliness, orderliness, trustworthiness, law observance, loyalty to society at large, absence of criminality, and so on'.

Both long-term productivity-enhancing welfare-state policies and policy actions that stimulate labour-force participation in the private sector, for instance among married women and various minority groups, also tend to expand the tax base in the long run, which helps finance the welfare state in the first place – an obvious example of a virtuous circle.[5]

It has also been argued that an even distribution of income mitigates social conflicts (Alesina and Rodrik, 1994), and that it tends to reduce the political pressure to redistribute disposable income further by way of distortionary political interventions (Meltzer and Richard, 1981; Persson and Tabellini, 1994). Another common view is that welfare-state arrangements make citizens more willing to accept reallocation of resources in response to changes in technology, product demand and international competition – and even contribute to making citizens more sympathetic to the market system.

Several of these asserted dynamic consequences of welfare-state arrangements may be regarded as improvements in the system of *property rights*, in the sense of assuring private agents that they can retain a large and stable fraction of the return to their own effort (Rebelo, 1991; Cashin, 1995). Of course, the taxes that finance the welfare state, in particular unpredicted changes in the tax rules, have effects on property rights in the opposite direction.

Welfare-state policies may also have profound long-term consequences for the role of the family in society. Some family-oriented welfare states on the European continent tend to support the traditional family, in the sense that married women are encouraged to work in their homes rather than in the open market. Examples of such countries are Austria, the Netherlands, Switzerland, and to a considerable extent also Germany.

The consequences for the labour-force participation of married women are more complex in 'individual-centred' welfare states, e.g., in the Nordic countries.[6] It is unavoidable that high marginal tax rates create substitution effects in favour of household work, i.e., against work in the open market.

But incentives in the opposite direction are created by subsidies to care of children, the sick and the elderly outside the household, i.e., positive cross-substitution effects on labour supply. In some countries, labour-force participation of married women is also stimulated by separate assessment of income taxes on husband and wife, which lowers the marginal income tax rate for the 'second' income earner in the household. Another example is positive 'liquidity effects' on labour supply due to a combination of high average tax rates and the provision of benefits 'in kind' that cannot be transformed into money income, which often makes it difficult to finance the family on the basis of one income earner only. Labour supply in some countries is also enhanced by tying the individual's right to social benefits to work – to *previous* work in the case of pensions, sickness benefits and paid maternity leave, to *current* work in the case of subsidized child care, and to the willingness of the individual to be available for *future* job offers in the case of unemployment benefits and social assistance.

All this means that the welfare state has quite ambiguous consequences for the labour market. In countries with a combination of high marginal tax and benefit wedges *and* strict work requirements, labour-force participation may very well be high, in particular for married women, but the average number of working hours per year of individuals may be rather low, in particular if the benefit systems are far from actuarially fair.[7] Strongly subsidized child care and old-age care may also result in a high birth rate in such societies – even for highly educated females.

It is, of course, a question of values whether we are in favour of family-oriented or individual-oriented welfare states – or if we prefer, in conformity with non-paternalistic principles, to opt for welfare-state arrangements that are intended to be neutral with respect to the division of labour between household work and market activities, and to the division of work between family members.

3 DYNAMIC PROBLEMS

The dynamic achievements of the modern welfare state discussed above should, of course, be compared with various dynamic problems. An obvious example is that the positive effects of subsidies on investment in human capital are counteracted by the reduced return on such investment because of the marginal tax and benefit wedges on labour income. The more progressive the tax system, the greater the probability that the *net* effect of these conflicting forces will be negative.

There appears to be broad agreement that high marginal tax wedges on the return on *physical assets* – in the absence of full loss-offset – will reduce the accumulation of such assets. A more important point is perhaps that high marginal tax rates on capital tend to distort the *allocation* of capital on different uses. The reason is various asymmetries of the taxation of different types of assets and asset holders that characterize the tax system in all countries. High tax rates create a strong leverage in these asymmetries. It is, by contrast, often argued that policies with negative effects on *domestic saving* do not harm domestic investment in physical assets in a world with free international capital mobility. This is, I believe, a mistaken view. One reason is that there seems to be a home bias regarding the supply of funds to physical investment, in the sense that foreign saving is not a perfect substitute for domestic saving when it comes to the financing of domestic investment. In particular, it is likely that small and medium-sized firms are favoured by domestically supplied financial capital – equity capital as well as loans – because of various information problems in capital and credit markets. For instance, providers of financial capital require detailed knowledge of the entrepreneurs to whom they supply funds, and this knowledge is difficult to acquire 'by long distance'. Moreover, private entrepreneurs, probably particularly small ones, are likely to have preferences for capital that is controlled either by themselves or by people whom they know. Thus, both capital taxes that deter private incentives to save, and welfare-state arrangements that reduce the need for household saving, would be expected to thwart the entry and growth of small private firms – also in countries with free international capital mobility. As a result, the level of GNP can be expected to fall, as will its rate of growth at least during a period of transition to a new steady-state growth path. Capitalism cannot exist without capitalists, and these will emerge only if there is domestic private saving.

More wide-ranging dynamic problems may also arise in connection with welfare-state policies. I have hypothesized elsewhere (Lindbeck, 1995; Lindbeck, Nyberg and Weibull, 1995) that full realization of various disincentive effects of taxes and benefits is likely to be delayed because habits and social norms, at least for a while, constrain individual behaviour. In this sense, social norms function as a form of 'social capital'. Before the build-up of generous welfare-state arrangements, work and saving were crucial for the living standard of the individual, indeed often even for his or her survival. It may be hypothesized that today's habits and social norms are, at least partly, a result of incentive and control systems in the past. But as increased marginal tax and benefit wedges have recently reduced the return on work, and made individual saving less imperative, it is likely that habits and social norms have gradually adjusted to the new incentive system. To begin with a few ('entrepreneurial') individuals may start breaking previous norms. As more and more individuals abandon previously obeyed social norms, the easier it will be for others to follow suit. In other words, it may be hypothesized that the social nature of norms can contribute to a dynamic process by which different individuals gradually adjust their behaviour to a new incentive structure, as earlier obeyed norms are abandoned. If these delayed effects are not anticipated by politicians when welfare-state arrangements are established, the welfare state will easily 'overshoot', in the sense that the disincentive effects will become greater than politicians would have tolerated initially (Lindbeck, 1994a).

It is also important to avoid the naïve belief that all types of social problems and conflicts can be effectively mitigated by welfare-state arrangements. Today, even the most advanced welfare states experience – indeed often increasingly so – pockets of poverty, social problems in connection with unemployment, unstable family relations, brutal urban environments, drug abuse, crime, etc. Certain kinds of economic crimes are even enhanced by high marginal tax rates. The reason is, of course, that the return to economic crimes is usually tax exempt, which means that honesty becomes 'expensive' in high-tax societies. This is bound to have negative effects in a long-term perspective on the supply of honesty. This is serious not only from an ethical point of view. Honesty may also be regarded as an important collective capital good in society – another example of how 'social capital' may depreciate if the incentive to keep it up deteriorates. As a result, some citizens (with weaker social norms than others) will certainly be tempted to cheat on taxes or benefits, work in the underground economy or even commit outright economic crimes. This is another example of how induced changes in social norms may, over time, create serious problems for the welfare state: an initially rather honest civilization may become increasingly dishonest because of the increased costs of honesty. I am afraid that this has already begun to happen in the high-tax Nordic countries in recent decades.

I hypothesized above that some welfare-state arrangements may raise the acceptance among citizens of continuing reallocation of labour. Nevertheless, we may note that resistance to such reallocations often emerges also in advanced welfare states. For instance, generous benefits mean that people may choose to stay where they are rather than shift to other jobs and geographical locations. We cannot even be sure that reductions in income inequality, when brought about by policy actions, will always mitigate political pressure for further redistributions through taxes, transfers and regulations. The 'appetite' for redistributions may even increase by the amount of redistributions implemented earlier. A reason may be that such policy actions tend to politicize distributional issues, and make people believe that income differences are 'arbitrarily' determined in the political process, rather than constituting an indispensable element of a well functioning market system. This is, in fact, my own interpretation of the Swedish experience of redistribution policy after the Second World War. It would seem that the political discussion in Sweden has increasingly focused on remaining inequalities, and the demands to reduce them, regardless of how small they have become. Thus, the often asserted negative relation between income inequality and distributional conflicts may not be monotone. However, this observation may not be a general pattern in the political process; the US experience may be a counterexample.

The possibilities of the emergence of such hazardous dynamics mean that vicious circles, and not just virtuous ones, may be generated by welfare-state arrangements. If the vicious ones, at some point in time, start to dominate, the welfare state may be undermined in the long run due to a combination of exploding welfare-state spending and an erosion of the tax base. A basic dilemma of the welfare state is exactly this: the more 'humane' it tries to be, the greater is the risk that it undermines its own economic foundations in the long run, and that it will not be able to live up to its promises.

The economic problems of the welfare state have, of course, been accentuated by the slowdown of long-term GDP growth during the last two decades, as well as by higher life expectancy. Both these developments may, in fact, have been boosted by the welfare state itself. We also know that the welfare-state crisis became acute in some countries in the 1980s and early 1990s in connection with strongly negative, short-term macroeconomic shocks, which threw large groups of citizens on to various safety nets, and induced others to withdraw from the labour force. These developments may also have speeded up the long-term weakening of social norms against living on various types of benefits (Lindbeck 1995).

If this is correct, it is important to take the warnings about the risk of delayed disincentive effects seriously. The problem is rather similar to environmental disturbances, which often also build up gradually with delayed effects. In both cases – the welfare state as well as the environment – the conclusion must be that the risks of serious, delayed and partly irreversible damage should make us cautious.

4 LESSONS FOR WOULD-BE WELFARE STATES

What, then, are the most important lessons for would-be welfare states – including both former socialist states (FSS), and middle-income countries outside Europe? These lessons have to be formulated, of course, against the background of both the previous welfare-state arrangements in these countries and the social problems that exist today.

Prior to their collapse, the socialist countries provided often quite elaborate 'cradle-to-grave' welfare states. Administration of these benefits, however, was often closely tied to the employment contract – partly by job guarantees, partly by employment-related benefits, including generous family benefits of various types (Krumm, Milanovic and Walton, 1994; Atkinson and Micklewright, 1992; Barr, 1994). Subsidies and direct provision of goods and services were frequently also tied to firms. Such arrangements are obviously not conducive to an emerging market system, as firms are then unable to give employment guarantees; nor can they easily finance social spending. It is also difficult to create a flexible labour market when benefits are tied to specific firms. For these reasons, it is hardly surprising that the governments in these countries have gradually taken over more of both the financing and the administration of welfare arrangements. Indeed, as unemployment benefits and social assistance hardly existed during the socialist period, such systems had to be constructed largely from scratch.

Several countries in Latin America also built up rather generous welfare states during the first decade after the Second World War (or even earlier). Often, however, the systems turned out to be unsustainable, cf. Mesa-Lago (1994). This has shown up in huge imbalances between revenues and spending in the social security systems in various years, and in expected aggregate actuarial imbalances of the systems over an extended future time span. This may be regarded as a result of the tensions between the generosity of the benefit systems and the limited economic resources of the countries concerned.

The 'dependency rate' of the benefit systems – i.e., the ratio of individuals living on transfers to those living on factor income – is often about the same in the FSS and in several middle-income countries outside Europe. The proportion of citizens above the age of 60 or 65, however, is usually much higher in the FSS. Indeed, this proportion today is about as high as in most OECD countries, where the ratio between the number of individuals of working age and pensioners is often as low as about 2, and is likely to fall even further in coming decades. A low retirement age in the FSS during the socialist period – often 60 years for men and 55 for women – has accentuated the problem. This means that welfare-state spending in these countries is to a large extent directed towards consumption for the elderly rather than towards investment in human capital among the young. The situation is quite different in several middle-income countries outside Europe, in particular in Pacific Asia, where the elderly, so far, comprise a much smaller fraction of the entire population.

When drawing on the OECD experience, it is important to recall that the generous welfare-state arrangements in these countries emerged only after about a century of successful economic growth. It is not self-evident that these countries would have been equally rich today if they had tried to set up comprehensive and generous welfare-state arrangements during the first decades of this century. These arrangements were also, to begin with, quite selective, i.e., strongly targeted, before comprehensive and 'universal' welfare states were established after the Second World War. Therefore, it is probably prudent for builders of future welfare states to limit their ambitions during the coming decades – not only so as to finance the systems, but also to avoid serious disincentive effects during the early phases of their economic development. It is also interesting to note that the recently successful economies in Pacific Asia, in terms of economic growth, have waited quite a long time before even contemplating the construction of elaborate welfare-state arrangements. One important reason why this has been feasible is, of course, that extended families are still an important source of income security in these countries.

There is, of course, a strong social case for building up, or improving, welfare-state arrangements today also in middle-income countries, including the FSS. The political forces that work in that direction are also strong. The most important *positive* lesson from the welfare-state experience in the OECD countries may be drawn from the above-mentioned achievements in terms of economic security and the mitigation of poverty. When trying to transmit this experience to would-be welfare states, it is important, however, to get the priorities 'right' from the beginning. A tradeoff certainly exists between increasing economic security for the majority, on the one hand, and mitigating poverty for a minority, on the other. Income security for the majority may be important for political stability, as well as for a wide acceptance of continuing adjustments of relative wages to efficiency criteria. Ethical considerations instead motivate a concentration of resources on relieving the poverty of those who are worst off in society. Moreover, many observers of conditions in middle-income countries today probably agree that *both* these ambitions are more important than equalizing the overall distribution of income, as measured, for instance, by the Gini coefficient. Both ethical considerations and concern for social and political stability provide, however, arguments for avoiding small groups of citizens becoming rich on the basis of socially dubious activities. To mitigate this problem requires, however, actions outside the area of welfare-state arrangements.

A special problem when trying to safeguard the incomes of the poorest segments of the population in the FSS is that the difference between the minimum benefits required to avoid severe poverty and the lowest wages in society tends to be very small in such countries. For instance, while the ratio of minimum wages to the social-assistance income level is often 2, 3, or even 4 in the OECD countries, it is not much higher than unity in some FSS (Krumm *et al.*, 1994, Table 2).

It is hazardous to suggest designs for the build-up of welfare-state arrangements in the middle-income countries. On the basis of experience in various OECD countries, and the situation that exists today in various middle-income countries, it may, however, be a good idea for these countries to concentrate, at least to begin with, on four types of welfare-state arrangements.

(i) Strictly targeted support for the poor, in the form of means-tested social assistance, partly perhaps 'in kind' to limit the negative effects on work. A basic reason for this proposal is, of course, that such support is rather inexpensive.

(ii) A rather low safety net in the form of flat-rate benefits tied to specific contingencies such as sickness, work injury unemployment and old age. Again, a reason for the proposal is that it is important to limit the financial costs for the government. Another reason is to limit the risks of serious disincentive problems, in particular in a long-run perspective.

(iii) Subsidies of services with strong elements of investment in human capital, such as prenatal care, maternity care and education – in particular for low-income groups. A main reason is, of course, to stimulate economic growth, but also to improve the position of low-productivity groups in the long run.

(iv) *Temporary*, rather than permanent, support for the unemployed, in the form of once-and-for-all severance pay when employees are laid off, assistance for individuals to become self-employed or start small firms, temporary public works programmes, and temporary training programmes tied to firms, instead of relying on permanent measures such as regular public-sector employment, public-works programmes of long duration, or early retirement. A rationale for this proposal is, of course, to avoid permanent expansion of public-sector employment and to mitigate tendencies to unemployment persistence.

As total government spending already hovers around 50 per cent of GNP both in several FSS and in some Latin American countries, i.e., somewhat above the OECD average, it may even be advisable to wind down some benefit programmes. The reason is not only to avoid financial difficulties for the public sector. Another reason is that quite strong incentives to work, save and invest may be necessary now in order to *restore* economically and socially efficient behaviour of individuals in some of these countries. In particular, as it is likely that such habits and norms have already been seriously damaged due to the poor incentive system in these countries during recent decades. It may also be particularly important in these countries to keep marginal tax rates rather low so as to combat the severe problems of economic crime.

Moreover, the truism that capitalism requires capitalists, and hence also private saving, is particularly important in the FSS, as there is very little accumulated private saving. It is, therefore, important that the new welfare-state arrangements in these countries are constructed in ways that do not harm private saving more than 'necessary'.

5 MARGINAL REFORMS

Reforms of and retreats from various welfare-state arrangements are under way in several OECD countries. The reform debate in these countries is also of interest for would-be welfare states. Let me start with what may be called 'marginal' reforms, subsequently shifting the focus to more 'radical' reforms. The former often aim at making the systems less generous, largely to avoid moral hazard and cheating, as well as to make the arrangements financially sustainable in a long-term perspective, while radical reforms aim at overhauling the basic structure of the welfare-state arrangements.

The most obvious marginal reform is perhaps to reduce benefit levels – not only in order to improve the financial position of the government, but also to provide coinsurance, and hence to mitigate moral hazard and to restore economic incentives. Stronger actuarial elements in social security systems would also improve economic incentives, as the (implicit) marginal tax wedge would then be reduced. It is important to note that strong actuarial elements are feasible also in the context of pay-as-you-go systems, by tying future benefits to the value of previously paid contributions. Such actuarial, contributions-defined pay-as-you-go systems are perhaps easiest to achieve for old-age and early retirement pensions.[8] Such systems will, however, as a rule not be consistent with requirements of balanced social insurance budgets.

Another problem in several countries is that individuals tend to shift between different benefit systems depending on which is the most favourable one. It is, therefore, useful to have the same replacement level in all benefit systems between which the individual can move at his or her own discretion – such as the sick-leave, work-injury, early retirement or unemployment benefit systems. Strict eligibility requirements for receiving benefits, and stiff controls that these requirements are satisfied, are also important, though the need for controls is smaller the lower the benefit levels. There are, of course, practical limits to controls, which are probably more effective against cheating than against moral hazard.

To avoid overinsurance, it is also useful to put caps on total insurance benefits, i.e., on the total level of compulsory *plus* private insurance benefits. Otherwise, the compulsory system will be exposed to negative external effects by moral hazard and cheating in the voluntary system. Such caps are not necessary in the old-age pension system, however, as moral hazard hardly arises in this case.

Another important problem is how to construct welfare-state arrangements that are reasonably robust to shocks due to demographic factors or productivity growth. A basic problem in this connection is the extent to which such adjustments should be automatic or discretionary.[9] In a pension system, for instance, an obvious method to achieve *automatic* adjustments to demographic changes is to tie the normal pension age to the life expectancy of the population. In order to provide a pension system with automatic protection against a slowdown in productivity growth, the pension benefits can be formally tied to the *per capita* disposable income, or *per capita* consumption of the active population, see Merton (1983). Similar automatic adjustment mechanisms may also be constructed for other parts of a social security system. For instance, either the contributions or the benefits of an unemployment insurance system may be automatically tied to the unemployment rate. In a sick-pay system, the contributions and benefits may be formally tied to the number of sick days in the population as a whole, etc. There are, of course, limits to such automatic adjustments of benefit levels if we are anxious to avoid creating severe hardship for some individuals.

Automatic adjustments have the advantage of being more predictable, and perhaps also politically easier to implement, than discretionary adjustments. In other words, automatic adjustment mechanisms may reduce the risk for discretionary political interventions in the rules of benefit systems, i.e., 'political risks' may be mitigated. It also becomes easier to keep the systems outside the yearly budget process, which is also likely to reduce the frequency of political intervention in the rules. A weakness of automatic adjustment mechanisms of this aggregate type is, of course, that they may make it difficult to establish a tight 'actuarial' relationship between contributions and benefits for the individual. *Relative* benefits for different individuals could, however, still be tied to previously paid contributions, even if average benefits are tied to the average disposable income (consumption) of the contemporary working population.

Incentive problems also extend to the case of the provision of *social services*, in the sense that it has turned out to be difficult to achieve efficiency while simultaneously guaranteeing freedom of choice when the government provides such services. The obvious way of dealing with this problem is either administrative reforms of public-sector agencies or the opening up of competition with private and cooperative institutions. The first option includes methods such as administrative decentralization, cash limits, better measurement of performance, and comparison of the performance of different units in the public sector (i.e., 'benchmark competition'). The second option requires free entry and an end to the discrimination of actual and potential competitors to public-sector agencies. To avoid distributional problems in connection with freer competition, a voucher system is perhaps the most obvious device.

Would-be welfare states should consider options like these at an early stage. It has turned out to be politically difficult to achieve the twofold objective of reforming the operation of government agencies and letting in competition, after the production of such services has already been monopolized by public-sector agencies. Serious protests from public-sector employees are more likely as a response to *cuts* in existing services and employment than to restraints in the build-up of such services in the first place.

6 RADICAL REFORMS

The considerations above focused on marginal reforms within an approximately given structure of welfare-stage arrangements. More recently, however, there has also been some discussion of radical reforms, i.e., changes in the basic structure of the welfare state. That discussion may also be of interest for would-be welfare states. Indeed, it should be easier to choose between alternative structures when a system is being built up, than to reform an old system to which people have already adjusted their lives. After all, social security systems are implicit long-term contracts between the government and the citizens and the political and social costs of breaking these contracts may be very high.

Examples of recently proposed radical alternatives are (i) to replace a system of income protection with a safety net that is common to all (flat-rate benefits), or vice versa; (ii) to shift from a pay-as-you-go to a funded social insurance system, possibly combined with partial or total privatization, while keeping insurance compulsory; (iii) to replace a complex social security system, in which benefits are tied to specific contingencies, with a 'negative income tax' (a so-called 'gradient system'); or (iv) to replace a traditional social security system with actuarially-based lifetime 'drawing rights', i.e., forced-saving accounts, whereby an individual is free to draw, at his or her own discretion, on an individual account, which is comprised of compulsory fees accumulated over the working life.

Each of these radical reforms has specific advantages and drawbacks. A shift to a common safety net, i.e., the 'back to Beveridge strategy', has the advantage of being financially inexpensive for the government. Such a system is also attractive if we want the individual to take considerable responsibility in the form of voluntary saving and insurance policies, which is often believed to reduce the risk that individuals will become pacified. The types of welfare-state benefits for which this type of arrangement would be feasible are transfer programmes rather than services such as health-care. A disadvantage of this strategy is, of course, that the administrative costs will often be higher than in existing social security systems.

An advantage of *funded systems*, as compared to pay-as-you-go systems is that the return to the individual's contribution is likely to be higher. (This assumes that the real return on a portfolio of assets is higher than the growth in the tax base of the pay-as-you-go system.) Aggregate national saving would also be expected to be higher, in particular during a transition period. It is also reasonable to assume that property rights are stronger in funded systems than in a pay-as-you-go system, in the sense that the political risks would be expected to be smaller, even though individuals would, of course, instead be exposed to more capital-market risks. In terms of an important concept in social psychology, the hypothesis is here that the political risks are smaller if the benefits are 'framed' in terms of the right to one's own saving rather than having vague 'rights' to transfers financed by others.

In addition to well-known transition problems, a government-implemented funded system also raises the difficult issue of who should administer and control the funds. It is theoretically possible for the funds to be managed in such a way that their managers, and hence also politicians and public-sector bureaucrats, do not interfere in either the allocation of the assets or the control of the firms in which the funds are invested. Theoretically it may, for instance, be possible to legislate that the funds should hold 'market portfolios', or invest only in mutual funds.[10]

But it is extremely naïve to believe that future politicians will necessarily stick to such rules. They can simply amend legislation in the future so as to control the composition of the funds and/or to exert power over firms. There are, in other words, severe risks that a funded, government-operated social security system will, in reality, sooner or later develop into a system with strong government control of both capital markets and individual firms. It is much easier for politicians to use an instrument that already exists, i.e., government-created funds, to exercise power over firms, than to engage in 'open' socialization with the *explicit* purpose of taking control of the private sector.

The Swedish experience is instructive from this point of view. When the supplementary pension system was introduced in Sweden in 1959, it was explicitly stated that the buffer funds created by the new system should *not* be used to buy shares in private firms. Nevertheless, new decisions have been taken over the years to do just that. Moreover, Swedish politicians have not chosen index funds or mutual funds, and the government-appointed boards of the funds have, in fact, used the voting rights of the shares held by the buffer funds to intervene in firms. From time to time, politicians and trade union leaders have also suggested that the pension funds should be used as instruments for centralized 'industrial policies'. Those who want to limit the risk of future socialization of firms, therefore, have good reason to object to a shift to a government-operated *funded* social-security system. This warning should be of particular interest for the FSS, as the citizens in these countries may be particularly anxious not to wind up in a socialist system again, after recently having escaped such a society.

What about a shift to a *negative income tax*, which is a popular idea among many economists? A main advantage would be that extremely high implicit marginal tax rates, i.e., poverty traps, may then be avoided for low-income earners. But such a system is very expensive because of the 'thickness' of the left tail in the factor-income distribution in most countries, which requires quite high tax rates on the rest of the population. As a result, the marginal tax distortions would simply move up along the income distribution, which might create more incentive problems than it solved.

There is, however, an even more serious problem with a negative income tax. It may create new generations of 'drifters', living on government handouts, as the benefits in such systems in fact constitute 'individual rights', rather than serving as income support based on specific contingencies. A negative income tax may, over time, result in a demise of habits and social norms that enhance work and saving, for instance among the young generation – even more so than social security systems in which the benefits are tied to well defined contingencies (Lindbeck, 1995). Considering that the FSS have been plagued with serious incentive problems for decades, it would seem that a shift to a negative income tax would be even more hazardous in these countries that in the rich OECD countries.

A system of *drawing rights*, finally, would allow the individual to draw on an account in the public sector for well defined contingencies, for instance, in connection with education, training, sickness or unemployment, though less would then be available later on, ultimately for pensions (Fölster, 1995). An advantage of such a system, if it is made strongly actuarial, is that it helps keep down marginal tax wedges. However, such a system requires complementary risk insurance, as different individuals are exposed to quite different risks – sickness, permanent invalidism, unemployment, etc. It would also be necessary to put a strict ceiling on how much the individual is allowed to draw before retirement age – to avoid myopic behaviour and free-riding. From the point of view of economic incentives, the main advantage of a system with drawing rights, as compared to an actuarially-fair pay-as-you-go system, seems to be that the less an individual has used other social systems earlier in his life, the higher his pension. In this way, a system of drawing rights pools accumulates saving for different types of contingencies, and hence also increases the freedom of choice for the individual. Experiences in Singapore and Malaysia suggest that a system of this type is at least administratively feasible.

7 CONCLUSION

When welfare-state arrangements are constructed or reformed, it is important to find a proper combination of redistribution, insurance and incentives. It is also important to choose a system that is reasonably robust to economic, demographic and political risks. In view of these complex considerations, it is natural that recent radical welfare-state proposals have included combinations of different elements. The most celebrated combination is perhaps a 'three-pillared system' consisting of: (i) tax-financed flat-rate benefits, i.e., a safety net, at the 'bottom' for well defined contingencies such as sickness, unemployment and old age – combined with discretionary social assistance for people, who, for various reasons, cannot support themselves; (ii) a supplementary system of mandatory social insurance designed for income protection, with strong actuarial elements in order to minimize tax wedges – possibly also some funding, provided it is possible to guarantee *both* individual ownership of the assets *and* privately operated funds; and, finally, (iii) voluntary saving and voluntary insurance policies 'at the top', which may include both collective and individual insurance. The first pillar, which may be strongly redistributive, need not be institutionally separate from the second, more actuarial, pillar; the two may be administratively combined.

A three-pillared system of this type would pool political risks and market risks. This is perhaps as much economic security as can be achieved in an uncertain world. To bring this about, however, requires not only profound economic analysis, proper insurance techniques and competent administration. It also, and perhaps above all, requires a good understanding of *political behaviour*. This is the case both when we try to understand how the present welfare-state problems have arisen, and when we consider reforms to mitigate these problems.

For instance, while the huge expansion of welfare-state spending after the Second World War certainly reflects high and rising demand among citizens for economic security and redistributions, the process cannot be fully understood without insights into the process of competition for votes among political parties. A traditional view of this issue is, of course, that government spending is stimulated by the fact that benefits are usually *specific*, while the financing of them is usually *general*. This view of the political process also helps explain why it is difficult to rewind government spending later on, in particular if individuals have already adjusted their behaviour, indeed their lives, to the benefit systems. An extreme example is a country where the majority of the electorate, as in Belgium, Norway and Sweden today, is tax financed – either by living on transfers or by being employed in government-service production. Is this a point of no return?

For these various reasons, reforms of and retreats from the welfare state may be politically very difficult – that is, if the country is not blessed with politicians with 'suicidal instincts', or if a serious financial crisis in the government does not 'force' politicians to reform and reduce welfare-state spending. A large 'package' of several simultaneous spending and tax cuts may also be easier to implement than a series of specific reforms. In the former case everybody would be a winner on some accounts and a loser on others. Indeed, if the package is large, it may even be impossible to identify winners and losers. This probably makes it easier politically to cut government spending, and hence to prevent an even more serious crisis for the welfare state in the future. The idea is, then, not to abolish the welfare state, but rather to make it sustainable in a long-term perspective.

Notes

1. I am grateful for comments on an earlier draft by Anders Björklund, Michael Bruno, Peter Diamond, Ulf Jacobsson, Hans-Werner Sinn and K. G. Scherman. Julie Sundquist has improved the language.
2. While the Gini coefficient for the overall distribution of yearly factor income of households is typically about 0.40–0.45 in the rich OECD countries, it is usually in the interval of 0.20–0.30 in the case of yearly disposable (i.e., post-tax post-transfer) income (Mitchell, 1991, p. 127). Suppose that the 'poverty line' is drawn at 40 per cent of median income, and that the 'poverty gap' is defined as the aggregate amount of income that would have to be given to households below the poverty line in order to bring their income up to this line. The relevant amount is typically 3.0–5.0 per cent of GNP in most OECD countries in the case of factor income. In the case of disposable income, the corresponding amount is as low as 0.1–1.2 per cent of GNP (Mitchell, 1991, pp. 57, 75).

   The figures refer to yearly income. We know less about the difference between the distribution of factor income and disposable income on a *lifetime income basis*.
3. In the United States, the 'marginal costs of public funds' are often estimated at about 1.2–1.3 dollars per dollar of additional spending, which means that higher government spending can be motivated if it is believed to be worth more than 1.2–1.3 dollars to society per extra dollar spent. By contrast, in Sweden during the 1980s, the marginal costs of public funds have been estimated at 2 or 3 dollars. Because of the limited domain of such analyses, in terms of the number of decisions studied, and also because of the methodological difficulties involved, we should probably regard calculations like these as experiments in quantification rather than as reliable estimates.
4. For illustrations in the case of Sweden, see Lindbeck (1997).
5. For recent emphasis on positive interrelations between social achievements and economic efficiency, see, for instance, Glyn and Miliband (1994).
6. For an analysis of issues like these in Sweden, see Freeman, Swedenborg and Topel (1996).
7. Sweden is a pronounced example. Labour-force participation is above 70 per cent for both men and women between 24 and 65 years of age, but the average number of hours *per year* for those who work was during the 1980s only about 1400 while typical figures for most other developed countries are between 1600 and 2000. (The *statutory* number of working hours per week, however, was not particularly low in Sweden.)
8. In a system of work-injury benefits, actuarial elements may be introduced by varying the contributions from firms in accordance with revealed work-

injury risks ('experience rating'). In the unemployment benefit system, actuarial elements may be instituted by differentiating the fees by sectors and professions in accordance with unemployment risks.
9. This issue is discussed in Diamond (1996).
10. This has been suggested by, for instance, Peter Diamond (1996).

References

Alesina, A. and D. Rodrik (1994) 'Distributive Politics and Economic Growth', *Quarterly Journal of Economics*, vol. 109, no. 2, pp. 465–90.

Atkinson, A. B. (1991) 'The Social Safety Net', *Welfare-State Programme Discussion Paper*, 66, STICERD, London School of Economics.

Atkinson, A. B. and J. Micklewright (1992) *Economic Transformation in Eastern Europe and the Distribution of Income* (Cambridge: Cambridge University Press).

Barr, N. (ed.) (1994) *Labor Markets and Social Policy in Central and Eastern Europe* (Washington, DC: World Bank).

Cashin, P. (1995) 'Government Spending, Taxes, and Economic Growth', *International Monetary Fund Staff Papers*, vol. 42, no. 2, pp. 237–69.

Coder, J., L. Rainwater and T. Sweeding (1989) 'Inequality among Children and Elderly in Ten Modern Nations: The United States in an International Context', *American Economic Review*, vol. 79, no. 2, pp. 320–4.

Diamond, P. (1996) 'Proposals to Restructure Social Security', *Journal of Economic Perspectives*, vol. 10, no. 3, pp. 67–88.

Freeman, R., B. Swedenborg and R. Topel (eds) *Reforming the Welfare State: The Swedish Model in Transition* (Stockholm and Cambridge, MA: NBER-SNS).

Fölster, S. (1995) 'Social Insurance Based on Personal Saving-Accounts: A Possible Reform Strategy for Overburdened Welfare States?' (Stockholm: 101), mimeo.

Glyn, A. and D. Miliband (eds) (1994) *Paying for Inequality* (London: IPPR/Rivers Oran Press).

Hagen, J. (1994) 'Crime, Inequality and Efficiency', in A. Glyn and D. Miliband (eds) *Paying for Inequality*.

Hassler, J. and A. Lindbeck (1997) 'A Note on Optimum Actuarial Fairness of Pension System', *Economics Letters* (forthcoming).

Haveman, R. and B. Wolfe (1993) 'Children's Prospects and Children's Policy', *Journal of Economic Perspectives*, vol. 7, no. 4, pp. 153–74.

Jäntti, M. and S. Danziger (1994) 'Child Poverty in Sweden and the United States: The Effects of Social Transfers and Parental Labor Force Participation', Academy of Finland (October), mimeo.

Krumm, K., B. Milanovic and M. Walton (1994) 'Transfers and the Transition from Socialism', *Policy Research Paper*, 1380 (Washington DC: World Bank).

Lindbeck, A. (1994a) 'Overshooting Reform and Retreat of the Welfare State', *De Economist*, vol. 104, no. 1, pp. 1–19.

Lindbeck, A. (1994b) 'Uncertainty under the Welfare State – Policy Induced Risk', *Geneva Papers on Risk and Insurance*, vol. 19, no. 73, pp. 379–93.

Lindbeck, A. (1995) 'Welfare State Disincentives with Endogenous Habits and Norms', *Scandinavian Journal of Economics*, vol. 97, no. 4, pp. 477–94.

Lindbeck, A. (1997) 'The Swedish Experiment', *Journal of Economic Literature*.

Lindbeck, A., S. Nyberg and J. W. Weibull (1995) 'Social Norms, Voting and the Welfare State', *Working Paper* (Stockholm: IUI).

Liungqvist, L. and T. Sargent (1996) 'Welfare States and Unemployment', in R. Freeman, B. Swedenborg and R. Topel (eds), *Reforming the Welfare State* (Stockholm and Cambridge, MA: NBER-SNS).

Meltzer, A. and S. Richard (1981) 'A Rational Theory of the Size of Government', *Journal of Political Economy*, vol. 89, no. 5, pp. 914–27.

Merton, R. (1983) 'On the Role of Social Security as a Means for Efficient Risk-bearing in an Economy where Human Capital is not Tradable', in Z. Bodie and J. B. Shoven (eds), *Financial Aspects of the US Pension System* (Chicago: University of Chicago Press).

Mesa-Lago, C. (1994) 'Social Welfare Reform in the Context of Economics–Political Liberalisation: Latin American Cases', Conference on 'Reform of the State in Latin America and Eastern Europe', Rio de Janeiro (June 24–26).

Mitchell, D. (1991) *Income Transfers in Ten Welfare States* (Aldershot: Avebury).

Milanovic, B. (1994) 'Poverty, Inequality and Social Policy in Transition Economies' (Washington DC: World Bank), mimeo.

Myrdal, G. (1944) *An American Dilemma* (New York: Carnegie Foundation).

Persson, T. and G. Tabellini (1994) 'Is Inequality Harmful for Growth?', *American Economic Review*, vol. 84, no. 3, pp. 600–21.

Rebelo, S. (1991) 'Long-Run Policy Analysis and Long-Run Growth', *Journal of Political Economy*, vol. 99, no. 3, pp. 500–21.

Wilson, W. J. (1987) *The Truly Disadvantaged: The Inner City, The Underclass and Public Policy* (Chicago: Chicago University Press).

2 Income Distribution Theory: A Survey of Selected Recent Contributions

Thomas Piketty
MASSACHUSETTS INSTITUTE OF TECHNOLOGY, USA, and CNRS–CEPREMAP, PARIS, FRANCE

1 INTRODUCTION

The field of income distribution theory has probably received more attention during the past five years than it had received during the previous 15–20 years. These developments were mostly motivated by the urgent need to move beyond representative-agent models and the development of new tools allowing tractable equilibrium modelling of heterogeneity between agents, but probably also by the dramatic recent development of income inequality both in developed and developing countries.

This survey is not intended to be exhaustive.[1] On the contrary, I choose to concentrate on three different sets of ideas that have been developed in recent research and which I view as important, while leaving untouched the rest of the literature. I summarize briefly the main theoretical ingredients of these different models, and I move on to the research agenda and especially the need for more collaboration with empirical research.

First, I show how credit-rationing modifies substantially the logic of the neoclassical accumulation/distribution model, by making the wealth distribution (and not only aggregate wealth) a key variable of the development process; I emphasize the distinction between 'poverty traps' and 'low-mobility traps' and the urgent need for further empirical work.

Next, I present the main ideas of recent work on local externalities and neighbourhood segregation (housing market vs zoning, social inefficiency, long-run effects), stressing the interaction with other levels of spatial segregation (firm, family) and the prospects for estimating the key parameters.

Finally, I show how recent work on mechanisms generating persistent inequality out of self-fulfilling beliefs (e.g., statistical discrimination, learning models) addresses the issue of efficient redistributive policy tools: transfers contingent solely on income vs quota-type affirmative action vs transfers contingent on income and race (or gender, or parental income).

The next three sections take these topics in turn.

2 CREDIT RATIONING AND INEQUALITY TRAPS

Credit or wealth constraints are said to arise whenever the opportunity to invest depends not only on the 'technological' viability of the investment (rate of return, risk, ability of the entrepreneur, ...) but also on the initial wealth (or collateral) of the would-be entrepreneur *per se*. Although the idea that such constraints are pervasive in capitalist economies dates back at least to Marx,[2] one had to wait for the development of information economics in the past 15 years to find formal theories describing precisely the microeconomic origin of these constraints. It is by now well understood that the source of credit constraints is the commitment power of initial wealth: without a sufficient personal stake in the project the would-be entrepreneur has no commitment that he or she will reveal the truth to the lender (adverse selection) nor that he or she will take the right actions to ensure the lender will be repaid (moral hazard). Depending on the exact technological and informational parameters, this will result in equilibrium into a credit-rationing curve $k(w,r)$: $k(w,r) \geqslant w$ is the maximal capital investment a would-be entrepreneur with initial wealth w can undertake when the interest rate is r, i.e. $k(w,r) - w$ is the maximal credit that lenders accept to offer.

In the past five years, these equilibrium credit-rationing models have been used as building blocks by a new generation of dynamic models of capital accumulation and income distribution. The general conclusion is that long-run output, capital stock and income distribution can now depend on the initial distribution of wealth as well as on transitory shocks, which stands in great contrast with Solow-type models. In the Solow model, the long-run capital stock *per capita* k^* (which is also the long-run average wealth) is uniquely determined by $sf(k^*) = \delta k^*$ in the case with linear savings,[3] and by $f(k^*) = \Theta + \delta$ in the case with dynastic preferences,[4] and this k^* is completely independent from the initial wealth distribution $F_0(w)$. Intuitively, this is because first-best credit makes wealth inequality irrelevant: efficient capital allocation implies that the rich and the poor work with the same amount of capital per labour unit, so that aggregate output only depends on aggregate wealth; the concavity of the production function then ensures global convergence of aggregate accumulation.[5]

The simplest novelty introduced by credit-rationing is the possible existence of poverty traps.[6] Consider for example a model with linear savings and a very extreme form of moral-hazard-induced credit-rationing: borrowers can always 'take the money and run' at no cost, so that in effect the credit market completely collapses ($k(w,r) = w$); further assume that each generation can either earn a subsistence income y or make a fixed investment I that yields a net return RI, with $RI > y$. Then at each period t, all agents whose initial wealth w_t is smaller than I earn y, while agents with $w_t \geq I$ earn RI, so that transitional equations can be written:

$$\text{If } w_t < l,\ w_{t+1} = (1 - \delta)w_t + sy$$
$$\text{If } w_t > l,\ w_{t+1} = (1 - \delta)w_t + sRl$$

If we assume the savings rate s to be small enough so that $sy + (1 - \delta I) < I$ and the rate of return R to be high enough so that $sRI + (1 - \delta)I > I$, then we have a poverty trap: poor dynasties starting with $w_0 < I$ earn a low income y and remain poor forever (w_t --> $w^0 = sy/\delta < I$), while rich dynasties starting with w_0 earn a high-income RI and remain rich (w_t --> $w^1 = sRI/\delta > I$). That is, if the initial distribution of wealth $F_0(w)$ is characterized by a mass $F_0(I)$ of poor dynasties and a mass $1 - F_0(I)$ of rich dynasties, then so will be the long-run distribution $F_\alpha(w)$: initial wealth inequality persists in the long run. Note that this persistence would immediately disappear with first-best credit: everybody would invest I irrespective of one's initial wealth, and all dynasties would converge to the same wealth level, for any initial wealth distribution. Note also that those poverty traps rely entirely on a threshold effect requiring a technological non-convexity: without the assumption of a fixed-size investment, poor dynasties could slowly accumulate by starting with small investment levels and eventually catch up with the rich.

However, an important finding of the recent literature is that we actually do not need non-convexities and threshold effects to conclude that initial inequality can persist in the long run. Consider a model where agents can invest at any level according to a production function $f(k)$, but where moral hazard in entrepreneurial effort leads to a credit-rationing curve $k(w,r)$ that becomes more binding as the market interest rate r goes up ($dk(w,r)/dr < 0$).[7] Risks from investment are imperfectly insurable (because of moral hazard), so that individual transitions $w_{t+1}(w_t)$ are stochastic. With suitable concavity assumptions, one can ensure that individual transitions $w_{t+1}(w_t)$ exhibit no threshold effect, i.e., that one can switch between any two wealth levels in a finite time with positive probability. If we assume that the interest rate r is exogeneously fixed, this ergodicity property is sufficient to ensure global convergence, i.e., the fact that the long-run distribution $F_{\alpha r}(w)$ does not depend on the initial distribution $F_0(w)$.

However things are different when the interest rate is endogenously determined by the supply and demand of capital. Note first that with credit constraints the equilibrium interest rate is not simply given by 'the' marginal product of capital, since the latter varies across production units. In other words the equilibrium interest rate r_t now depends on the entire wealth distribution $F_t(w)$ at period t. One can then show that depending on the exact initial distribution $F_0(w)$ there will exist different possible long-run distributions $F_{\alpha 1}(w)$, $F_{\alpha 2}(w)$ associated with different long-run interest rates.[8] The intuition is the following: initial distributions with a large mass of low-wealth agents lead to a high demand for capital and to high interest rates, which in turn imply that it takes a long time for low-wealth agents to accumulate and rebuild their collateral, so that the initially large mass of poor agents is self-reproducing; conversely, low initial interest rates lead to high wealth mobility, high accumulation and low equilibirum interest rates. Such a multiplicity will arise whenever an interest rate rise strengthens credit constraints more than it strengthens the accumulation of the rich, i.e., whenever $|dk(w,r)/dr|$ is large enough. The steady states with higher interest rates have at the same time less wealth mobility and a lower aggregate output and capital stock.[9]

The key difference between this type of 'low-mobility trap' and the inequality traps described earlier is that the latter can be eliminated once and for all by pushing all poor agents above the threshold, whereas the former is more perverse and requires continuous downward pressures on the interest rate (through monetary or credit policy) to shift the economy to a lower interest rate, higher mobility development path.

This phenomenon of low-mobility traps is actually very general, and it has first been pointed out by Banerjee and Newman (1993) in a context that is slightly different from the one we have just described. Banerjee and Newman consider a dynamic accumulation/distribution model with a fixed exogenous interest rate r, but with an endogenous wage rate v_t playing a role that is similar to the endogenous interest rate in the previous discussion. In their model, the wage rate is the equilibrium market price of monitored labour: they consider a world where moral hazard-induced credit constraints prevent poor agents from investing in large projects but where rich agents can use a technology to monitor poor agents working as wage earners. That is, there are three possible occupations in their model (unlike in the previous model where everybody was an entrepreneur): wage earners (who are too poor to make any investment on their own), self-employed (who finance and run their own investment) and entrepreneurs (who finance large investments and monitor wage earners).[10] The equilibrium wage rate v_t is determined by the equality between the number of agents 'choosing' to become wage earners and the number of wage earners required by entrepreneurs, and thus depends on the entire wealth distribution $F_t(w)$. One can easily see how this can generate long-run effects of the initial wealth distribution: an initially large mass of poor agents with no other option than becoming a wage earner leads to a low wage rate and little upward mobility for wage earners, while an initially small mass of poor agents leads to high wage rates and high mobility between wage earners and self-employed, which reproduces the forces leading to high wage rates.

At this stage, it is fair to say that the properties of credit-rationing models of income distribution are well understood at a theoretical level. However, much more empirical work remains to be done in order to convince ourselves that these inequality and mobility traps are indeed relevant and that some specific policies of credit subsidies or wealth redistribution might be appropriate. First, we need to know more about the magnitude of actual credit constraints: we know that they exist from indirect evidence such as that about parental wealth and children's education investment,[11] but to my knowledge there exists no systematic study about the actual policies of existing credit institutions (how do collateral requirements differ across investment projects, across countries?).[12]

Next, we need to know whether these credit constraints are sufficiently large so that their interaction with actual wealth distributions can generate traps of the type described above. We already know that this is plausible: historians cite France vs England. Note, however, that this empirical work can more easily be done for traps based on accumulation thresholds, since they do not require looking at the formation of prices on the capital and labour markets.

3 LOCAL SEGREGATION

The importance of social segregation in spatially distinct neighbourhood has been stressed by sociological research for a long time.[13] However it is only in the past few years that formal economic models of income distribution have started to integrate the determinants and consequences of spatial segregation. These models tell us under what conditions laissez-faire spatial segregation is socially inefficient and identify the exact parameters that we need to estimate in order to know in which case we are.

Consider first the following transparent model due to Benabou (1993a): agents must choose to live in one of two spatially distinct neighbourhoods and whether to obtain a low education (cost C_L) or a high education (cost C_H); these costs $C_L(x)$ and $C_H(x)$ depend negatively upon the fraction x of one's neighbours choosing to obtain a high education, reflecting the positive external effects of education on one's neighbours (in the classroom, as a role model, ...). Whether or not it is socially optimal to get all agents choosing a high education to live in the same neighbourhood depends on the slope of the total educational cost function $C(x) = xC_H(x) + (1 - x) C_L(x)$: if $C(x)$ is convex, then for any given optimal number of high-education agents it is less costly to divide them equally between the two neighbourhoods, and conversely segregation is optimal if $C(x)$ is concave.

The key point is that whether segregation or integration will prevail in laissez-faire equilibrium depends on a different condition: Benabou shows that whenever $C_H'(x) < C_L'(x)$, i.e., the marginal benefits of having more educated neighbours are higher if you choose high education, then integration is inherently unstable and market forces push towards stable segregation. The intuition is that if the two neighbourhoods have initially a marginally different composition, this condition implies that high-education agents are ready to pay a marginally higher rent to live in the better neighbourhood, which leads to more segregation, and so on. The reason why the conditions for social optimality and decentralized equilibrium are different is that high-education agents only take into account their marginal benefits of moving to a better neighbourhood and do not internalize the marginal costs they impose on their initial neighbourhood by diminishing the fraction of high-education agents. The failure of the price system is that the housing market does not charge the true social costs of moving: market rents are the same for everybody, whereas a socially-optimal price system should charge a higher rent to high-education movers to a high-education area (or, alternatively, a lower rent to high-education movers to a low-education area). These two conditions also highlight what typical situations lead to inefficient segregation: if $C_H'(x) < C_L'(x)$ but both slopes are very close, then $C(x)$ will be convex if $C_H(x)$ and $C_L(x)$ are convex, i.e., if the benefits of living with educated people exhibit decreasing returns; conversely if these returns are increasing segregation will be socially optimal, and so will be the decentralized equilibrium.[14]

In Benabou's model, the forces behind segregation are the pure forces of local externalities (peer effects) and the housing market. This can be extended in several directions: first, segregation could be supported by other institutions than a competitive housing market, such as the possiblity for local communities to enact zoning regulations, which will in general exacerbate inefficient segregation.[15] Next, individual motives for segregation can be more complex than direct peer effects: if each community decides how much fiscal revenue to allocate to schools, then this creates an incentive to locate in a wealthy neighborhood, even if there are no direct peer effects in the classroom.[16] Whether segregation will take place and whether it is efficient then depend on the shape of the marginal benefits of having better-funded schools, just as in the Benabou model. Note also that forces behind inefficient segregation always tend to be magnified by imperfect capital markets: if one adds to the Benabou model that agents are intially unequal and face credit constraints, then poor agents might be unable to move to a better neighbourhood even if $C_H'(x) > C_L'(x)$, i.e., even if their marginal benefits of moving are higher. Dynamic extensions of these models also help to identify other key parameters: Benabou (1993b) shows that even in cases where for a given initial level of human capital inequality segregation leads to higher output, segregation can actually be dynamically inefficient because by increasing future human capital inequality it reduces long-run output and growth; the magnitude of these different effects depends on the exact elasticities of the production function.[17]

Just as for the topic of the previous section, these theories of local segregation tend to be ahead of measurement: the Benabou model provides a powerful rationale for radical policies like generalized busing or housing policies, but we do not know whether the right parameter conditions are met in practice. At least, past research tells us that this is plausible: there is a long tradition of empirical research arguing that direct financial transfers to the schools of poor neighbourhoods have a limited effect on educational achievement, thereby suggesting that the 'quality' of one's classmates matters more than the amount of money allocated to schools and that only busing or housing policies can counteract these peer effects.[18] The availability of large panel data sets with information about several generations and about neighbourhoods now makes possible to better estimate the magnitude of neighbourhood effects: Cooper *et al.* (1994) find in PSID data that for a given parental income group the intergenerational correlation of incomes can vary by a factor of 2 depending on the average income of the parents' neighbourhood. However these results do not allow us to distinguish between different channels of neighbourhood effects: more micro data about educational achievement are needed to estimate the parameters identified by the theory.

The models described above all deal with a specific level of local externalities (namely, neighbourhood and schooling) and analyze the endogenous division of the population between different groups and the consequences for the dynamics of inequality. The same task can be undertaken for other levels of local externalities, like the family and the firm. At the level of the family, Meyer (1995) shows how divorce leads to a higher correlation of income and human capital levels between spouses, because more information about others' permanent attributes have been accumulated by the age of divorce. She also shows that almost half of the total increase of US household income inequality in the past 20 years is due to the increase in the correlation between spouses' incomes, and that almost 40 per cent of the rise in this correlation is due to this 'divorce effect'. Kremer (1995) suggests that a cumulative mechanism might exist along similar lines: higher human capital inequality increases the incentives to marry with someone of similar human capital level, which in turn generates higher human capital inequality between children, and so on. Kremer illustrates these perverse dynamics by contrasting the US case with that of Brazil.

At the level of the firm, Kremer and Maskin (1995) show that higher human capital inequality also increases the incentives of high-skill workers to break away from low-skill workers and work together. If human capital acquisition is influenced by one's co-workers (just as by one's neighbours and one's parents), then this can also generate perverse, cumulative dynamics. They show that this process might be quite relevant to account for the recent evolution of US wage inequality.[19]

4 SELF-FULFILLING INEQUALITY AND REDISTRIBUTIVE TOOLS

One of the most widely held economic principles about inequality and redistribution is that if governments want to reduce inequality they should do so through a system of taxes and transfers conditional solely on incomes obtained on the market, and not by trying to influence directly the productive sphere and the formation of prices. Of course, the existence of imperfections such as credit constraints or local externalities can justify using more complex tools such as credit subsidies or housing policy. However we observe many other redistributive tools in the real world, many of which seem hard to justify on economic grounds. For example, it is not obvious why quota-type affirmative action is an efficient way to redistribute towards minorities, as opposed to direct income transfers.

This latter issue has been addressed by Coate and Loury (1993). They start with a model of persistent inequality borrowed from the statistical theory of discrimination:[20] two racial groups (say, the blacks and the whites) have the same distribution $G(c)$ of cost c to become a qualified worker, but employers only observe a noisy signal θ of workers' qualification; under appropriate assumptions there exists a discriminatory hiring policy (θ_B,θ_w) which is self-fulfilling: employers promote to qualified tasks black workers with a $\theta \geq \theta_B$ and white workers with a $\theta \geq \theta_w < \theta_B$, which induces black workers to become qualified less often than the whites (the threshold cost c_B is lower than c_w), which in turn validates employers' discriminatory priors.

Coate and Loury then ask: what policy can break this inefficient equilibrium? The ideal policy would be to force employers to use the same testing requirements $\theta_B = \theta_w$, which would immediately annihilate racial inequality. However they argue that this is not enforceable, and that in practice affirmative action policies look much more like quotas: employers must end up with the same distribution of black and white workers in their qualified and unqualified tasks. Coate and Loury then distinguish between two cases. First, they show that if initial discrimination is not complete, in the sense that a positive fraction of black workers ends up in qualified tasks, then quota-type policies are generally dominated by a policy of state-financed income subsidy to black workers promoted to qualified tasks, which would gradually eliminate discrimination. The intuition is that quotas can lead to 'patronizing' hiring policies whereby employers reduce their standards θ_B so much in order to meet the quota that black workers have even less incentive to become qualified than in the previous situation. However, if we start from a situation where θ_B is so high that no black worker is allocated to qualified tasks (complete discrimination), then quota-type affirmative action is the only way to make progress. In any case, note that the optimal policy tool (race-specific income subsidies to promotion or quotas) would be difficult to justify without a model of racial inequality based upon self-fulfilling beliefs.

As is always the case with statistical discrimination, one can apply this same logic to other observationally distinguishable groups than blacks and whites. For example, Acemoglu (1994) shows that in a model where employers observe imperfectly whether unemployed have paid the cost to recover their skills, an equilibrium where unemployed do not incur this cost and are discriminated against by employers can be supported by self-fulfilling beliefs; he then shows how this can justify policies of positive discrimination towards long-term unemployed, although such policies would seem inefficient in a model where the latter are simply less productive.

I believe that one can learn a lot by applying this same methodology to similar issues: the fact that persistent inequality can be generated through various mechanisms of self-fulfilling beliefs can possibly justify the existence of many other redistributive tools that would otherwise appear seriously inefficient. For example, one can show that the (rational) process of learning the relative importance of individual effort and pre-determined factors (luck ...) for becoming rich can generate persistent inequality between otherwise identical dynasties: 'left-wing' dynasties believe less in effort and are less often upwardly-mobile than 'right-wing' dynasties, whatever the truth might be.[21] Such a situation can generate a rationale for negative marginal income tax rates, of the type used in the United States with EITC,[22] in order to induce those dynasties that are viewed by the majority as underestimating effort to put more effort and learn that it pays off. In a world where persistent inequality is simply the product of fixed ability differentials, such negative marginal rates seem hard to justify: most distributive justice theories would prescribe that transfers decline monotonically with market income.[23]

At this stage, it is still the case that looking at the way redistribution is actually carried out raises a lot of unexplained puzzles. In general, direct income transfers raise much less enthusiasm than their presumed efficiency properties would suggest: French farmers do not want income transfers in exchange for producing less, they want to be able to produce and sell their production at a 'fair' price; similar types of behaviour exist within the unskilled almost everywhere.[24] This is probably the single largest gap between economic theory and the way economic agents behave. The right answer has probably something to do with the fact that agents care about 'status', and that the latter is largely correlated with labour market earnings. Whether formal models can help us to make progress on this front remains to be established. Unlike the first two topics covered in this survey, this is an area where empirical knowledge seems to be ahead of theory.

Notes

1. See the relevant chapters in A. B. Atkinson and F. Bourguignon (eds), *Handbook of Income Distribution* (Amsterdam: North Holland), forthcoming 1998, for surveys designed to cover the entire literature.
2. According to Marx and many other socialist theorists, initial wealth and capital ownership *per se* determine power relationships on the workplace: this could not happen in a world of neoclassical, first-best credit markets where initial wealth *per se* is irrelevant from the viewpoint of productive efficiency. Given the underdeveloped financial systems surrounding them,

nineteenth-century theorists do not even refer to the concept of credit constraints, although it is implicit in their analysis.

3. Where s is the savings rate and δ is the depreciation rate.
4. Where θ is the rate of time preference.
5. With linear savings, all individual wealth levels converge towards the same wealth level $w^* = k^*$, irrespective of $F_0(w)$. With dynastic preferences, any distribution $F(w)$ whose average wealth equals k^* is a steady-state distribution. In both cases, wealth dispersion is irrelevant for long-run output and capital stock. Note that things would be different with a convex, exogenous savings function $S(y)$, see Bourguignon (1981) (this case is somewhat similar in spirit to the case of poverty traps described below).
6. A formal dynamic model of such poverty traps was first proposed by Galor and Zeira (1993), who choose to interpret the fixed-size investment as a human capital investment. The model that follows is essentially similar to theirs.
7. For an endogenous derivation of such a curve, see Piketty (1992), whose moral-hazard credit model is taken from Aghion and Bolton (1991).
8. See Piketty (1992).
9. This is obviously not the only development pattern that the interaction between equilibrium interest rate, wealth distribution and credit constraints can generate. For example, Aghion and Bolton (1991) do not consider the long-run effects of initial wealth dispersion and concentrate on the endogenous Kuznets curve implied by credit constraints and a dropping interest rate (at a low development stage, interest rates are high and inequality rises, before the rich accumulate, the interest rate drops and inequality diminishes).
10. On the concept of poverty implied by this process of occupational 'choice', see Banerjee and Newman (1994). This typology of occupational choice based solely upon endogenous incentive constraints and the wealth distribution has been extended by Legros and Newman (1994): they allow poor agents to form partnerships to be able to invest, in contrast to 'hierarchical' firms where one rich agent makes the investment and monitors poor wage earners. They show that hierarchical firms will tend to dominate in equilibrium even though partnerships lead to higher output (there is no labour wasted in monitoring) and are incentive-compatible, essentially because rich agents use hierarchical firms to extract a larger share of a smaller pie.
11. There exists a long tradition of sociological research showing that for given school tests at the age of 10 children from lower parental strata tend to end their education earlier. Obviously, this does not distinguish between credit constraints and differences in motivation and 'reference group'. See, e.g., Boudon (1973).
12. For example the recent empirical literature on the 'credit crunch' shows that investment behaviour depends crucially on the current net wealth and that the toughness of these credit constraints varies substantially along the business cycle and across different types of firms, but without analyzing the actual credit policies of banks. On this literature, see Bernanke and Gertler (1993).
13. Dating back at least to the Chicago School of sociology between the two world wars.

14. Assume for example $C_L(x) = (1 - a)C_H(x) - c$, with a sufficiently close to 0. Then $C''(x) = C_H(x)''(x) - ad^2((1 - x)C_H(x))/dx^2$, which is arbitrarily close to $C_H''(x)$.
15. Zoning regulations allow local communities to restrict access to their neighbourhood to agents meeting specific criteria of income, age, children, landowner/tenant status ... See Durlauf (1993) and Fernandez and Rogerson (1993a) for such models.
16. See Fernandez and Rogerson (1993b) and Benabou (1993a, 1993b) for an explicit modelling of this fiscal channel for segregation.
17. See also the dynamic model of Fernandez and Rogerson (1993b), who calibrate their model to US data to estimate the output gain of a switch from local education financing to national education financing.
18. The Coleman Report (USGPO 1966) first pointed out the limited effects of financial tranfers to poor schools on educational achievement. This literature has generally been used to argue that we should stop wasting money and forget about altering human capital inequality, although another reading is that it points towards more radical policies. See however Card and Krueger (1992) for a criticism of these estimates: they find much larger effects by using after-school wages rather than standardized tests.
19. Kremer and Maskin show that in almost every production sector the variance of the distribution of firm-level mean wages has increased much more rapidly than the mean variance of the firm-level distribution of wages. Kramarz, Lolliven and LePele (1995) obtain similar conclusions with French data.
20. See Arrow (1973) and Phelps (1968).
21. For such a model based upon rational Bayesian learning, see Piketty (1995). See also the quasi-rational model of Roemer and Wets (1994), where agents learn about the convex relationship between human capital investment and market income through linear extrapolation of the (human capital investment, income) pair of their social neighbourhood.
22. EITC (Earned Income Tax Credit) is the rapidly growing US system of subsidies to low market incomes. In 1996, the transfer will be equal to 40 per cent of earned incomes below \$9110 per year (a maximum transfer of \$3644) before declining at a 21 per cent rate between \$11 900 and \$29 200 per year. Thus the \$0–9110 income interval benefits from a 40 per cent negative marginal tax rate. The effects on labour market participation seem substantial (see Eissa and Liebman, 1995).
23. In a Mirrlees-type framework with pure productivity differentials, both the Rawlsian and the utilitarian optima involve positive marginal rates along the entire tax schedule (though not necessarily monotonic).
24. For an analysis of similar behaviour, see Kahneman *et al.* (1986) and Akerlof and Yellen (1990).

References

Acemoglu, D. (1994) 'Public Policy in a Model of Long-Term Unemployment', Cambridge, MA: MIT mimeo.

Aghion, P. and P. Bolton (1991) 'A Trickle-Down Theory of Growth Development with Debt Overhang', LSE, mimeo.

Akerlof, G. and J. Yellen (1990) 'The Fair Wage–Effort Hypothesis and Unemployment', *Quarterly Journal of Economic*, vol. 10, pp. 255–83.

Arrow, K. (1973), 'The Theory of Discrimination', in Ashenfelter, D. and Rees, A. (eds) *Discrimination in Labor Markets* Princeton: Princeton University Press).

Banerjee, A. and A. Newman (1993) 'Occupational Choice and the Process of Development', *Journal of Political Economy*, 101 (April), pp. 274–99.

Banerjee, A. and A. Newman (1994), 'Poverty, Incentives and Development', *American Economic Review*, vol. 84–2, pp. 211–16.

Benabou, R. (1993a), 'Workings of a City: Location, Education, Production', *Quarterly Journal of Economics*, vol. 108, pp. 619–53.

Benabou, R. (1993b), 'Heterogeneity, Stratification and Growth', New York University, mimeo.

Benabou, R. (1994), 'Human Capital, Inequality and Growth: the Local Connection', *European Economic Review*, vol. 38, pp. 817–26.

Bernanke, R. and R. Gertler (1993), 'The Financial Accelerator and the Flight to Quality', Princeton and New York Universities, mimeo.

Boudon, R. (1973) *L'inégalité des chances* (Paris: Armand Colin, Collection 'U').

Bourguignon, F. (1981) 'Pareto-Superiority of Unegalitarian Equilibria in Stiglitz's Model of Wealth Distribution with Convex Savings Function', *Econometrica*, vol. 49, pp. 1469–75.

Card, D. and A. Krueger (1992) 'Does School Quality Matter?', *Journal of Political Economy*, vol. 100, 1–40.

Coate, S. and G. Loury (1993) 'Will Affirmative-Action Policies Eliminate Negative Stereotypes?', *American Economic Review*, vol. 83, pp. 1220–40.

Cooper, S., S. Durlauf and P. Johnson (1994) 'On the Transmission of Economic Status across Generations', University of Wisconsin, mimeo.

Durlauf, S. (1993) 'A Theory of Persistent Inequality', University of Wisconsin, mimeo.

Eissa, N. and J. Liebman (1995) 'Labor Supply Response to the EITC', Harvard University, mimeo.

Fernandez, R. and R. Rogerson (1993a) 'Keeping People Out: Income Distribution, Zoning and the Quality of Public Education', New York University, mimeo.

Fernandez, R. and R. Rogerson (1993b) 'The Political Economy of Education Finance Reform', mimeo.

Galor, O. and J. Zeira (1993), 'Income Distribution and Macroeconomics', *Review of Economic Studies*, vol. 60, pp. 35–52.

Kahneman, D., J. Knetsch and R. Thaler (1986), 'Fairness as a Constraint on Profit-Seeking: Entitlements on the Market', *American Economic Review*, vol. 76, pp. 728–41.

Kramarz, F., S. Lolliven and L. LePele (1995) 'Wage Inequalities and Firm-Specific Competition in France, Paris: INSEE, mimeo

Kremer, M. (1995), 'The Dynamics of Inequality: US vs Brazil', mimeo.

Kremer, M. and E. Maskin (1995), 'Segregation by Skill and the Rise in Inequality', Harvard University and MIT, mimeo.

Legros, P. and A. Newman (1994) 'Wealth Effects and the Theory of Organisation', Columbia University, mimeo.

Meyer, C. (1995), 'Income Distribution and Family Structure', PhD dissertation, MIT.

Phelps, E. (1968) 'The Statistical Theory of Racism and Sexism, *American Economic Review*, vol. 62, pp. 657–61.

Piketty, T. (1992), 'Imperfect Capital Markets and Persistence of Initial Wealth Inequalities', *Working Paper*, LSE/STICERD TE/92/255; revised version, 'The Dynamics of the Wealth Distribution and the Interest Rate with Credit-Rationing', *Review of Economic Studies*, vol. 64, 1997, pp. 173–89.

Piketty, T. (1995), 'Social Mobility and Redistributive Politics', *Quarterly Journal of Economics*, vol. 110, pp. 551–84.

Roemer, J. and R. Wets (1994), 'Neighbourhood Effects on Belief Formation and the Distribution of Education and Income', University of California at Davis.

USGPO (1966) *Equality of Educational Opportunity* (Washington, DC: US Government Printing Office).

3 The International Evidence on Income Distribution in Modern Economies: Where Do We Stand?

Timothy M. Smeeding
SYRACUSE UNIVERSITY, USA

and

Peter Gottschalk
BOSTON COLLEGE, USA

1 INTRODUCTION[1]

Interest in cross-national comparison of personal income distributions, low relative incomes, and income inequality in general has grown dramatically during the past five years. Interest in cross-national distribution research did not come about by accident; several factors helped propel this line of research in the 1980s and 1990s. First of all, income distributions in the United States, the United Kingdom, and in several other nations began to trend toward greater inequality in a systematic and secular pattern, and the inequality-generating pressures of a rapidly internationalizing highly technical economy were felt in several modern nations. Second, the former state socialist nations of Central and Eastern Europe (CEE) began a still continuing process of economic and social adjustment and transition to a new socioeconomic order. While this transition is still underway, CEE nations have experienced large changes in both real income levels and in income distribution. Third, along with the rise in inequality, a growing interest in the question of 'fairness' *vis-à-vis* 'budget pressures' was present in the national political debates of the late 1980s and early 1990s, thus making 'income distribution' a legitimate realm of political inquiry.

Finally, the emergence of comparable cross-national data on distribution allowed for comparisons of similarities and differences across countries and over time. Similarities and differences in experiences help us understand how market forces, demographic forces and public policy affect the relative economic status of various groups in each nation.

This brief chapter summarizes and provides limited updates on a small part of what was learned in a large study undertaken for the OECD (Atkinson, Rainwater, and Smeeding, 1995), and a subsequent review article (Gottschalk and Smeeding, 1996). It also adds recent material for CEE nations (Torrey, Smeeding and Bailey, 1996) and for Taiwan (Republic of China).

Lessons learned from international income comparisons are heavily dependent on the underlying quality and comparability of the income data on which they rest. While all estimates of 'income' are subject to choice of data and measurement techniques, many of these choices lead to findings which, on closer examination, are found to be mere statistical artifacts rather than genuine economic regularities. The value of empirical contributions has more often been found in the theoretical processes used to explain them than in the empirical observation itself. It can be argued that the contribution of Kuznets' Presidential Address to the American Economic Association lay in his analytical framework of income distribution rather than in the much celebrated Kuznets curve indicating that inequality first rises and then falls as a country develops. While several recent writers claim to have evidence which contradicts the Kuznets curve (e.g., Milanovic, 1995), advances in the theory of income distribution have not moved much beyond Kuznets over the past 40 years (Atkinson, 1994).

This chapter starts therefore from a position of caution as to what can be achieved by a summary of the empirical evidence. Not the least of the reasons for this caution are the difficulties in making choices about concepts of measurement. Because of space constraints, we are unable to document all of the limitations and footnotes that go into the data sets presented here. In particular, we have not been able to verify the quality of the CEE data sets by comparing them with administrative records due mainly to the paucity of these records. However, the quality of data from the Luxembourg Income Study for OECD nations can be more fully investigated in Atkinson *et al.* (1995, Chapters 2, 3 and Appendices). We begin with our choice of measures and a more general listing of cautions in Section 2. The second difficulty in writing a paper on 'empirical facts' is that these have many dimensions. Here we have chosen to concentrate on the comparison of two dimensions: market and disposable income inequality across countries, and time. Section 2 covers the specific terms and definitions used to make these comparisons.[2]

Section 3 summarizes, for a range of nations, the extent of income inequality in the 1980s and early 1990s and its trend. One question to be asked is: can one identify distinct groupings of countries with different degrees of inequality? Section 4 briefly discusses the trend in inequality in recent years, and asks if there is a world-wide trend toward greater inequality or whether a particular set of countries is different. Section 5 addresses some of the factors that seem to have affected inequality: differences in market incomes, demographic factors, and then government intervention (direct taxes and transfers). The final section (6) summarizes the chapter and offers suggestions for additional research.

2 CHOICES AND MEASURES

There are currently no international standards for income distribution which parallel the international standards used for systems of national income accounts.[3] Hence, researchers need to decide what they want to measure and how far they can measure it on a comparable basis. The Luxembourg Income Study (LIS) offers the reader many choices of perspective in terms of country, income measure, accounting unit, and time frame, but its relatively short time frame (1979–93 for most nations, but 1968–95 for five countries) and limited number of observation periods per country (three – five periods per country at present) currently limits its usefulness for studying longer-term trends in income distribution. The purpose of this section of the chapter is to explain the choices we have made in our use of LIS. The choices others have made to study longer-term trends in income distribution are discussed in Gottschalk and Smeeding (1997).

2.1 Choices: Inequality of What among Whom on What Terms?

Our attention is focused primarily on the distribution of *disposable money income*, that is income after direct taxes and including transfer payments. Several points should be noted:

a. Income rather than consumption is taken as the indicator of resources, although there may be both theoretical and empirical arguments favouring use of the latter.
b. The definition of income falls considerably short of the Haig–Simons comprehensive definition, typically excluding much of capital gains,

imputed rents, home production, and most of income in-kind (with the exception of near-cash benefits).

c. No account is taken of indirect taxes or of the benefits from public spending (other than cash and near-cash transfers) such as health care, education, or most housing subsidies.
d. The period of income measurement is in general the calendar year with income measured on an annual basis (although the UK evidence relates to weekly or monthly income).

Thus, variables measured may be less than ideal and results may not be fully comparable across countries. For example, one country may help low-income families through money benefits (included in cash income), whereas another provides subsidized housing, child care, or education (which is not taken into account). While a recent study (Smeeding *et al.*, 1993) finds that the distribution of housing, education and health care benefits reinforces the general differences in income distribution for a subset of the western nations examined here, there is no guarantee that these relationships hold for alternative countries or methods of accounting.[4] Still this study shows that countries which spend more for cash benefits tend to also spend more for non-cash benefits. Because non-cash benefits are more equally distributed than are cash benefits, levels of inequality within countries are lessened, but the same rank ordering of these countries with respect to inequality levels that is found here using cash alone persists when non-cash benefits are added in.

Market income, which includes earned income from wages and salaries and self-employment, cash property income (but not capital gains or losses) and other private cash income transfers (occupational pensions, alimony, and child support), is the primary source of disposable income for most non-elderly families. To reach disposable income, governments add public transfer payments (social retirement, family allowances, unemployment compensation, welfare benefits) and deduct personal income tax and social security contributions from market income. Near-cash benefits – those which are virtually equivalent to cash (food stamps in the United States and housing allowances in the United Kingdom and Sweden) are also included in the disposable income measure.[5] And differences between disposable and market income capture the net effects of income redistribution.

The question of distribution 'among whom' is here given the simplest answer – among individuals. When assessing disposable income inequality, however, the unit of aggregation is the household: the incomes of all household members are aggregated and then divided by an equivalence scale to arrive at individual equivalent income. The choice of the household, rather than a narrower unit such as the spending unit or the family, is open to debate. It captures the economies of scale inherent or implicit in shared living arrangements, but it assumes a degree of income-sharing within the household that may not be realized. Moreover, the choice of unit may affect comparisons across countries in light of different household structures. For the most part, the household – all persons sharing the same housing unit regardless of familial relationship – is the common unit of analysis. However, for Sweden and Canada more restrictive nuclear family (Sweden) and economic family (Canada) definitions of the accounting unit are necessary (see Atkinson, Rainwater and Smeeding, 1995, Chapter 2, for additional details). These restrictions probably overstate the amount of household-based inequality in each of these two nations.[6]

2.2 Measurement Approach and Comparability

The approach adopted here, based in large part on data from LIS, overcomes some, but not all, of the problems of making comparisons across countries and across time that plagued earlier studies. Some problems, e.g., the use of data from different types of sources, still remain. But most of the data are now drawn from household income surveys, or their equivalent, and in no case are synthetic data used.[7] The main qualification concerns the French data, which come from tax records that have been augmented to reflect income transfer receipt.

One major advantage of LIS is the availability of micro-data. The aim of the LIS project has been to assemble a single data base containing survey data from many countries that is as consistent as possible. Access to the micro-data means that it is possible to produce results on the same basis, starting from individual household records, and to test their sensitivity to alternative choices of units, definition, and other concepts. It is therefore possible to make any desired adjustment for household size. Aggregate adjustments, such as that from pre-tax (market income) to post-tax (disposable) income are not necessary, although in some cases imputations are necessary at the household level.[8] The data all cover, at least in principle, the whole noninstitutionalized population as well.

The aim of the LIS project is to increase the degree of cross-national comparability, but complete cross-national comparability is not possible, even if we were to administer our own surveys in each nation. Comparability is a matter of degree, and all that one can hope for is to reach an acceptably high level. It is left to the reader to decide if the level of comparability found in this study is acceptable. Moreover, many of the cross-national results provided here have been reviewed by a team of national experts – statisticians, social scientists and policy analysts – prior to their publication by OECD and in other forums. This painstaking two-year process helped improve the quality of the analysis while also testing the mettle of both the analysts and the reviewers. In some nations, we only update the OECD results to a later year using the same national data base. Finally, our results for CEE nations have been reviewed by teams of country experts, but not by national authorities.

3 INCOME INEQUALITY IN 25 NATIONS

The LIS data sets have been used here to compare the distribution of disposable income in 25 nations over a 5–10-year period.[9] The numbers presented are taken from the most recent LIS data and correspond generally to the results found in Atkinson, Rainwater and Smeeding (1995), which use earlier years' LIS data in most cases. Figure 3.1 shows the percentiles of the distribution as percentages of the median, where P_{10} is considered 'low,' P_{90} 'high'. The ratio of high to low (decile ratio) is also shown. For instance, the high to low ratio in Russia is 6.83, indicating that a person in a high-income family at the 90th percentile enjoys almost seven times the income of a low-income family of equivalent size at the 10th percentile.

Russia has the highest decile ratio at 6.84 followed by the United States (5.67) with the second largest value recorded in Figure 3.1, the next largest being Australia with a value of 4.26. The lower part of the distribution of disposable income as shown under the low column appears to be substantially different in Russia (35) and in the United States (37) with the closest other nations being Australia (45) and Canada (47). Low-income units have living standards in excess of 50 per cent for most other nations, up to 59 per cent in Belgium, Luxembourg and the Netherlands and 65/66 per cent in the Czech and Slovak Republics. No doubt this difference owes in part to the relatively low values for P_{10} for the US earnings distribution, which is attributable to both low wages and to the weakness of the US incomes package for families with children and the aged at this income level (Rainwater and Smeeding, 1995; Gottschalk and Smeeding, 1997; Smeeding, Rainwater and Torrey, 1993). In Russia the basic safety net to the poor and the aged and nominally fixed state-sector wages have been ravaged by inflation and the socioeconomic upheaval.

The relative incomes of the rich are highest in Russia, where a person at the 90th percentile has 2.39 times the median person's income and nearly seven times as much as a low-income person. The value of US relative income at the 90th percentile point is 2.07 times the median, while that

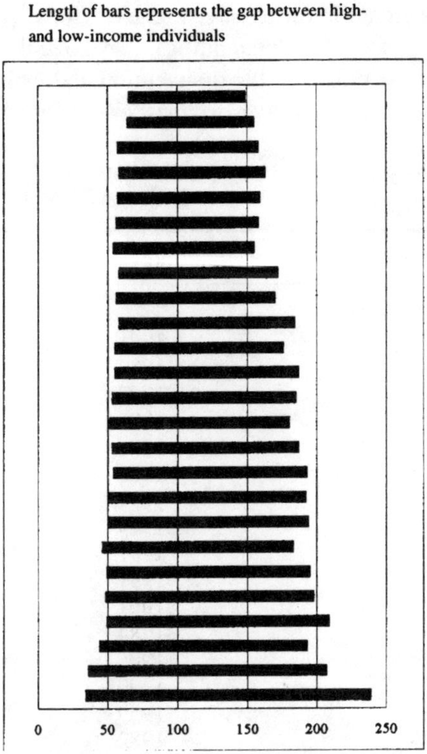

Country	*Low*[a]	*High*[b]	*Ratio of high to low*[c]
Slovak Republic 1992	66	149	2.25
Czech Republic 1992	65	155	2.36
Finland 1991	58	158	2.71
Belgium 1992	59	163	2.76
Sweden 1992	58	159	2.77
Norway 1991	57	158	2.79
Denmark 1992	55	155	2.84
The Netherlands 1991	59	172	2.94
Germany 1984	57	170	2.98
Luxembourg 1985	59	184	3.12
Italy 1991	56	176	3.14
Austria 1987	56	187	3.34
Switzerland 1982	54	185	3.43
Hungary 1991	52	180	3.46
New Zealand 1987/88	54	187	3.46
France 1984	55	193	3.51
Poland 1992	51	192	3.76
United Kingdom 1986	51	194	3.80
Canada 1991	47	183	3.86
Republic of China/Taiwan 1991	50	195	3.90
Spain 1990	49	198	4.04
Ireland 1987	50	209	4.18
Australia 1989	45	193	4.26
United States 1991	37	207	5.67
Russia 1992	35	239	6.84
Average[a]	53	182	3.53

[a] Relative income for individuals who are lower than 90 per cent of the individuals in the country and higher than 10 per cent of the individuals, as a percentage of the national median.
[b] Relative income for individuals who are higher than 90 per cent of the individuals in the country and lower than 10 per cent of the individuals, as a percentage of the national median.
[c] Ratio of 90th to 10th percentiles, or decile ratio.
[d] Simple average, excluding United States.

Source: Authors' tabulation of data in the Luxembourg Income Study.

Figure 3.1 The gap between low- and high-income individuals, number given as percentage of median in each nation

found in Ireland is 2.09. Other nations with P_{90} values nearly twice the median include Spain (1.98) and Taiwan (1.95). The distribution at the top is noticeably less unequal in the Czech and Slovak Republics and in Scandinavia (Denmark, Finland, Norway and Sweden), followed by Belgium and Germany.

While percentile ratios have some obvious appeal (e.g., insensitivity to top coding, ease of understanding), they have the disadvantage of focusing on only a few points in the distribution and lack a normative basis. Table 3.1 presents an alternative Lorenz-based summary measure of inequality,

Table 3.1 Measures of inequality in OECD countries, in transition economies, in Taiwan and Israel

Country	*Year*	*Gini (1)*[a]	*Gini (2)*[b]
A. OECD countries			
Finland	1991	.223	.223
Austria[c]	1987	.227	.227
Sweden	1992	.229	.229
Belgium	1992	.230	.230
Norway	1991	.233	.233
Luxembourg	1985	.238	.238
Denmark	1992	.240	.239
Germany (West)	1984	.250	.249
Italy	1991	.255	.255
Netherlands	1991	.271	.268
Canada	1991	.286	.285
France	1984	.295	.294
United Kingdom	1986	.304	.303
Spain	1990	.308	.306
Australia	1989	.309	.308
Switzerland	1982	.323	.311
Ireland	1987	.330	.328
United States	1991	.343	.343
B. CEE Transition countries			
Slovak Republic	1992	.189	.189
Czech Republic	1992	.208	.207
Hungary	1991	.289	.289
Poland	1992	.291	.290
Russia	1992	.437	.393
C. Taiwan and Israel			
Republic of China/Taiwan	1991	.302	.300
Israel	1992	.305	.305

[a] Gini (1) = Gini coefficient for equivalent disposable income (EI) where EI = DPI/S^E, S = family size, E = .5, person weighted, bottom coded at 1 per cent mean DPI.
[b] Gini (2) = Gini (1) top coded at 10 times median disposable income.
[c] Austria excludes the self-employed.

Source: Authors' tabulation of data in the Luxembourg Income Study.

the Gini coefficient, with countries grouped according to type (OECD, CEE, Taiwan, Israel).[10]

Among the OECD nations, the lowest Gini is found in Finland, followed by most, but not all, Scandinavian nations. Austria's figures must be treated with caution because of their exclusion of self-employment income, but they and the smaller Benelux nations come next, followed by West Germany, Italy, and The Netherlands. There is then a gap of 0.015 points to Canada and France. The United Kingdom, Spain, and Australia are next, with another gap of 0.014 to Switzerland, Ireland, and finally the United States. As measured by these Ginis, the range of inequality across OECD nations runs from 0.223 (Finland) to 0.343 (United States) or by as much as 54 per cent.

Turning to the CEE nations, income inequality for persons in the Czech and Slovak Republics is most similar to that found in the Scandinavian economies while Hungary and Poland are similar to France, Canada, Australia and the United Kingdom. Russia had the highest Gini as well as the highest rich to poor ratio of all countries for which we have LIS data in the 1990s. This is partially the result of some very high incomes since the Gini changes by a large fraction when we impose a top code of 10 times the median adjusted income in Russia, while other nations' estimates change little, if at all. Russia still has the highest Gini and the ranking of nations is unaffected.

Based on these data, it appears that there is a wider range of disposable income inequality in the five CEE transition countries, including Russia, than in the major and much richer OECD nations based on these preliminary results. Finally, the Republic of China and Israel have inequality levels near the middle of the OECD range, with Ginis very similar to that found in the United Kingdom.

3.1 Absolute Comparisons of Income Inequality

Since countries differ substantially in terms of real GDP *per capita*, most authors have made comparisons across nations in nominal or relative terms. Measures of real or absolute income differences across nations are much more difficult because they require comparisons of purchasing power of currencies across nations. One problem is that the purchasing power parities (PPPs) used to compare real levels of GDP *per capita* or total consumption (including government spending on health, education, transportation) across nations are not designed for adjusting measures of disposable personal income such as those examined here. Nonetheless, such comparisons are at least implicitly made by analysts from rich nations who argue that the higher the average standard of living in a particular nation, the better off are its citizens. For example, because the United States real GDP *per capita* in 1993 was $24 750 as compared to say $17 750 in the United Kingdom, $15 230 in Finland, $18 050 in The Netherlands, and $18 070 in Italy, the United States is, 'on average,' better off than these nations (World Bank, 1995). It is interesting to ask how far that average advantage carries when one takes account of the wider dispersion in overall distribution in the United States. What has been implicitly assumed by analysts is that the higher US average standard of living extends to all levels of the income distribution.

We investigate this question by converting the median incomes of a set of rich nations, on which the percentile points in Figure 3.1 are based, into real US 1991 dollars using the Penn World Tables' purchasing power parities (Summers and Heston, 1991, see Figure 3.2). We then recompute median, high, and low incomes as a fraction of the US median. We show both the real US dollar gap (Panel A) and the resulting comparisons across countries at several percentile points with the United States set at 100 (Panel B).[11]

The real dollar gaps in Panel A are much closer at the bottom end of the scale than are those in Figure 3.1, because almost all of the nations shown in Figure 3.1 and Figure 3.2 are 'poorer' than the United States in terms of real GDP per person. Stated differently, both low and high disposable incomes fall as a per cent of the US median income. Of course, the rates of high to low income stay the same with both ends of the distribution being converted to US dollars using the same scale. As is often claimed, the United States has the highest median ('average') standard of living of the countries compared here (Panel B, middle column). The rankings of nations at the 50th percentile are therefore similar to those found when using GDP *per capita* (e.g., World Bank, 1995). However, the wider distribution of US incomes means that 'low-income' persons living in households at the P_{10} level in the United States had lower living standards than did similarly situated persons in each of the 10 other nations in the early 1990s. Despite the fact that the median American enjoyed a standard of living far above the median Finn (whose income per equivalent adult was only 77 per cent as high), Dutch (78 per cent as high), or Italian person (75 per cent as high), low-income Americans – at P_{10} – had living standards that were 22 per cent below that of low-income Finns, 24 per cent below low-income Dutch, and 15 per cent below the average income of the bottom quintile Italian. Only the Australians had incomes that were near those of the Americans at low income levels.

Real income comparisons move in both directions, however. At the other end of the scale, 'high-income' Americans enjoyed real living

A The real dollar gap between high- and low-income individuals (United States median = 100)

Country	*Low disposable income*[a]	*High disposable income*[b]	*Ratio of high to low incomes*
Finland 1991	45	122	2.74
Belgium 1992	49	135	2.76
Sweden 1992	49	136	2.77
Norway 1991	46	128	2.79
Denmark 1992	48	136	2.84
The Netherlands 1991	45	134	2.94
Italy 1991	42	132	3.14
Canada 1991	45	174	3.86
Australia 1989	38	161	4.26
United States 1991	37	207	5.67
Average[e]	45	146	3.12

Length of bars represents the gap between high- and low-income individuals

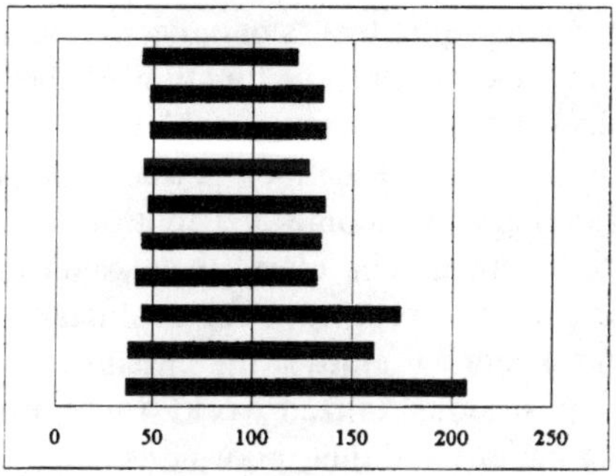

B Ratio of real income to US real income (United States = 100 at each point)

Country	*Low disposable income* (P_{10})	*Incomes at the median*[c] (P_{50})	*High disposable income*[b] (P_{90})	*Income of the rich* (P_{95})
Finland 1991	122	77	59	57
Belgium 1992	133	83	65	62
Sweden 1992	134	85	65	63
Norway 1991	125	81	62	59
Denmark 1992	131	88	66	62
The Netherlands 1991	124	78	64	64
Italy 1991	115	75	64	63
Canada 1991	123	95	84	82
Australia 1989	103	83	78	77
United States 1991	100	100	100	100
	123	83	67	65

[a] Relative income for individuals who are below 90 per cent of the individuals in the country and more affluent than 10 per cent of the individuals in the country. Numbers give real income (1991 US dollars) as a percentage of the US median.
[b] Relative income for individuals who are more affluent than 90 per cent of the individuals in the country and below 10 per cent of the individuals in the country. Numbers give real income (1991 US dollars) as a percentage of the US median.
[c] Numbers give real income (1991 US dollars) of the median individual in each country as a percentage of the US median.
[d] Numbers give real income (1991 US dollars) at the 95th percentile (individuals are more affluent than 95 per cent of the population) as a percentage of the US 95th percentile.
[e] Simple average, excluding United States.

Source: Authors' tabulation of data in the Luxembourg Income Study.

Figure 3.2 Real income distribution comparisons, all figures in 1991 US dollars

standards far above those experienced in other nations. At the P_{90} level, the real income of Americans was 50 per cent more than the average incomes of the rich in the other nations studied. At the very top of the distribution, the rich (P_{95} level), these differences remained the same or were further magnified.

Although we would argue that economic wellbeing in the most developed countries is most crucially a function of the individual's relative position in the distribution of income, real levels of living are also important in comparing income and wellbeing. Such comparisons allow one to balance off differences in income distribution with differences in real overall spendable income. The claim that 'America enjoys the highest standard of living in the world' must be evaluated alongside the equally valid claim that America enjoys the greatest level of real income inequality in the post-industrialized world – with their rich far better off than rich in other nations and their poor not so well off as are the poor in other nations.

In closing, we must reiterate a point made in passing above. Because countries differ in the way that they finance goods such as health care and education, and because they differ in the extent to which specific types of consumption are tax-subsidized, e.g., owned vs rented housing, these PPPs are less than ideal for adjusting disposable income for total control over resources – standard of living – across countries. The 'real income' measures above should therefore be seen as measures of net spendable income rather than measures of total consumption, the largest difference between the two concepts being goods and services such as health care, child care and education, which are provided at different prices and under different financing schemes in different nations.

Finally, we stress that we have not overcome any of the problems associated with PPP comparisons. All that we have done is to apply the PPP methodology to median disposable incomes and to different points in the income distribution.

4 THE COMPARATIVE TREND IN INCOME INEQUALITY

In this section we lay out the facts of how income inequality has changed over the past 15–25 years in major modern nations. The empirical evidence concerning recent trends in income inequality in different nations is summarized in Table 3.2.[12] While the various studies surveyed use different income and inequality measures and cover different periods, they are sufficiently robust to paint a picture of overall changes in inequality during the 1980s and into the early 1990s in a large number of nations.[13] These series give a reasonable span of years and the data themselves are internally over time. They, therefore, give an indication of the relative trends in different countries. We summarize these changes in Table 3.2 using a

Table 3.2 Changes in market and disposable income inequality[a]

Country[b]	*Years change*	*Market income inequality*[c]	*Disposable income inequality*
United Kingdom	1981–1991	+++	++++
United States	1980–1993	+++	+++
Sweden	1980–1992	+++	+++
Czech Republic	1980–1992	na	+++
Hungary	1989–1992	na	+++
Poland	1987–1992	na	++
Australia	1980/81–1989/90	++	++
Denmark	1981–1990	++	++
New Zealand	1981–1989	+	++
Japan	1981–1990	+	++
Slovak Republic	1980–1992	na	+
Netherlands	1981–1989	+	+
Norway	1982–1989	+	+
Belgium	1985–1992	+	+
Finland	1981–1992	+++	0
Canada	1980–1992	+	0
Israel	1979–1992	+	0
Ireland	1980–1987	+	0
West Germany	1983–1990	+	0
France	1979–1989	0	0
Republic of China	1981–1991	0	0
Portugal	1980–1990	0	0
Spain	1980–1990	n/a	0
Italy	1976–1991	–	–

[a] Degree of change is based on Table A-1 and is coded as follows:

Designation	*Interpretation*	*Range of change in Gini*
–	small decline	–5 per cent or more
0	zero	–4 to +4 per cent
+	small increase	5 to 10 per cent
++	moderate increase	10 to 15 per cent
+++	large increase	16 to 29 per cent
++++	extremely large increase	30 per cent or more

[b] For a complete listing of country sources, see Gottschalk and Smeeding (1997, tables 4 and B-1)

[c] Most studies show changes in market income inequality, while still others do not discuss market income changes at all. The latter are marked 'na'.

simple summary score based on the Gini coefficients that are used in all studies reviewed here. Countries are listed in order of change in disposable income inequality, from largest to least change. Where they are available from the same studies, we also present data on the trend in market income inequality in each nation.

Both the United Kingdom and the United States experienced a substantial rise in inequality during the 1980s, with the increase in the United Kingdom being much greater over this time period. Whereas trends in earnings inequality were similar in the United States and the United Kingdom, the time paths for changes in the distribution of family income were markedly different. In the United Kingdom income inequality fell through the mid-1970s but the Gini coefficient rose by more than 30 per cent between 1978 and 1991. This is almost double the increase over two decades in the United States, and more than double the decline in the United Kingdom from 1949 to 1976.

While starting from a much lower level of inequality, Sweden experienced a pattern of change in inequality similar to that in the United Kingdom, downward until 1981, then upward in the 1980s, with the sharpest increases in the early 1990s. The Swedish Gini increased by about 20 per cent from 1980 to 1992, though the Swedish income distribution remained considerably more equal than either that of the United States or the United Kingdom, in spite of these changes.[14]

The Czech Republic experienced a somewhat larger 25 per cent rise in inequality, more than that found in Sweden and the United States over exactly the same period. While 'market' income inequality in the Czech Republic was unmeasurable in 1980 because of the absence of a true labour market, this change in disposable income inequality over this period is less than that found in the United Kingdom (Torrey, Smeeding and Bailey, 1997). The changes experienced by Hungary and Poland – 28 and 12 per cent, respectively, over a shorter period (three and five years, respectively) – are closer to our expectations. While the Hungarian change is very large, the change found in Poland is not much different from that found in the United Kingdom over the 1981–6 period or in Sweden from 1988 to 1992.[15]

In Australia, Denmark and Japan (and in Poland, though over a shorter period), the upward trend over the 1980s is slightly less than that experienced in the United States and Sweden. The same is true in New Zealand, though all of the increases here came during the late 1980s (Saunders, 1994). In Belgium, The Netherlands, the Slovak Republic and Norway, the overall increase in inequality was just about 5 per cent from 1980 to 1990. In many nations – Canada, Ireland, Israel, Portugal, Taiwan, Finland

and France – there was little or no change in the 1980s and early 1990s. And income inequality actually declined slightly in Italy during the 1980s.

Our overall assessment is that any 1970s trend toward greater equality has ended in virtually all of the nations studied here, with the single exception of Italy. And there is a tendency for those nations with the most recent data to show rising disposable income inequality. Certainly market income trends show this type of change in most nations observed here. It may well be that the nations which have so far shown resistance to rising disposable income inequality may soon exhibit such trends.

It is also noteworthy that there appears to be no apparent relation between the *trend* over the 1980s and the *overall level* of inequality at the start of the period. Inequality has increased both in the United States, with a very high level of inequality even before the increase, and in Sweden, which started from a much lower level of inequality. Inequality has fallen in Italy, but risen in the United Kingdom, both occupying intermediate inequality positions in the mid-1980s (Figure 3.1).

Nor is there a consistent 'group country' story. Among the Scandinavian nations, Sweden experienced a rapid rise in inequality in the early 1990s, while Finland did not. In Europe we find large secular increases in inequality in the United Kingdom, small increases in Belgium and in The Netherlands, but stasis in Germany, Denmark, Portugal, Ireland and France, with secular decreases in Italy and Denmark. Canada experienced only mild increases in inequality of family income while the United States experienced much larger increases despite similar market forces affecting market incomes in both countries (Hanratty and Blank, 1993). And finally, if there is a regional pattern, it is to be found among the CEE nations, with inequality rising in Poland, Slovakia and the Czech Republic at the upper end of the range found in Western nations over similar periods, while Hungarian inequality appears to have risen more rapidly than in these other nations.

5 EXPLORING DIFFERENCES IN LEVELS AND TRENDS

The story of why we observe these differences in levels and trends in inequality is necessarily incomplete because of the confluence of market, demographic, institutional and policy changes. The inclusion of multiple income sources received by multiple individuals thwarts attempts to identify the causal links that lead to variations across countries and over time in the distribution of total post-tax and transfer family income. There is ample evidence that family members take account of all sources of income available to the family in deciding not only how much each member might work in a market setting, but also how to structure living arrangements. Moreover, governments themselves react differently to market income changes via changes in redistribution (tax and transfer) policy, and via other policies (e.g., macroeconomic policy or micro-policies such as government employment). This leads to decision-making processes that are much too complex to be treated in a unified causal framework at this time. We therefore limit ourselves to a simple descriptive exercise that focuses on the difference in inequality before and after government redistribution.

5.1 Differences in the Level of Inequality of Market Income and Disposable Income

Table 3.3 and Figure 3.3 show the Gini coefficient for market income (pre-tax and transfer) and for disposable income (post-tax and transfer). The difference between these two Ginis represents both the behavioural effect of taxes and transfers as well the direct effects of redistribution.

First of all, we note that the disposable personal income Gini (DPI) is not closely related to the level of inequality of market income (MI), both of which vary substantially across nations. Countries are ranked according to the DPI Ginis in Table 3.3, which also indicates the MI Gini, and differences between MI and DPI. This difference reflects the net effects of direct taxation (income taxes and employee social security taxes) and government transfer benefits and runs from 0.023 (Taiwan) to 0.245 (Sweden). The relationship between DPI and MI can be more clearly seen in Figure 3.3. For example, Finland, Italy, and Taiwan all have some of the lowest levels of inequality of market income (around 0.33), but they differ substantially in inequality of disposable income, with Finland achieving the lowest level (0.233) followed by Italy (0.255), and finally Taiwan with a DPI inequality measure of 0.302, not much different from the MI measure of 0.325. The lack of any clear pattern between inequality of market and disposable income is apparent in the low correlation between these two series (multiple correlation coefficient of 0.282). Similarly, Hungary, France, Poland and Canada all have DPI Ginis in the 0.285–0.295 range, but MI Ginis that run from 0.415 to 0.470.

These data suggest that there is a wide variety of experiences which underlies the differences between market income and disposable income inequality. Some of these differences may reflect differences in the willingness of governments to alter the pre-fiscal distribution of income. While differences may also reflect different behavioural responses to redistributive policies, we believe that much of the pattern reflects policy

Table 3.3 Inequality in disposable and market income and income redistribution in 24 nations

Country[a]	*Year*	*Abbreviation*	*DPI Gini*	*MI Gini*	*Difference*	*Income redistribution*[b]
Slovak Republic	1992	SR92	0.189	0.404	0.215	53.1
Czech Republic	1992	CZ92	0.208	0.413	0.206	49.8
Finland	1991	FI91	0.223	0.337	0.114	33.9
Sweden	1992	SW92	0.229	0.474	0.245	51.6
Belgium	1992	BE92	0.230	0.456	0.226	49.6
Norway	1991	NO91	0.233	0.378	0.145	38.4
Luxembourg	1985	LX85	0.238	0.380	0.142	37.4
Denmark	1992	DK92	0.240	0.436	0.196	45.0
Germany	1984	GE84	0.250	0.428	0.178	41.6
Italy	1991	IT91	0.255	0.330	0.075	22.8
Netherlands	1991	NL91	0.270	0.414	0.143	34.5
Canada	1991	CN91	0.286	0.415	0.129	31.1
Hungary	1991	HU91	0.289	0.493	0.204	41.4
Poland	1992	PL92	0.291	0.446	0.156	34.9
France	1984	FR84	0.295	0.470	0.175	37.2
Taiwan	1991	RC91	0.302	0.325	0.023	7.0
United Kingdom	1986	UK86	0.304	0.488	0.185	37.8
Israel	1992	IS92	0.305	0.453	0.147	32.6
Spain	1990	SP90	0.308	0.429	0.121	28.1
Australia	1990	AS90	0.309	0.437	0.128	29.3
Switzerland	1982	CH82	0.323	0.406	0.083	20.4
Ireland	1987	IR87	0.330	0.503	0.174	34.5
United States	1991	US91	0.343	0.449	0.107	23.7
Russia RLMS	1992	RL92	0.440	0.549	0.110	20.0

[a] Austria is omitted.
[b] Income redistribution is measured by the percentage reduction from MI Gini to DPI Gini (i.e. [(MI – DPI)/MI]) 100.

Source: Luxembourg Income Study.

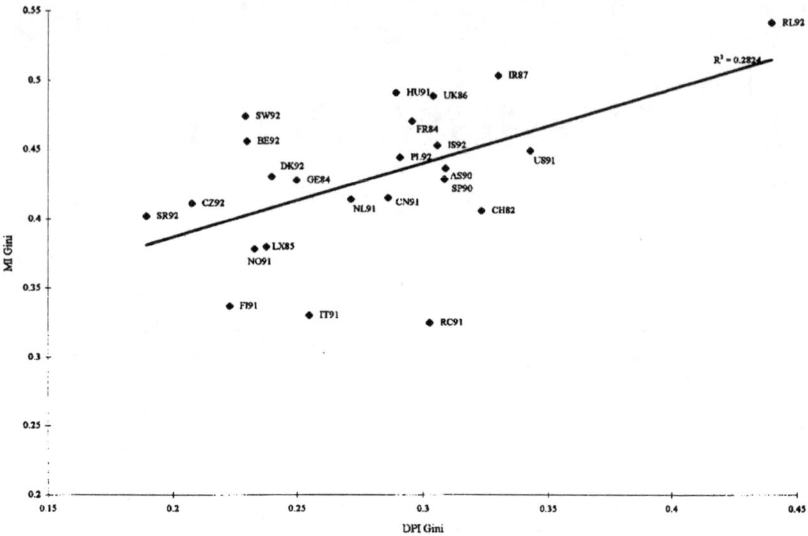

Source: Authors' tabulations of Luxembourg Income Study.

Figure 3.3 Market income and disposable income inequality

differences, which explicitly and implicitly offset both MI and especially DPIs, though this would have to be shown.

5.2 Changes in Inequality over Time

Changes in earned income inequality appear to be the prime force behind changes in market income inequality during the 1980s in the nations studied here.[16] With earnings at or above roughly 70 per cent of market income in most modern nations, this is to be expected. Other market forces (such as capital income) and non-market forces, both demographic and social, also affected market income inequality, though to a lesser degree.

But market income changes do not tell the whole story. By the mid-1980s, more than 25 per cent of all households in major OECD nations depended on something other than earnings as the primary source of their incomes. In nations such as the United Kingdom, The Netherlands and Sweden, this figure reached 30 per cent of income (Atkinson, Rainwater and Smeeding, 1995, Table 8). The redistributive effects of government are therefore important in explaining trends in inequality as well as the level of inequality at any point in time.

The crude evidence in Table 3.2 indicates that the trends in market income inequality mirror the trends in disposable income inequality in most nations. In some countries, especially Finland, but also in Israel, Spain, Ireland, Canada and Germany, government redistribution appears to have muted the trend in market income inequality. In other nations, notably the United Kingdom, New Zealand and Japan, the trend in disposable income inequality is more pronounced than is the trend in market income inequality.

Our reading of the limited cross-national information on changes in tax and transfer structures is that changes in taxes paid and transfers received were largely offsetting to the changes in the distribution of pre-tax and transfer incomes. This would occur automatically in countries with progressive tax and transfer systems. How much of these changes came from explicit policy changes as compared to changes in the economic behaviour of households is an important question that remains to be answered. The link between changes in tax and transfer policy and changes in the distribution of disposable income is certainly not well understood at this stage in the literature.

6 SUMMARY AND RESEARCH IMPLICATIONS

We find a wide range of levels of income inequality across the 25 nations studied here. The range of inequality among OECD nations is very large, and the range among CEE nations appears to be even larger. Comparisons of real income differences across countries are also instructive and can add a great deal in cases where one wishes to compare nations with similar overall levels of production and economic output (*per capita* GDP). Government redistribution has a measurable effect on overall income inequality, reducing market income-based measures compared to disposable income measures in every nation. However, countries with very similar disposable income inequality often have very different inequality of market income and vice versa. These differences are yet to be explained.

Trends in overall income inequality diverge across nations in interesting ways. One finds large increases in inequality among very different nations: two Anglo–Saxon nations (the United Kingdom, the United States), one Scandinavian nation (Sweden), and three CEE nations (Czech Republic, Hungary, Poland) exhibit the largest increases in measured income inequality from roughly 1980 to 1992. In contrast, other Anglo–Saxon (e.g., Canada), European and Scandinavian (e.g., Finland) nations have experienced a much lesser change in inequality. And many nations have shown no measurable change in inequality during the 1980s.

Additional research is needed to further investigate the patterns found here to provide a better overall theory of income distribution, and to build better structural models of income distribution and redistribution that can be applied across and within nations. Atkinson's (1994) self-characterization of his review of the economic theory of income distribution is 'a prospectus for a yet-unwritten book rather than a self-contained essay,' a statement that we heartily endorse.

Notes

1. We would like to thank, without implication, colleagues who have contributed to our work in this area: Anthony B. Atkinson, Lee Rainwater, Barbara Torrey and Debra Bailey. We would also like to thank Ann Wicks, Rick Joy, Inge O'Connor and Debra Bailey for assistance in preparing this manuscript. Smeeding is grateful for financial support provided by the Russell Sage Foundation and by the National Science Foundation under No. SBR-9022192, and No. SBR-9511521. We retain responsibility for all errors of omission or commission.
2. In order to realize the full range of choices and their potential applications, the larger studies need to be consulted (Atkinson, Rainwater and Smeeding, 1995, Chapters 2, 3, Appendices 2–6; Gottschalk and Smeeding, 1997).
3. For a discussion of the problems of comparability across countries, see, among others, Atkinson, Rainwater and Smeeding (1995); Buhmann *et al.* (1988). The issue of international standards for income distribution studies is also being addressed by the Luxembourg Income Study Project.
4. Smeeding *et al.* (1993) covers Australia, Canada, West Germany, United Kingdom, The Netherlands and the United States around 1980.
5. In many of the CEE nations, we have the option of adding production for own consumption (mainly among rural farm families), the value of goods produced and bartered, and in-kind transfers (food, appliances, etc.) received from outside the household. However, these amounts are not included here.
6. Our comparisons of income distribution, and of the effect of taxes and transfers on inequality, use equivalence scales to adjust families for differences in economic need as reflected by family size. These scales have been found to systematically affect the level of overall inequality, but not its pattern. See Atkinson, Rainwater and Smeeding (1995), Chapter 4). See also Buhmann *et al.* (1988).
7. Synthetic data may well give a more accurate picture of the distribution; they are not, however, typically available as micro-data. It should also be noted that Australian, Canadian and United States LIS-based estimates are based, respectively, on 33, 25, and 20 per cent subsamples of the original surveys.
8. For example, the after-tax data for Australia, New Zealand, the United States and other nations used below are obtained using a tax imputation

model at the level of the individual household to estimate direct taxes. In France, LIS uses INSEE computations of transfer receipt to the tax records.

9. We compare incomes by considering household disposable income (or market income) per equivalent adult, using an 'intermediate' equivalence scale of household size raised to the power of a half (or S^E where $E = 0.5$). Thus, adjusted income equals unadjusted income divided by S^E. Many recent cross-national studies of inequality and poverty have used this value for E (e.g., Atkinson, Rainwater and Smeeding, 1995; Hagenaars *et al.*, 1994).
10. Two sets of figures are presented, each bottom coded at 1 per cent of median disposable income; the other top coded at 10 times median income.
11. Such comparisons can clearly not be made by *all* countries shown in Figure 3.1. For instance, real GDP *per capita* in Poland and Hungary and Slovakia were only 25 per cent of US GDP *per capita* in 1993 (World Bank, 1995). In future analyses, we intend to add more countries to this comparison. Atkinson (1995) makes a similar comparison for European nations.
12. These trends are drawn from numerous primary studies which are summarized in Gottschalk and Smeeding (1997).
13. It should be emphasized that these figures are not comparable across countries. One can draw no conclusions from these estimates about the relative degree of inequality in different countries. In each case, the estimates are drawn from national studies of income inequality which are not designed for purposes of international comparison, and they are not necessarily based on the same concepts of income or method of calculation. While we have used the LIS data for inequality comparisons across a subset of these nations, where other national studies were not available, the LIS data are less complete in terms of years studied than are those from the other national studies cited here. Where LIS trend data is available, however, it supports the findings shown in Table 3.2.
14. Were we to show not percentage change, but percentage point change in inequality, Sweden might fare a bit better than shown here. A 15 percentage point change in the Swedish 1991 Gini of 0.229 or 0.034, is less than a 10 per cent change in the US. 1991 Gini of 0.343.
15. While the Polish data are consistent from 1987 to 1992, it is not entirely clear that the Polish household budget survey has adequately captured changes in entrepreneurial incomes since 1990. Thus, the Polish results must be cautiously interpreted.
16. This conclusion draws heavily on Gottschalk and Smeeding (1997), who in turn base their conclusions on material from Gottschalk, Gustafsson and Palmer (1997), OECD (1994), Gardiner (1993), Ploug and Kvist (1994), Messere (1994) and Commission of the European Communities (1993a, 1993b).

References

Atkinson, A. B. (1994) 'Explaining the Distribution of Income', mimeo prepared for the J. Rowntree Inquiry into Income and Wealth (Cambridge: University of Cambridge).

Atkinson, A. B. (1995) 'Income Distribution in Europe and the United States', *LIS Working Paper*, 133 (October).

Atkinson, A. B., L. Rainwater and T. Smeeding (1995) *Income Distribution in OECD Countries: Evidence from the Luxembourg Income Study (LIS)* (Paris: OECD).

Buhmann, B., L. Rainwater, G. Schmaus and T. Smeeding (1988) 'Equivalence Scales, Well-Being, Inequality and Poverty: Sensitivity Estimates Across Ten Countries Using the Luxembourg Income Study (LIS) Data Base', *Review of Income and Wealth*, vol. 34, pp. 115–142.

Commission of the European Communities (1993a) *Social Protection in Europe, 1993* (Brussels: Directorate General for Employment, Industrial Relations and Social Affairs).

Commission of the European Communities (1993b) 'Recent Reforms in Social Protection Systems in the Community', in *Social Protection in Europe*, Chapter 2 (Brussels: Directorate General for Employment, Industrial Relations and Social Affairs), pp. 31–40.

Gardiner, K. (1993) 'A Survey of Income Inequality Over the Last Twenty Years – How Does the United Kingdom Compare?', *Welfare State Programme Discussion Paper*, WSP/100 (London: London School of Economics).

Gottschalk, P. and T. Smeeding (1997) 'Cross-National Comparisons of Earnings and Income Inequality', *Journal of Economic Literature*, vol. 35, pp. 633–86.

Gottschalk, P., B. Gustafsson and E. Palmer (eds) (1997) *The Distribution of Economic Welfare in the 1980s* (Cambridge: Cambridge University Press).

Hagenaars, A., K. de Vos and A. Zaidi (1994) 'Patterns of Poverty in Europe' *mimeo* (Netherlands: University of Leiden), mimeo.

Hanratty, M. and R. Blank (1993) 'Down and Out in North America: Recent Trends in Poverty Rates in the US and Canada', *Quarterly Journal of Economics*, vol. 10, pp. 233–57.

Messere, K. C. (1994) *Tax Policy in OECD Countries: Choices and Conflicts* (Amsterdam Publications BV).

Milanovic, B. (1995) 'Determinants of Cross-Country Income Inequality: An Augmented Kuznets' Hypothesis', in *Income Distribution During the Transition, Research Project Paper*, vol. 5 (Washington, DC: World Bank).

Organization for Economic Cooperation and Development (OECD) (1994) 'New Orientations for Social Policy,' *Social Policy Studies No. 12* (Paris: OECD).

Ploug, N. and J. Kvist (eds) (1994) *Recent Trends in Cash Benefits in Europe* (Copenhagen: Danish National Institute of Social Research).

Rainwater, L. and T. Smeeding (1995) 'Doing Poorly: The Real Income of American Children in a Comparative Perspective', *Luxembourg Income Study Working Paper*, 127, Center for Policy Research, The Maxwell School, Syracuse University.

Saunders, P. (1994) 'Rising on the Tasman Tide: Income Inequality in Australia and New Zealand in the 1980s', *SPRC Discussion Papers*, vol. 49, University of New South Wales.

Smeeding, T., P. Saunders, J. Coder, S. Jenkins, J. Fritzell, A. Hagenaars, R. Hauser and M. Wolfson (1993) 'Poverty, Inequality and Family Living Standard Impacts across Seven Nations: The Effect of Noncash Subsidies', *Review of Income and Wealth*, vol. 39, no. 3, pp. 229–56.

Smeeding, T., L. Rainwater and D. Torrey (1993) 'Going to Extremes: The US Elderly in an International Context', *Luxembourg Income Study Working Paper*, 89, Center for Policy Research, The Maxwell School, Syracuse University.

Summers, R. and A. Heston (1991) 'The Penn World Table (Mark 5): An Expanded Set of International Comparisons, 1950–1988', *Quarterly Journal of Economics* (May), pp. 327–68.

Torrey, B., T. Smeeding and D. Bailey (1997) 'Rowing between Scylla and Charybdis? Income Transitions in Central European Households', forthcoming in an untitled National Academy of Sciences book on economic transformation of households and health.

World Bank (1995) *The World Bank Atlas 1995* (Washington, DC: World Bank).

4 Openness and Within-Country Inequality[1]

Susan Horton
UNIVERSITY OF TORONTO

Ravi Kanbur
THE WORLD BANK

and

Dipak Mazumdar
UNIVERSITY OF TORONTO

1 INTRODUCTION

Increasing globalization is a fact of life. Dramatic reductions in transportation and communication costs, and colossal increases in capital flows, are knitting together the world economy as never before. Although some of the recent trends are not dramatically different from the past,[2] there are some new patterns, such as the marked rise in manufacturing exports by a group of developing countries in East Asia. Should other developing countries, particularly those in Africa, go against the grain of this globalization, or should they work towards complementing it? While resisting global trends is most likely a futile activity, the issue of complementary policies is important because, in our view, closer integration of the world economy poses significant tradeoffs – while it holds out the prospect of higher growth it also carries dangers of increasing inequality in the short to medium run, particularly because of the interaction of globalization and new technology with existing skill and educational inequalities.

This chapter, for reasons of space, does not deal with the large issue of the impact of trade on inter-country or inter-regional equality, but focuses instead on inequality within individual developing countries. We focus on inequality and not on poverty, and on trade as opposed to other aspects of openness, whilst recognizing that it is difficult to separate the effects of trade from those of capital mobility for example. Section 2 of this chapter lays out some of the main conceptual issues in the notion of a tradeoff between growth and equity in the post-war literature. Then, in Section 3, we review some of the evidence, arguing that it is supportive of those who contend that trade liberalization, in the presence of structural rigidities and skill-enhancing technological change, can exacerbate inequity within countries. Section 4 turns to policy implications, and Section 5 concludes the chapter.

2 IS THERE A GROWTH–EQUITY TRADEOFF?

Ever since Kuznets' (1955) classic statement, analysts have been considering the proposition that the process of economic growth may be accompanied by systematic changes in inequality. Kuznets' paper marks, perhaps, the start of a sceptical attitude towards the 'trickle down' view that dominated immediate post-war thinking. Kuznets' original model was similar in spirit to that of Lewis (1954) – in which labour moved from a low-paying agricultural/rural/informal sector to a high-paying industrial/urban/formal sector, everything else being held constant. As a result, measured inequality would increase in the early stages as a small number of workers secured a much higher standard of living. While Kuznets complemented this basic framework with a rich discussion of other mechanisms, including policy interventions to redistribute income, the subsequent literature focused on the 'reduced form' relationship between *per capita* income in a country and relative income inequality in that country. The best known example of this strand of the literature is the paper by Ahluwalia (1976), which tested the relationship on cross-country data and claimed to have established an 'inverse-U' relationship where income inequality first increased and then decreased as growth in *per capita* income took place. An influential book on the policy implications of this line of thinking was the famous *Redistribution with Growth* (Chenery *et al.*, 1974).

The publication of *Redistribution with Growth* can also be seen, in one sense, as a culmination of the critique of the 'trickle down' hypothesis, which held that growth by itself would alleviate poverty. Chenery *et al.* (1974), influenced by the increase in inequality experienced during the Brazilian growth 'miracle', cautioned that inequitable growth might well leave the position of the poor unaffected, or even make it worse. The policy conclusions were interventionist in nature – both in terms of direct redistribution of income through taxation, but also redistribution of physical and human assets through land reform, basic education, and the like.

In the late 1970s and 1980s the academic literature questioned the empirical basis of the 'Kuznets hypothesis' (see, for example, the overviews in Fishlow (1995), or Anand and Kanbur (1993a, 1993b), thereby implicitly questioning the notion of a tradeoff. As Bruno *et al.* (1995) conclude from this literature, 'the "stylized fact" that distribution must get better before it gets worse turns out not to be a fact at all'. In the policy arena, towards the end of the 1970s, macroeconomic crisis revealed the weaknesses of the policies (originally introduced with support from international agencies) being followed by many developing countries. These policies, which discriminated against agriculture and protected state-owned enterprises, were argued to be both inefficient and inequitable. The notion of a tradeoff thus became less prominent – policy reform could lead to both higher *per capita* income and more equality, given how far inside the 'policy frontier' countries found themselves. Two examples of this literature are de Melo and Robinson (1982) and Kanbur (1987), which both argue that devaluation of an overvalued currency can, in certain conditions, improve both efficiency and equity.

In the late 1980s and early 1990s, the academic literature turned another interesting corner. Instead of testing (unsuccessfully) for a relationship where inequality increased with *per capita* income, a number of analysts started examining, at a theoretical level, the possibility that structural inequalities might impede growth. The arguments stemmed both from constraints in the credit market, and from political economy arguments which suggested that high inequalities might well lead to the adoption of inefficient distortionary policies. The theoretical literature (e.g., Banerjee and Newman, 1993; Bencivenga and Smith, 1991; Persson and Tabellini, 1994) has been supported to some extent by empirical work which attempts to link inequality at the start of a period to growth in that period (Alesina and Rodrik, 1994; Persson and Tabellini, 1994), but the strength of the evidence is by no means clear (Fishlow, 1995).

Simultaneously with this development of academic thinking on policy reform in the face of macroeconomic crisis, and on the impact of inequality on growth, work was also proceeding in the policy arena which argued that there was no necessary conflict between growth and poverty reduction (which may be related to – but is not synonymous with – the conflict between growth and equity). The best statement of the view that policy could promote both growth and poverty reduction, is perhaps to be found in the World Bank's *World Development Report* on Poverty (World Bank, 1990). As noted in the Foreword:

> A review of development experience shows that the most effective way of achieving rapid and politically sustainable improvements in the quality of life for the poor has been through the two-part strategy. The first element of the strategy is the pursuit of a pattern of growth that

> ensures productive use of the poor's most abundant asset – labour. The second element is widespread provision to the poor of basic social services, especially primary education, primary health care, and family planning. The first component provides opportunities; the second increases the capacity of the poor to take advantage of these opportunities. The strategy must be complemented by well-targeted transfers, to help those not able to benefit from these policies, and by safety nets, to protect those who are exposed to shocks.

While there are many elements in the pursuit of a pro-poor pattern of growth, it is clear that the 1990 *World Development Report*, and subsequent World Bank publications such as *Adjustment in Africa* (World Bank, 1994), view an outward-oriented strategy which encourages exporting and integration into the global economy as being crucial. The reasoning is that exposing the economy to the international market test will force increasing demand for abundant factors of production and, since this includes labour, the poor will benefit. The East Asian experience is a constant source of inspiration for this line of argument, including in *The East Asian Miracle* study (World Bank, 1993).

And yet, recently, there has been a growing acceptance of some of the problems of the line of argument which goes: greater openness – trade liberalization – higher returns to tradeable production – reduced inequality and/or poverty. In the policy arena, the 1995 *World Development Report* on Workers in an Integrating World (World Bank, 1995), sounds a warning:

> Some groups of relatively poor workers have experienced large gains in the past thirty years – especially in Asia. But there is no worldwide convergence between rich and poor workers. Indeed, there are risks that workers in poorer countries will fall further behind, as lower investment and educational attainment widen disparities. Some workers, especially in sub-Saharan Africa, could become increasingly marginalised. And those left out of the general prosperity in countries that are enjoying growth could suffer permanent losses, setting in motion intergenerational cycles of neglect.

While accepting this possibility, however, the 1995 *World Development Report* nevertheless concludes that 'preserving open trading relations' and 'domestic policies that promote labour-demanding growth' are central to equitable growth.

The analytical literature has also emphasized some of the complications, best summarized by Bruno *et al.* (1995):

> One should be clear about what can and cannot be concluded from our results. Let us reiterate that it would not be correct to say that growth always benefits the poor, or that none of the poor lose from pro-growth policy reforms. Here we are only looking at broad aggregates ... even in countries with initially low inequality and a growth process which brings rapid and sizable gains to most of the poor, some will not be in a position to take advantage of the new opportunities, and some may well lose.

The losses to the poor from policy reform, even when the reform benefits growth, has been emphasized by those who focus on the poorest of the poor, including both international organizations such as UNICEF (e.g., Cornia *et al.*, 1987) and NGOs (e.g., Oxfam, 1995). The debate between those who argue that policy reform does not, or need not, adversely affect the poor, and those who believe that it does, has become increasingly acrimonious and devoid of mutual comprehension. But perhaps one way of bridging the divide is to take the lead of Bruno *et al.* (1995) and see one side as claiming that aggregate poverty is not affected (as argued by Demery and Squire, 1995), and the other side as emphasizing a disaggregated approach that forces attention on the losers from the reform process.

For example, the simple analysis in Kanbur (1987) on the impact effects of expenditure switching and expenditure reduction, or the analysis of devaluation in de Melo and Robinson (1982) would suggest benign distributional effects in aggregate. But there are at least three dimensions of disaggregation which may help to explain the growing perception among the NGO community that the effects are not quite so benign. The first disaggregation, straightforwardly, is that the non-tradeable sector is heterogeneous, including both the highly paid parastatal employees, and the urban poor, as is the tradeable sector, which includes smallholder cash crop growers, plantations, mining and the emerging financial sector. One would expect, then, that a significant number of urban poor would lose out, and that inequalities may increase as those with access to credit, the better educated, etc., take much better advantage of the emerging opportunities. In fact, the increases in inequality observed in Ghana, and documented in Demery and Squire (1995) and Demery, Sen and Viswanath (1995) support this line of argument, as do empirical results for Latin America in de Janvry and Sadoulet (1995).

The second disaggregation is by gender. The problem for the first-cut analysis in Kanbur (1987) and similar works is that in an African context it is often the case that food crops are both non-tradeable internationally and the domain of women, while internationally traded cash crops are the domain of men. This would not matter if income pooling were the rule in the household. But there is growing evidence that such income pooling is not the norm, and that a bargaining model much better describes intrahousehold allocation processes (see Alderman *et al.*, 1995). In such a situation, improving the terms of trade of cash crops *vis-à-vis* food crops might actually worsen the position of women and children. The theory of such effects is analyzed, for example, by Haddad and Kanbur (1994). The role of food crops, and the worsening position of women following on from increased outward orientation of an economy has been claimed by many NGOs who deal directly with the plight of poor women (e.g., Oxfam, 1995).

A third disaggregation concerns expenditure reduction, in particular cuts in public expenditure. Ferroni and Kanbur (1991), Berg (1994) and Sahn (1992) have pointed to the complex evolution of total public expenditures, and their composition in Africa and Latin America in the 1980s. But it is clear that this analysis is at too aggregative a level. The NGOs and critics of policy reform have been picking up, through their ground-level work, the victims of public expenditure cuts which, even if they were targeted in general away from the poor, in their execution did in fact affect some poor or almost poor. It is this emphasis of one side on the disaggregated effects with a focus on the losers, and the other side's recourse to the aggregate effects which weigh the gainers against the losers, which has probably led to a failure of dialogue.

After all this, where would we say the literature currently stands? Our position would be the following. There seems to have been an evolution from the immediate post-war focus on growth and 'trickle down', through the concern with the growth–equity relationship in the 1960s and 1970s to the view in the 1980s and 1990s that policy reform can provide both growth and equity, with the latter view being challenged by strong critics of the outward-oriented model of development. Most recently, however, concern on the inequality increasing effects of globalization and openness has grown, and we turn now to consider this evidence.

3 TRADE LIBERALIZATION AND INEQUALITY

A recent literature for the United States has focused on the widening of wage differentials by skill and education since the 1970s (Murphy and Welch, 1992; Goldin and Margo, 1992; Katz and Murphy, 1992). This widening has been quite marked: according to Katz and Murphy (1992), 'weekly wages of young male college graduates increased by 30 per cent relative to young males with twelve or fewer years of schooling from 1979 to 1987'. Increases in differentials were also observed for older workers relative to younger ones, and inequality within narrow skill and demographic groups also rose. A related phenomenon of widening distribution has also been observed for the United Kingdom over the period 1980–92 (Lindley, 1997). This increase in differentials was surprising in view of what Goldin and Margo (1992) dubbed 'the great compression' from 1940 to 1970.

There has been much interest in explaining the causes of these changes. Katz and Murphy (1992) show that the changes are predominantly associated with increases in demand for more educated and more skilled workers. Several different explanations for these demand shifts have been advanced. Revenga (1992) and Wood (1994) discuss the effects of import competition on low-paid import-competing sectors, particularly in manufacturing. Others argue that technological change with a bias towards greater education and skills, such as the 'information revolution' is responsible (Berman, Bound and Griliches, 1994). Of course, both these forces were in play during the 1980s, and may have reinforced each other. Finally, ILO (1995) blames inadequate growth, in turn related to biases associated with a lack of international coordination of macro-policy.

Another aspect of changing wage distribution has been the reversal after the mid-1970s of the gains in employment and relative earnings by black Americans which had begun in the mid-1960s. Bound and Freeman (1992) find that a number of factors were involved, including loss of jobs in manufacturing (some of which may be related to trade), falling minimum wages, a drop in union density and an increase in the supply of black relative to white college graduates. It is less clear whether native North Americans have suffered the same reversal in earnings. Studies cited in Patrinos (1994) suggest that differentials in the United States narrowed over the 1960s and 1970s, in part due to improvements in educational attainment by native Americans. In Canada, however, the part of the earnings gap for native Canadians not explained by measured characteristics tends to rise with educational level, and the gap in earnings not explained by characteristics has increased since the 1970s (Patrinos, 1994).

Given these changes in wage distribution in developed countries, it is of interest to see how this extends to developing countries. The conventional wisdom here is well stated by Bruno *et al.* (1995):

> Trade theory would predict that protection lowers the reward for the most abundant (most equally distributed) factor of production and increases returns to scarce factors, which are likely to be the more inequitably distributed. Presence of protection indeed seems to worsen income distribution (Bourguignon and Morrison, 1990).

Wood (1995) argues in greater detail as follows:

> Heckscher–Ohlin theory asserts that countries export goods which use intensively those factors of production which are relatively abundantly endowed, and import goods which use intensively factors which are relatively scarce at home. Trade thus increases demand for abundant factors, because of the expansion of export sectors, and reduces demand for scarce factors, because of the contraction of import-competing sectors, with corresponding effects on factor prices. In developing countries, where unskilled labour is abundant and skilled labour is scarce, trade tends to raise unskilled wages and lower skilled wages, and hence to narrow the gap between them.

So much for the theory. What about the evidence? There is, in fact, a substantial literature suggesting that the returns to skill and/or overall wage inequality have risen in developing countries in the wake of trade liberalization. Wood (1995) presents an excellent up-to-date review. The evidence for Hong Kong, Korea, Singapore and Taiwan was reviewed by Wood (1994), who questioned, on empirical grounds, the conventional wisdom that wage differentials had in fact narrowed as a result of external liberalization. The complex interactions between demand-side and supply-side factor is illustrated by the following quotation from Wood (1995):

> Skill differentials in Korea widened in the mid-1970s, because of the heavy and chemical industry drive, but narrowed again throughout the 1980s, when there was rapid expansion of higher education (as well as a rise in union power from 1987). In Singapore, where higher education also expanded rapidly in the 1980s, skill differentials widened in 1981–6, probably in reaction to their forcible compression by government wage policy during 1979–81, but narrowed again during the rest of the decade. In Taiwan and Hong Kong, however, where higher education expanded less rapidly (and where labour markets were more or less free of institutional influences), wage inequality rose during most of the 1980s.

Robbins (1995a, 1995b) finds that wage differentials rose accompanying trade liberalization in Chile, Costa Rica, Colombia and possibly the Philippines and Argentina, but not Malaysia. For Mexico, the studies of Feenstra and Hanson (1995), Revenga and Montenegro (1995) and Alarcon and McKinley (1995) show widening wage differentials by skill accompanying trade liberalization. Robbins (1995a) also uses the methodology of Katz and Murphy (1992) to examine the returns to skill in a non-parametric framework, and tries to separate supply and demand shifts. He concludes that demand effects predominate in explaining widening differentials, and are only partially offset by supply effects (the increased supply of relatively educated labour). There is some suggestion in Robbins (1995a) and Feenstra and Hanson (1995) that liberalization of labour market regulation may also be part of the explanation of the increasing inequality.

Going beyond wage differentials, there is an accumulating body of evidence on changes in the overall distribution of income accompanying trade liberalization. Berry (1995) summarizes the results for a number of studies in Latin America. He concludes that the income distribution worsened in Argentina, Chile, Colombia, the Dominican Republic, Ecuador, Mexico and Uruguay, with a strong suggestion that the policy package accompanying trade liberalization is implicated. The evidence is especially strong for Chile, where the deterioration is very marked, and for Mexico, where the Gini coefficient of wage and salary distribution rose from 0.419 in 1984 to 0.519 in 1992. Costa Rica is the only case where income distribution apparently did not change, and this is clouded somewhat by a break in the income statistics that coincided with the onset of reform. It should be noted that the Berry (1995) line of argument stands somewhat counter to that of Morley (1994), which links increases in inequality to recession. Berry (1995), while accepting the hypothesis, questions some of Morley's (1994) evidence and concludes that factors other than the economic cycle have been important.

For Africa, there is very little in the way of evidence on wage inequalities. Demery, Sen and Viswanath (1995) consider the growth, poverty and inequality consequences of adjustment policies (in which trade liberalization is a prominent feature) on income distribution using household survey data for a handful countries:

> The failure to adjust in Côte d'Ivoire was associated with a narrowing income distribution, declining incomes being experienced by the non-poor more than the poor. But there is no comfort in this message. Consider the experience of the four countries which achieved above average success in their adjustment (Ethiopia, Ghana, Nigeria and Tanzania). All these countries experienced widening income distributions in the process of recovery. And the evidence suggests that income distribution within rural areas deteriorated. Just why this is the case is unclear. It is possible that some of the poor were simply not affected either way by these changes. And this 'disjointedness' would lead to

increasing inequality – the non-poor and some poor experiencing increasing incomes, but other poor groups (the poor not articulated with markets and infrastructure) being left behind. Clearly there is need for further research into the determinants of income inequality change in Africa in the 1980s.

With regard to evidence on discrimination in developing countries, there are very large gaps in earnings and effects of differences in poverty. Patrinos (1994) summarizes results for differentials by caste in India, and by ethnic origin in China. There are cases where earnings differentials have narrowed over time, such as the relative earnings of African in Kenya over the period 1914–76 (Bigsten, 1988, cited in Patrinos, 1994), of coloured citizens in South Africa (Moll, 1992, cited in Patrinos, 1994), and of Malays (bumiputras) in Malaysia under the New Economic Policy (NEP) (Ariffin *et al.*, 1995; although Tzannatos, 1991, argues that reverse discrimination in higher education under the NEP did not reduce inequality and harmed the poor). There is little evidence of what has happened over time to ethnic differentials where governments have not actively intervened, nor of what has happened in the recent past. This is an area of potential concern, given the disturbing trends in the United States.

Another strand of research points out the importance of agricultural policy accompanying the expansion of manufacturing exports. Some studies (Mazumdar, 1995; Mazumdar and Basu, 1994) argue that land reform in Japan, Korea and Taiwan, and interventionist and protectionist agricultural policies in East and Southeast Asia in general, were important components of the relatively equitable income distribution outcomes. Pricing policies which favoured farmers, combined with technological advances improving productivity, were important in pushing up the supply price of labour to the industrial sector, at the same time as manufacturing exports shifted out labour demand. Land reform and agricultural intervention have been much less important in Latin America and Africa than in Asia, and may be another factor in the less benign income distribution outcomes.

While there is indeed need for further research on all regions of the world, there does seem to us to be sufficient grounds for concern about the links between globalization, greater integration of economies into the global system, and growing inequality within developing countries. While Wood's (1995) conclusion is narrowly focused on wage differentials, it has wider significance:

> All this time series evidence is open to doubts, which are as serious for the studies which are consistent with the conventional wisdom that

external liberalisation reduces wage inequality in developing countries as for those that contradict it. But it would be hard to avoid the conclusion that the outcome has varied. In some countries, increased openness to trade has been associated with the narrowing of skill differentials. However, there are enough cases where the opposite has happened to make it seem unlikely that the conventional wisdom is the whole story, and hence to make it necessary to look for some more comprehensive explanation.

We turn now to these alternative ways of looking at the consequences of trade liberalization, and their implications for policy.

4 ALTERNATIVE EXPLANATIONS AND POLICY IMPLICATIONS

It is unlikely that any economy in the world will be able to resist the trend of globalization of the world economy. But what are the consequences of this trend? The benefits to the world economy in terms of higher growth are not to be doubted. But, as the 1995 *World Development Report* notes, there is a chance that some countries, and some groups within countries are likely to be left behind, so that increased growth is likely to be accompanied by increasing inequality. In this chapter we have been considering the effect on inequality within developing countries. Basic trade theory suggests that greater openness to trade will lead to reduced inequality. Yet the evidence suggests that greater openness has, in a significant number of cases, been accompanied by increasing inequality. Why? And what are the policy implications of a view of the world which, in light of the evidence, departs from conventional theory?

Wood (1995) divides possible explanations into the categories of 'unconventional Heckscher–Ohlin' and 'non-Heckscher–Ohlin' explanations. Among the more plausible in the first category is one which subdivides labour into different skill categories. Thus, following Wood (1994), suppose we think of the labour force as having either no education (A), basic education (B), or advanced education (C), and assume that category A are unemployable in manufacturing. Then if a country has a relatively large supply of B, reduction of trade barriers will raise the demand for labour of type B relative to types A and C. This will reduce the differential between B and C, and thus reduce inequality, but increase the gap between A and C, thus increasing inequality – the latter effect may well dominate. Another explanation in this category starts with the observation that, in the standard Heckscher–Ohlin model, a relative decline in the terms of trade of labour-intensive goods globally would reduce the wages of unskilled workers in countries where this factor was more abundant. Wood argues that this explanation has some empirical support since, in the 1980s, there was a rapid increase in the manufactured exports of some developing countries.

Among the 'non-Heckscher–Ohlin' explanations one that is most plausible is that of 'skill-enhancing trade' (Robbins, 1995a). In this view, increased capital goods imports following trade liberalization would be associated with increased returns to skilled labour which is complementary to capital (Hamermesh, 1993; Stokey, 1994). These theories are consistent with some versions of endogenous growth theory emphasizing increasing returns (Romer, 1986). Leamer (1995) provides further analysis, arguing that importation of new technology which was sectorally biased (in an economy which was diversified) or factorally biased (for an economy which was specialized) could lead to a widening of differentials between skilled and unskilled labour. As Robbins (1995a) notes, 'the indirect effects associated with capital, technology and knowledge flows will tend to raise the returns to schooling in the short and medium run. While this explanation may not fit all circumstances, it may explain increasing inequality in Chile, for example.'

Another explanation not directly related to Heckscher–Ohlin theory is that the changes in inequality are transitory and associated with the change away from a distorted trade regime and the growth of new opportunities. Finally, it is possible that the trade effects are being swamped by even larger skill-enhancing effects of new technologies.

More research is needed to develop explanations for the trend towards greater inequality, in the wake of greater openness, in many developing countries. It clear that technology and globalization are combining in ways that magnify, more than ever before, the effects of differences in levels of skill and schooling. Since we believe that globalization cannot be resisted indefinitely, we conclude that equalizing the distribution of skills and education will be the key to taking advantage of globalization while minimizing its effects on inequality. In fact, the evidence from developed countries, and developing countries, is that when differences in schooling levels were being narrowed rapidly, wage inequality was also being narrowed. The aggregative evidence for the United States and East Asia has been referred to in the previous sections.

Another powerful source of support for this line of argument comes from evidence on relative earnings differentials between men and women, which have by and large narrowed with the narrowing of the education gap and reduction of discrimination. For the United States gains in women's relative education, combined with shifts to white collar employment, were important in causing the 10 percentage point increase in women's wages relative to men's over the period 1880–1930. These same factors, plus the fall in family size, were responsible for that same 10 percentage point increase in women's relative earnings which occurred within one or two recent decades in several Asian countries (Horton, 1996).

Pro-active intervention to reduce inequalities in skill levels is called for by an emerging situation where any degree of inequality of skills is likely to be magnified by the new trends in globalization. But another dimension is highlighted more than it would be otherwise. This is a strengthened argument for redistributing the primary incomes to achieve a more equal final distribution of income, during the phase where inequalities of skill persist, and their interactions with globalization and new technologies intensify inequality of the distribution of primary incomes. Of course, it is well understood that such attempted redistributions have efficiency costs. Following the classic work of Mirrlees (1971), a literature has developed which considers the implications of balancing out efficiency and equity concerns (see, for example, the survey in Tuomala, 1990, and Kanbur, Keen and Tuomala, 1994). In this literature, some attention has been paid to the implications of greater 'inherent inequality' on nature of the redistribution that is optimal. Mirrlees (1971) himself noted that greater inequality in the distribution of earnings capacity led to generally higher marginal tax rates in the optimum which balanced efficiency and equity appropriately. Kanbur and Tuomala (1994) confirm this, but also show that as the degree of inherent inequality increases, the steepness with which optimal marginal tax rates rise with income also increases. In an ordinarily recognizable sense, therefore, the optimal pattern of taxation becomes more redistributive as inherent inequality increases. Since we have argued that globalization and new technology act together to magnify the inequality inherent in disparate skill levels, economic analysis does indeed rationalize a more redistributive stance *vis-à-vis* the primary distribution of income. This argument is further strengthened by dynamic considerations which transmit inequality from generation to generation, amplified by imperfections in credit markets.

Another area where policy intervention is likely to be important is in agriculture. The previous section referred to the importance of land reform and agricultural policy in assisting equity in East Asia. Inequality in access to land is particularly high in Latin America, which has an adverse effect on the income of unskilled labour. In Africa, progress on rural and unskilled incomes is hindered by the lack of technological innovation in rain-fed agriculture, and in some of the coarse grains important in African climatic conditions. Investment in agricultural technology in Africa is likely to have a very high payoff both in terms of long-run growth, and progress on inequality. These policy prescriptions are not very different from those of Chenery *et al.* (1974) discussed in Section 2. But perhaps now the easier gains – of moving to the policy frontier – have already been exploited.

5 SUMMARY AND CONCLUSION

This chapter starts with the assumption that no developing (or developed) country can for long insulate and isolate itself from the inexorable trends of globalization and new technology. The only thing to do, therefore, is to be aware of the consequences and to design policy that will respond to these trends. The consequence we have highlighted is the link between openness to trade and increasing inequality within developing countries. We have argued that despite a basic theoretical prediction that greater openness to trade of a developing economy will reduce inequality, because it will increase demand for unskilled labour (the most abundant factor), the evidence points to the strong possibility of increasing inequality in the face of trade liberalization which opens the economy to more competition from the global market place. Whatever the consequences of this for growth, and they can be beneficial, the implications for inequality are not necessarily benign. This conclusion, in turn, has several implications. First, it sounds a note of caution on a seeming consensus in the recent literature, that growth and decreasing inequality can and do go hand in hand. This consensus, which can itself be seen as a reconciliation between the 'trickle down' views of the immediate postwar era and the 'Kuznets hypothesis' views which emerged as a challenge to that orthodoxy, must now, it seems to us, be subjected to further serious analysis and debate. Certainly, the current inequality outcomes in developing countries, in the wake of trade liberalization, and in the context of labour markets where skill distributions are highly uneven, call for such a reexamination. If a reexamination passes muster, and we are confident that it can, it would seem to call, on the basis of standard welfare economic analysis, for more pro-active intervention in both equalizing the distribution of skills, and in redistributing the primary distribution of income.

Notes

1. The authors would like to thank Gerry Helleiner, Ishrat Husain, Lant Pritchett and participants at the IEA session for their comments on an earlier draft.
2. It is interesting to note that although the ratio of trade to GDP world-wide in 1991 was twice as high as in 1950, it was only one and a half percentage points higher in 1993 than in 1913 (Mazumdar, 1995, using data from Pritchett, 1995).

References

Ahluwalia, M. (1976) 'Inequality, Poverty and Development', *Journal of Development Economics*, vol. 3, no. 4, pp. 307–42.

Alarcon, D. and T. McKinley (1995) 'Widening Wage Dispersion Under Structural Adjustment in Mexico', *Discussion Paper*, FC1995-4, Centre for International Studies, University of Toronto.

Alderman, H. *et al.* (1995) 'Unitary versus Collective Models of the Household: Is it Time to Shift the Burden of Proof?', *World Bank Research Observer*, vol. 10, no. 1, pp. 1–19.

Alesina, A. and D. Rodrik (1994) 'Distributive Politics and Economic Growth' *Quarterly Journal of Economics*, vol. 109, pp. 465–90.

Anand, S. and R. Kanbur (1993a) 'The Kuznets Process and the Inequality–Development Relationship', *Journal of Development Economics*, vol. 40 (February), pp. 25–52.

Anand, S. and R. Kanbur (1993b) 'Inequality and Development: A Critique', *Journal of Development Economics*, vol. 41 (June), pp. 19–43.

Ariffin, J., S. Horton and G. Sedlacek, (1995) 'Women in the Labour Market in Malaysia', in S. Horton (ed.), *Women and Industrialization in Asia* (London: Routledge).

Banerjee, A. and A. Newman (1993) 'Occupational Choice and the Process of Development', *Journal of Political Economy*, vol. 101 (April), pp. 274–99.

Bencivenga, V. and B. Smith (1991) 'Financial Intermediation and Endogenous Growth', *Review of Economic Studies*, vol. 58 (April), pp. 195–209.

Berg, E. (1994) 'Poverty and Structural Adjustment in the 1980s: Trends in Welfare Indicators in Latin America and Africa', *Development Alternatives International*, Bethesda, Maryland.

Berman, E., J. Bound and Z. Griliches (1994) 'Changes in the Demand for Skilled Labour within US Manufacturing; Evidence from the Annual Survey of Manufacturing', *Quarterly Journal of Economics*, vol. 109 (May).

Berry, A. (1995) 'The Social Challenge of the New Economic Era in Latin America', *FOCAL/CIS Discussion Paper*, FC 1995–8, University of Toronto.

Bigsten, A. (1988) 'Race and Inequality in Kenya, 1914–1976', *Eastern Africa Economic Review*, vol. 4(1).

Bound, J. and R. B. Freeman (1992) 'What Went Wrong? The Erosion of Relative Earnings and Employment Among Young Black Men in the 1980s', *Quarterly Journal of Economics*, vol. 107 (February), pp. 201–32.

Bourguignon, F. and C. Morrison (1990) 'Income Distribution, Development and Foreign Trade: A Cross-Sectional Analysis', *European Economic Review*, vol. 34 (September), pp. 113–32.

Bruno, M., M. Ravallion and L. Squire (1995) 'Equity and Growth in Developing Countries: Old and New Perspectives on the Policy Issues' (Washington, DC: World Bank), mimeo.

Chenery, H. *et al.* (1974) *Redistribution With Growth* (New York: Oxford: Clarendon Press).

Cornia, G., R. Jolly and F. Stewart (1987) *Adjustment With a Human Face* (Oxford: Clarendon Press).

de Janvry, A. and E. Sadoulet (1995) 'Poverty, Equity and Social Welfare in Latin America: Determinants of Change over Growth Spells' *Issues in Development Discussion Paper*, 6 (Geneva: International Labour Office).

de Melo, J. and S. Robinson (1982) 'Trade, Adjustment Policies and Income Distribution in Three Archetype Developing Economies', *Journal of Development Economics*, vol. 10, no. 1, pp. 67–92.

Demery, L., B. Sen, and T. Vishwanath (1995) 'Poverty, Inequality and Growth' (Washington, DC: World Bank), mimeo.

Demery, L. and L. Squire (1995) 'Poverty in Africa: An Emerging Picture' (Washington DC: World Bank), DC: mimeo.

Feenstra, R. and G. Hanson (1995) 'Foreign Investment, Outsourcing and Relative Wages', in R. Feenstra, G. Grossman and D. Irwin (eds) *Political Economy of Trade Policy: Essays in Honour of Jagdish Bhagwati* (Cambridge, MA: MIT Press).

Ferroni, M. and R. Kanbur (1991) 'Poverty Conscious Restructuring of Public Expenditure', in A. Chhibber and S. Fischer (eds), *Economic Reform in Sub-Saharan Africa* (Washington, DC: World Bank).

Fishlow, A. (1995) 'Inequality, Poverty and Growth: Where Do We Stand?' (Washington, DC: World Bank), mimeo.

Goldin, C. and R. Margo (1992) 'The Great Compression: The Wage Structure in the United States at mid-Century', *Quarterly Journal of Economics*, vol. 107 (February), pp. 1–34.

Haddad, L. and R. Kanbur (1994) 'Are Better Off Households More Unequal or Less Unequal?', *Oxford Economic Papers*, vol. 46 (July), pp. 445–58.

Hamermesh, D. (1993) *Labour Demand* (Princeton: Princeton University Press).

Horton, S. (1996) (ed.) *Women and Industrialization in Asia* (London: Routledge).

ILO (1995) *World Employment, 1995* (Geneva: ILO).

Kanbur, R. (1987) 'Measurement and Alleviation of Poverty: With an Application to the Impact of Macroeconomic Adjustment', *IMF Staff Papers*, vol. 34, no. 1, pp. 80–5.

Kanbur, R. and M. Tuomala (1994) 'Inherent Inequality and the Optimal Graduation of Marginal Tax Rates', *Scandinavian Journal of Economics*, vol. 8, no. 2, pp. 191–211.

Kanbur, R., M. Keen and M. Tuomala (1994) 'Labour Supply and Targeting in Poverty Alleviation Programs, *World Bank Economic Review*, vol. 8(3), pp. 191–212.

Katz, L. and K. Murphy (1992) 'Changes in Relative Wages, 1963–1987: Supply and Demand Factors', *Quarterly Journal of Economics*, vol. 107 (February), pp. 35–78.

Kuznets, S. (1955) 'Economic Growth and Income Inequality', *American Economic Review*, vol. 45, no. 1.

Leamer, E. (1995) 'A Trade Economist's View of US Wages and "Globalisation"', Anderson Graduate School of Management, University of California at Los Angeles, mimeo.

Lewis, W. (1954) 'Economic Development With Unlimited Supplies of Labour', *The Manchester School*, vol. 22, no. 2.

Lindley, R. (1997) 'The International Economic Framework and European Labour Market Conditions', E. Amadeo and S. Horton (eds), *Labour Market Flexibility and Productivity in Latin America* (London: Macmillan).

Mazumdar, D. and P. Basu (1994) 'Macroeconomic Policies, Growth and Employment: The East and Southeast Asian Experience' (Washington DC: World Bank), draft.

Mazumdar, D. (1995) 'Labour issues in the World Development Report: a Critical Assessment', Toronto: Centre for International Studies, University of Toronto.

Mirrlees, J. (1971) 'An Exploration in the Theory of Optimal Income Taxation', *Review of Economic Studies*, vol. 38, pp. 175–208.

Moll, P. G. (1992) 'The Decline of Discrimination against Coloured People in South Africa, 1970 to 1980', *Journal of Development Economics*, vol. 37, no. 2.

Morley, S. (1994) 'Poverty and Inequality in Latin America: Past Evidence, Future Prospects' (Washington, DC: Overseas Development Council).

Murphy, K. and F. Welch (1992) 'The Structure of Wages', *Quarterly Journal of Economics*, vol. 107 (February), pp. 286–326.

Oxfam (1995) *The Oxfam Poverty Report* (London: Oxfam Publications).

Patrinos, H. A. (1994) 'The Costs of Ethnicity: an International Review' in G. Psacharopoulos and H.A. Patrinos (eds), *Indigenous People and Poverty in Latin America* (Washington DC: World Bank).

Persson, T. and G. Tabellini (1994) 'Is Inequality Harmful for Growth?', *American Economic Review*, vol. 84 (3), pp. 600–21.

Pritchett, L. (1995) 'Capital Flows: Five Stylized Facts for the 1990s' (Washington DC: World Bank), unpublished draft prepared for meeting on 'Managing economic reform under capital flow volatility' (31 May 1995).

Revenga, A. (1992) 'Exporting Jobs? The Impact of Import Competition on Employment and Wages in US Manufacturing', *Quarterly Journal of Economics*, vol. 107 (February), pp. 225–84.

Revenga, A. and C. Montenegro (1995) 'North American Integration and Factor Price Equalization: Is there Evidence of Wage Convergence between Mexico and the United States?' (Washington, DC: World Bank), mimeo.

Robbins, D. (1995a) 'Earnings Dispersion in Chile after Trade Liberalization', Harvard University, mimeo.

Robbins, D. (1995b) 'Schematic Summary of Findings for Country Wage and Employment Structure Studies', Harvard University, mimeo.

Romer, P. (1986) 'Increasing Returns and Long-run Growth', *Journal of Political Economy*, vol. 94 (October), pp. 1002–37.

Sahn, D. (1992) 'Public Expenditures in Sub-Saharan Africa During a Period of Economic Reforms', *World Development*, vol. 20, no. 5, pp. 673–93.

Stokey, N. (1994) 'Free Trade, Factor Returns, and Factor Accumulation', University of Chicago, mimeo.

Tuomala, M. (1990) *Optimal Income Tax and Income Distribution* (Oxford: Clarendon Press).

Tzannatos, Z. (1991) 'Reverse Racial Discrimination in Higher Education in Malaysia: Has it Reduced Inequality and at What Cost to the Poor?' *International Journal of Educational Development*, vol. 11, no. 3.

Wood, A. (1994) *North–South Trade, Employment and Inequality* (Oxford: Clarendon Press).

Wood, A. (1995) 'Does Trade Reduce Wage Inequality in Developing Countries?' Institute of Development Studies, University of Sussex, mimeo.

World Bank (1990) *World Development Report: Poverty* (New York: Oxford University Press).

World Bank (1993) *The East Asian Miracle: Economic Growth and Public Policy* (New York: Oxford University Press).

World Bank (1994) *Adjustment in Africa: Reform, Results and the Road Ahead* (New York: Oxford University Press).

World Bank (1995) *World Development Report: Workers in an Integrating World* (New York: Oxford University Press).

Part II
Development Issues

5 Does History have Useful Economics? Lessons from Europe's Golden Age (1950–73)[1]

Gianni Toniolo
UNIVERSITÀ DI ROMA TOR VERGATA, ITALY, AND DUKE UNIVERSITY, USA

> If we know what an economic miracle is, we ought to be able to *make* one. (R. E. Lucas, Jr, 1993).

1 FOUR STYLIZED FACTS ABOUT EUROPE'S GOLDEN AGE

Between 1890 and 1992, the real GDP of Western Europe grew at an average annual rate of 2.3 per cent, or 1.7 per cent per annum *per capita*. This performance is roughly consistent with Kuznets' expectations about the secular trend in 'modern economic growth.' If, however, as in Table 5.1, this past century is divided into four intervals, only the first (1890–1913) and the last (1973–92) exhibit growth rates that are roughly equal to the average for the whole period. The other two subsets are far off the average in a spectacular way: during 1913–50 the European economy distinctly underperformed while the opposite was the case in 1950–73 when product and productivity grew at rates never before or since experienced.

More technically, Crafts and Mills (1996) have shown that the rate of growth achieved between 1951 and 1973 did not statistically belong to the long-run trend in Europe's modern economic growth. In fact, so impressive was the achievement of the European economy in the quarter century following the 'reconstruction' that the period has often been referred to as the 'Golden Age.' The word 'miracle' was also often used.

Table 5.1 Western Europe's growth, 1890–1993 (average annual rates of growth)

Period	*Real GDP*	*Real GDP per capita*	*Real GDP per man/hour*
1890–1993	2.5	1.9	2.6*
1890–1913	2.6	1.7	1.6
1913–50	1.4	1.0	1.9
1950–73	4.6	3.8	4.7
1973–93	2.0	1.7	2.7**

* 1890–1987
** 1973–87.

Definition: GDP and population are aggregates for 12 countries (Austria, Belgium, Denmark, Finland, France, Germany, Italy, Netherlands, Norway, Sweden Switzerland, United Kingdom, all adjusted for boundary changes)

Sources: 1870–1989; Maddison (1991); 1989–93; OECD (1993).

Four 'stylized facts' of the Golden Age stand out.

(i) The Golden Age was mostly a European phenomenon: North America, Australia and Latin America show much less pronounced growth acceleration during 1950–73.
(ii) High growth rates, relative to previous and subsequent records, characterized almost all the individual European economies, regardless of their social, political and economic institutions. Authoritarian regimes, both right- and left-wing, were able to achieve spectacular results during 1950–73: growth rates of *per capita* GDP in Eastern Europe were roughly as high as those prevailing in the West (e.g., Ofer, 1992) while the Iberian economies under Salazar and Franco were among fastest growers in the West. It is only after 1973 that communist countries were increasingly unable to keep pace even with Western Europe's reduced growth rates.
(iii) European unemployment reached its lowest secular level during the Golden Age. In most countries, the 'conquest of full employment' was a distinct feature of the period, when compared with previous and subsequent records.
(iv) While there are strong doubts about the existence of a process of universal convergence, subsets of countries exist forming distinct 'convergence clubs' (Andres *et al.*, 1996; Broadberry, 1996). During the Golden Age Europe and North America belonged to the same club, so that the former as a whole caught up with the latter, thereby

more than making good the previous divergence. Within Europe, the Golden Age was strongly characterized by both β and σ convergence, to use Barro and Sala-i-Martin's (1991) terminology. In other words, during 1950–73 we observe both a pronounced tendency for initially poorer European countries to grow faster than richer ones and a decline in the cross-sectional scatter of *per capita* output growth. As a result, in 1973 the dispersion in *levels* of *per capita* income among European countries was much less pronounced than it had been in 1950 (Crafts and Toniolo, 1996).

The above-mentioned 'stylized facts' are specific to the Golden Age. Dating from around the so-called 'first oil shock': (i) Production and productivity growth levelled off around the secular trend, while at the same time volatility increased. (ii) The slow-down affected market and socialist economies alike. The latter's performance was particularly poor, when compared to the record of the previous period. (iii) Unemployment rates almost trebled in the 1980s relative to the 1960s. (iv) β convergence was weaker after 1973.

2 ECONOMISTS' EXPLANATIONS OF THE GOLDEN AGE – OLD...

Growth accounting was an intellectual product of the Golden Age. Denison (1967) pioneered the development of empirical methods to break down and quantify the contribution of individual inputs to output growth. This approach provided a powerful boost to empirical research. Huge amounts of data were collected, problems of cross-sectional and time-series comparisons were solved, clever ways of treating data were found. Measures of total factor productivity (TFP) were introduced, paving the way to a large body of literature seeking to break down Solow's residual into individual 'sources of growth' as in Denison's (1967) pioneering work. Kuznets' general finding that 'material' inputs 'explained' about one-third of output growth was confirmed for the Golden Age. As for capital, the treatment of physical inputs is today still considered acceptable while that of human capital is less than adequate since it ignores training, re-training and the role of externalities (Oulton and O'Mahony, 1994). More generally, the measure of economies of scale – accounting for over 20 per cent of output growth – is not fully convincing, given the author's Solowian framework (Rossi and Toniolo, 1996).

The growth accounting literature could only suggest hypotheses about the causes of the Golden Age, not test them. Denison and others showed that no single variable, individually taken, had an overwhelming explanatory power as a 'source of growth', a finding that should have warned against the largely 'mono-causal' explanations that bloomed in the same years and are briefly reviewed in what follows.

2.1 An Investment Boom

Maddison (1959, 1964) argued that since a huge increase in the ratio of investment to GDP was one of the macroscopic novelties of the decades under examination, investment itself must have been the main cause of the astonishing performance of the European economy. Assuming incorporated technical progress, Maddison sees investment as the main factor behind productivity growth. The latter, together with increased capacity, allowed for supply to meet the buoyant post-war demand – in its turn stimulated by investment – while at the same time maintaining price and balance of payment equilibria.

Denison's growth accounting results are sufficient to cast considerable doubt on the investment boom argument. Inputs of physical capital 'explained' only 17 per cent of *per capita* output growth. Accounting based on the new growth theory places greater emphasis than Denison on the role of physical investment, but it still 'explains' only a small fraction of output growth. Moreover, the rate of growth of total non-residential capital stock (1950–73) of a sluggish performer such as the United Kingdom was only slightly lower than Germany's and higher than France's or the Netherlands' (Maddison, 1995: 41).

2.2 Export-led Growth

Lamfalussy (1961, 1963) argued that Continental Europe's rapid economic growth was driven by its extraordinary export performance. This approach, also embraced by Beckerman (1962) and subsequently put forth by Thirlwall (1979), came to be known as the 'export-led growth' explanation of the Golden Age.

Balassa (1979) showed that only minor differences existed in the initial competitive positions of fast-and slow-growing countries: if this is the case, the question about the setting-in of the export-led growth remains unanswered. More recently, Krugman (1989) has persuasively argued that it is possible that a faster growth rate of productive potential results in faster export growth. If such is the case, the country concerned increases its world market share and seems to face higher income elasticities of demand for its exports while all the difference originates on the supply side. The causation process remains obscure.

2.3 Unlimited Supply of Labour

A low wage/productivity ratio stemming from the specific features of Continental Europe's labour market was one of the key factors in the export-led growth explanation of the Golden Age. Large reserves of agricultural or foreign labour constitute a key factor also in Kaldor's (1966) story. He argued that dynamic economies of scale, in the form of Verdoorn's law, exist in the manufacturing sector. When the latter face a highly elastic supply of labour, the country involved experiences higher rates of growth than the others, since the transfer of labour does not impede the growth of output in the sectors that give it up.

The role played in this explanation of the Golden Age by an army of underemployed workers implies an element of catch-up which is overlooked by Kaldor and his pupils (Cripps and Tarling, 1973). Moreover, econometric research has not been kind to the existence of Verdoorn's law (Gomulka, 1971; Rowthorn, 1975, Chatterji and Wickens, 1983), cutting the grass at the very root of Kaldor's proposition. Something of it remained, however, namely the intuition – unsatisfactorily specified as it was – that increasing returns may be crucial to a theory of economic growth.

Kindleberger's (1967) version of the unlimited supply of labour hypothesis is more appealing. His contention (1967, p. 3) was that 'the major factor shaping the remarkable economic growth which most of Europe has experienced since 1950 has been the availability of a large supply of labour'. A Lewis (1954)–Fei and Ranis (1964) growth model provided the theoretical underpinning for arguing that an elastic labour supply skewed income distribution in favour of profits, thereby sustaining unusually high investment ratios.

From an empirical point of view, statistical evidence about the association of high growth rates of output and of labour supply is stronger for the 1950s, the period covered by Kindleberger, than for the 1960s (Toniolo, 1971). At the same time it has been argued that post-war mass migrations were indeed the effect rather the cause of high growth in the recipient regions (Postan, 1967). As far as theory is concerned, today's mainstream economists have difficulties in accepting the Lewis model. For instance, Layard and his co-authors (1991, pp. 100–9) show that in a standard static bargaining model framework of the NAIRU model, the profit share is independent of the bargained wage and of union power, while at the macro-level unemployment adjusts to bring the target real wage into line with the feasible real wage.

2.4 New Stances in Demand Management

Demand management was, according to Boltho (1982) the true novelty of the Golden Age, while cheap labour and technology were not. According to the author, the virtue of the new economic policies was to stabilize expectations, thereby creating an environment more conducive to investment (and possibly consumption) growth than that of the interwar years (Boltho, 1982, Maddison 1960, 1991).

This hypothesis was tested by Kormendi and Meguire (1985), who found that higher output variance was positively rather than negatively related to growth. At the same time, they found that greater variation in unanticipated money did reduce growth. Thus a predictable monetary stance seems to have a favourable impact on growth while the smoothing of the cycle does not seem to be relevant. Unanticipated monetary shocks were certainly more a feature of the inter-war than of the post-war years and this may indeed go some way in explaining the different economic performance of Europe in the two periods. On factual grounds it should be noted that monetary policies of Germany and Italy, the two fastest growers, can hardly be described as Keynesian 'fine tuning'. On the other hand, while misguided monetary and fiscal policies were indeed among the main causes of slow growth during the interwar years (Temin, 1989) they amplified exogenous shocks, rather than created them (Feinstein *et al.*, 1996). The economic environment affecting investor and consumer expectations in the post-1918 and post-1945 periods differed in a much deeper way than just demand management.

2.5 The End of Perverse 'Distributional Coalitions'

Olson (1982) explained the rapid growth of the 1950s and 1960s as well as the subsequent slow-down as the end and re-birth of distributional coalitions.

Olson's contribution had the great merit of introducing political economy considerations into the debate. More specifically, institutions are explicitly brought to bear. This is precisely the area where research into the causes of the Golden Age has been weak and where economic historians, among others, may contribute considerable value added. However, while *a priori* plausible, Olson's explanation was met with two kinds of criticism. It has been argued that interest associations pursuing selfish interests do not necessarily threaten growth (Unger and van Waarden, 1994). Moreover Olson's thesis does not seem to sit well with facts. Paque (1994) argues persuasively that the institutional structure of the German labour market in the 1920s resembled much more that of Germany in the 1950s than that of the United Kingdom at any time in this century. Unger and van Waarden (1994, p. 10) go as far as to argue that war, foreign occupation and political disruptions 'seem to have furthered the development of association rather then weakened it'. Finally, econometric evidence has not been too kind to Olson's proposition. Crafts (1992) tried to add various measures of corporatism to a conventional catch-up model without being able to increase its explanatory power. In the same vein, a variable measuring time elapsed since the last interruption of democracy proved to be insignificant in a similar convergence model (Castels and Dowrick, 1990).

3 ...AND NEW

Explanations of the Golden Age advanced by 'old' economists undoubtedly point to relevant aspects of the story but have failed to satisfactorily account for the causes of such an important phenomenon. What explanatory impact can so far be credited to the 'new growth theory'? The appearance of latter is particularly intriguing to economic historians on two accounts. (i) It rigorously formalized and gave theoretical respectability to a view long held by economic historians (such as Gerschenkron) that modern economic growth rests on increasing or constant returns to the accumulation of reproducible factors of production. (ii) The variables emphasized by the new growth economists – i.e., education, training, property rights, institutions – typically require for their specification and testing the economic historian's idiosyncratic skills.

For the purpose of this chapter, the main novelties of the new growth economics are: (a) the treatment of catch-up as conditional convergence, (b) the emphasis on broad investment (incorporating human capital accumulation), and (c) the emphasis on institutions.

The 'new growth economics' was born and came of age at a time when the European supergrowth of 1950–73 was a fact of the past. Thus it either concentrated on the very long run (as in Barro and Sala-i-Martin, 1991) or referred to more recent supergrowth stories, or 'miracles' (as in Lucas, 1993). Specific application to the causes of the Golden Age is found primarily in the work of Nick Crafts (1995; Crafts and Toniolo, 1996) and his collaborators (Crafts and van Ark eds, 1996; Crafts and Toniolo eds, 1996).

Table 5.2 Comparison of 'sources of growth' estimates, 1950–73 (West German advantage over United Kingdom, % per year)

	'Old' growth accounting	*'New' growth accounting*
Backwardness	0.53	1.18
Investment	0.52	0.73
Human capital	–0.01	0.51
Other TFP	1.70	–0.02

Source: Crafts (1994, p. 438).

Crafts (1995) has summarized the contribution of new growth theory to our understanding of the Golden Age in the following two points: (i) acceleration growth is 'attributed largely to greater investment in both physical and human capital rather than greater scope for catch-up in terms of larger income gaps', (ii) more of the acceleration in growth is attributed to human capital and less to TFP growth' (see Table 5.2).

The catch-up element requires further consideration from both theorists and historians if it is to fit with the above-mentioned absence – both in the secular and in the post-war data – of world-wide convergence. The challenge to the theorist lies in developing growth models able to predict both that *some* poorer countries close the gap with richer ones and that others maintain the gap unchanged (or even allow for its widening). Referring to South-East Asia, Lucas (1993: 269) argued that 'A successful theory of economic miracles should ... offer the possibility of rapid growth episodes, but should not imply their occurrence as a simple consequence of relative backwardness'. For the economic historian, 'conditional' convergence calls for more refined analyses of Gerschenkron's (1963) 'virtue of backwardness'. To use a more modern concept, social capability for growth (Abramovitz, 1986) is where we should look in more depth. According to Crafts (1995a) it is the unsatisfactory way in which the catch-up element is embodied in new growth models that leads otherwise robust regression models based on the 'new growth' approach to 'underpredict European growth during the Golden Age and to overpredict growth in the interwar period' (Crafts, 1995, p. 439).

As for the other main ingredients of the new growth theory, there is widespread agreement that they are often not adequately specified and their empirical proxies are unsatisfactory. Let us refer to just one example. The splitting of human capital formation into two main sources – formal education and on-the-job training – was an important step towards a better specification of this variable. But the new growth theory is still weak about the interactions of the two, and of these with technical change. If codified knowledge is of increasing importance in our societies (David, 1994), its development does not flow from R&D only. It has been argued, for instance, that a most fundamental aspect of learning is the transformation of tacit into codified knowledge and the latter's spiral movement back to where new kinds of tacit knowledge are developed (Nonaka, 1991). If this is the case, the feature of the networks that transfer knowledge back and forth from the various points of its formation becomes crucial. Property right access and protection – emphasized but naïvely treated by the new growth theory – are certainly important, but so is trust. The study of national systems that, at various points in time, have been more or less successful in creating legal systems, social policies and a climate of trust inducive to growth is indeed where economic historians can make an important contribution to the new growth theory. The fact that this contribution has so far neither been solicited nor offered may explain why the latest developments in growth economics have failed, like the older ones, to contribute more than growth accounting and convergence stories to our understanding of the causation process of the rise and demise of Europe's Golden Age.

4 THE GOLDEN AGE AND THE LONG RUN

The causes of the Golden Age are rooted in Europe's previous history. The coincident coming about of a set of propitious circumstances was at the root of the Golden Age. These did not simultaneously materialize by chance but as the result of a stream of events seeded in the history of Europe.

If 'a country's potential for growth is strong not when it is backward in all respects but when it is technologically backward but socially advanced' (Abramovitz, 1990: 3), then to understand the reasons for the Golden Age occurring at a specific point in time and space, we must pin down what made 'social capability' for growth so strong then rather than either previously or afterwards.

If none of the explanations reviewed in Sections 2 and 3 proved to be satisfactory individually, taken together they provide the main ingredients of the Golden Age. High investment rates were instrumental to the transfer of technology; exports added to scale economies; abundant labour allowed both its cheap reallocation to technologically advanced industries and wage moderation; demand management stabilized expectations and thus reinforced the investment drive. To these, one should add an adequate stock of human capital as well as apt institutions, as stressed by the 'new growth theory'. A crucial question, however, remains: what made the above-listed ingredients – most of which had been there for a long time – catalyze into the 'social capability for growth' that generated the Golden Age?

The specific factors that triggered the super-growth of the 1950s and 1960s can be appreciated when taking a longer-run perspective. Three sets of facts – the first specifically economic, the second economic and institutional, the third broadly socio–political – appear to be strong candidates to the role of peculiar growth-enhancing factors of the Golden Age. They are briefly sketched in what follows.

4.1 Human Capital and Technology Transfer

In 1950, capital per worker in the United States was about three times higher than that in the largest European countries (Table 5.3). The gulf would appear even wider if Italy were included or if machinery and equipment only were considered. The United States enjoyed a leadership in human capital as well, but in this area the European disadvantage was of minor proportions. This was a situation where a major opportunity for rapid catch-up growth existed in the laggard countries by adopting the leader's technology, adoption that would not be frustrated by an inapt labour force. But why was the potential for rapid growth not grasped by Europe then or in the 1920s? The reasons lay partly in what will be said below about the post-war settlements and the overall issue of European stability, partly in the nature of technology and consumer demand.

Table 5.3 Stock of physical and human capital per head in three large European countries in 1950 (United States = 100)

	*Physical capital**	*Human capital***
	(1)	(2)
United Kingdom	21.2	94.0
France	31.3	85.0
Germany	31.7	92.3

Notes:
* Stock of machinery and non-residential structures per worker.
** Years of education per person aged 15–64.

Source: Maddison (1995, pp. 36–7).

At the time the First World War broke out in Europe, the introduction of Ford's moving assembly line inaugurated the age of mass production in America. The consumer revolution that followed in the 1920s depended both on low production costs made possible by the new process technology and by a rapidly expanding demand for consumer durables. Supply- and demand-side factors were mutually reinforcing in a virtuous circle. Neither factor was equally favourable in Europe. On the supply side instability was an important, if hardly quantifiable, obstacle to the adoption of the latest American mass production techniques. As for demand, most of Europe was lagging behind the United States in *per capita* income by about 20 years and therefore it had not yet entered the stage when income elasticity of demand for consumer durables is exceptionally high. In the richest European country, Britain, Fordism was introduced in the late 1920s (Lewchuck, 1992). In Germany and France, mass production techniques were adopted in the 1930s when demand for consumer durables was picking up. These promising developments were cut short by the Second World War.

At the end of the conflict, the situation in Europe was uniquely suited for rapid adoption of American mass production technology. While the accumulation of physical capital had suffered a major setback in the previous decade, human capital had continued to grow (Table 5.3). Output per worker was low due to inadequate capital–labour ratio, but the latter could be raised rapidly thanks to the high quality of the labour force. As Barro and Sala-i-Martin (1991) have pointed out, the potential for catch-up is likely to be a function of the gap between steady-state and actual output per worker. In 1950, this gap was very large in Europe. At the same time the available technology happened to be of the kind required to meet the demand for mass consumption goods that could be expected to boom given Europe's *per capita* income at the beginning of the 1950s, roughly the same as America's around 1920.

The advanced versions of Fordism and Taylorism then available in America suited post-depression post-war European rationalism. The experience of reconstruction reinforced the idea that some sort of soft planning was good for growth. An unsophisticated consumer required large quantities of fairly homogeneous goods rather than quality diversification.

4.2 The Post-war Settlement

The 'second post-war settlement' has been seen as the trigger of the rapid growth of 1950–73. The received wisdom is that it created an international economic environment conducive to growth via stable expectations and decreasing international transaction costs. In each country there was also a domestic side to the 'settlement', not very well known outside the specialist circle of national historians. Recent research (Eichengreen, 1996) is trying to establish that the two sides – international and domestic – were mutually reinforcing.

Wage moderation was crucial in stimulating both the demand and the supply of investment – demand by making investment profitable, supply by making available the profits to finance it (e.g., Glyn, Hughes, Lipietz and Singh, 1990). However, as Eichengreen (1996) pointed out, wage moderation could not take place unless commitment and coordination problems were solved. A set of domestic institutions was developed, or rather adapted, to facilitate the solution of those problems.

Assuming that welfare is maximized when a cooperative equilibrium exists whereby both capitalists and workers agree to defer current compensation in return for future gains, Eichengreen (1996) observes that such equilibrium may be impossible to sustain since the sequences of commitments makes it time-inconsistent. If liquidity is needed for new investments then workers must exercise moderation *now* in order for capitalists to invest *later*. Once wage restraint is obtained, however, capitalists are better off by reneging on their agreement to invest, paying out dividends instead. A binding contract is therefore needed between the two social groups to overcome the dynamic inconsistency problem, rendering both groups better off. Eichengreen (1996) argues that the social and economic institutions developed in most European countries after the Second World War can be thought of as mechanisms to enforce this agreement. In particular, institutions were developed or adapted to (a) monitor the compliance of capitalists to their deferred contribution to the bargain and disseminate evidence that reduced the risk that shirking went unnoticed; (b) create bonds (benefits) that would be lost in the event of reneging; (c) precommit unions to wage moderation.

Eichengreen (1996) quotes the Dutch, German, Austrian, Norwegian and Belgian cases as particularly apt to fit his model, while he sees France and Italy as outliers to it. It may, however, be argued that the latter Latin countries also developed their own informal incomes policy. Both had strong communist-led unions that exercised great moderation, particularly in Italy, both had rather centralized wage-setting mechanisms, both introduced various kinds of bonds as inducement to avoid renegation on the informal social pact. In both countries, and particularly in Italy, the state – a major employer and producer – played a role that cannot be overlooked.

The post-war informal institutional arrangements show strong path-dependence from previous ones. Eichengreen (1996) rightly argues that institutions are resistant to change: they coordinate the action of a large number of individual parties, most of whom must be convinced that change is in their own interest. It may be added that they establish patterns of behaviour, interpersonal links and connections with other institutions that display very high transaction costs to transformation. The post-war situation provided an excellent opportunity for robust adaptation to new circumstances rather than for radical change.

The role of domestic institutions in promoting growth was reinforced by international ones. The Marshall Plan provided the initial condition for the wage moderation in that it allowed population in the lowest income quartile to avoid extreme hardship if not starvation. This made unions more willing to make the first move in the above-mentioned dynamic game. In other words, the Marshall Plan provided the first bond, or incentive, to play by the new informal rules. Thus, international institutions not only promoted growth via international trade but contributed to the efficacy and strength of domestic ones that in their turn made the dismantling of pre-war and wartime barriers attractive.

4.3 The Stability Issue

An economist's story may well stop here. There is, however, a further question. Was the above-mentioned equilibrium growth pattern the cause or the effect of social and political stability that is so strictly intertwined with 'social capability for growth'? Surely, success created social consensus. But how did stability and consensus come about in the first place? The question is not one that growth economists can afford to overlook. European societies had long been divided and highly ideological. The blame for the unsatisfactory first post-war settlement cannot be laid at the door of incompetent politicians only: its outcome was deep-seated in Europe's politics and society. Some important changes in the latter must have taken place for the second settlement to produce such a different result in terms of stability and consensus. In other words: how could Western Europe 'achieve political and social stability by mid-twentieth century after two great destructive wars and the intervening upheaval'? (Maier, 1987, p.154).

By the end of the nineteenth century, Europe's liberal capitalism was floundering under the weight of its own success: industrial development had resulted in the creation of an *élite* working class, conscious of its actual economic and potential political roles. Organized labour movements, socialist and to some extent catholic parties challenged the social legitimacy of the system on grounds of both electoral representation and income distribution. Moreover, during the 1880s and 1890s, the ability of nineteenth-century liberal capitalism to 'deliver the goods' was questioned. The social justification of capitalist entrepreneurship itself was contested.

Maier's (1987) persuasive intuition is that reversing the crisis of European liberal capitalism took half a century and two atrocious wars. To recreate stability, the *élites* – old and new – of Western European societies had to solve two related sets of problems: those of legitimation and those of production.

The problem of social legitimation of entrepreneurial capitalism was solved in the 1920s. 'The Left never again challenged the premise that production was a question of managers and engineers with the same vigour that they had immediately after the first war' (Maier, 1987, pp. 166–7). However, the problem of output growth and high employment was not solved in the 1920s and 1930s. It was on this ground that liberal capitalism came to be challenged, both from 'within' and from 'without'.

'Only by the 1950s were afflictions that undermined capitalist stability effectively overcome as a whole. The cumulative achievement required the institutional flux that was left in the wake not of one but of two wartime upheavals' (Maier, 1987, p. 162). The military, political and social situation of 1945 was more favourable than that of 1919 to the creation of preconditions to stability precisely because it came at the end of a long and tragic historical process. If international leadership was so important, it took two wars for America to emerge as the only great power in the West. If the European Left was less threatening it was because reaction to Fascism and Nazism had given the Second World War much larger popular support than the first, which was felt to be an upper-class affair. For quite the same reasons, Catholicism was more ready to contain the radical flux from within and to appeal at the moderate electorate of the centre. After depression and wars a need was universally felt to pause, reconstruct and lead 'normal' lives. The very success of reconstruction – the speed of which took everybody by surprise – showed the enormous gains that could be derived from adopting America's productive ideology.

It can be said then that the Golden Age bloomed when the 'times were ripe', not by a historical accident but at the end of a long process of search for new stable equilibria in Europe.

5 DOES HISTORY HAVE USEFUL ECONOMICS?

Is there a general message in this story? Needless to say, history does not need to have useful economics. But so much better if it does.

5.1 Humility and Cross-fertilization

The case of Europe's Golden Age has attracted a terrific amount of interest from economists over the past 40-odd years. Nevertheless, at least one-third of its causes are still econometrically unexplained. This should be enough to inject the profession with a sound dose of humility while at the same time stimulate new research. Economists and economic historians together may reduce what was once called 'the measure of our ignorance', particularly by making better use of the notion of path-dependence, by refining measurement techniques, by understanding and specifying in each individual case or epoch the notion of 'social capability'.

5.2 Climbing the Causation Ladder

Explanations provided by economists of this long episode of super-growth tend to capture only the last liners in the causation chain. To be sure: it is important to show – as only economists can – that investments, exports, technology, human capital and institutions did cause growth and, if possible, to quantify the contribution of such factors. But questions remain unsolved further up the causation chain: Why did investment and exports boom in 1950–73, rather than earlier or later? Why were technology transfer and human capital so productive then? What made for the emergence and sustainability of particularly efficient economic institutions? The lesson here is that these are issues the economist may legitimately discard, not overlook. Her own job is to use theory and econometric techniques to sort out causal links between quantifiable economic variables. And we have seen how little consensus there still is in the profession about causality at this level. The economist, however, cannot ignore that her answers are often one or two steps away from 'ultimate' causes. In particular, she cannot do so when she claims, not without justification, that her discipline is the 'queen of social sciences', equipped to provide broad explanations for complex social phenomena.

5.3 History and Government Consultants

History does have lessons for development consultants to governments as well. In their profession, disregard for the historical pattern leading to current economic conditions and institutional webs may result in colossal failures. An example from the Golden Age may illustrate the point. Immediately after the war, the military occupation authorities in Germany aimed at destroying not only monopolies but corporatist practices as well (for instance, they sought to replace centralized with decentralized wage bargain). There were, to be sure, overwhelming political reasons for this stance. However, this was 'sound' economic advice as well. As we have seen, however, corporatist practices had a long tradition in Germany. The government was part and parcel of the wage-setting mechanism. A web of institutional and personal links existed that made corporatist *modus operandi* socially acceptable. The whole post-war idea of a 'social market economy' was rooted in German history. And we have seen how important these practices were, according to Eichengreen, to build the informal institution so important to create the virtuous wage–investment circle. The political economy of growth may indeed require of government consultants a more sophisticated understanding of economic history than they are currently ready to admit.

Note

1. This chapter draws on research done jointly with Nick Crafts for a project of the Centre for Economic Policy Research (CEPR), London, the results of which are contained in Crafts and Toniolo (1996). My intellectual debt to Nick is enormous.

References

Abramovitz, M. (1986) *Quantitative Aspects of Europe's Postwar Growth* (Cambridge: Cambridge University Press).

Abramovitz, M. (1990) 'Catching up, Forging Ahead and Falling Behind', *Journal of Economic History*, vol. 46, pp. 385–406.

Andres, J., R. Domenech and C. Molinas (1996) 'Growth, Convergence and Macroeconomic Performance on OECD Countries: A Closer Look', in Crafts and van Ark (eds), *Quantitative Aspects*.

Armstrong, P., A. Glyn and J. Harrison (1991) *Capitalism Since 1945* (Oxford: Blackwell).

Balassa, B. (1963) 'Some Observations on Mr. Beckerman's Export Propelled Growth Model', *Economic Journal*, vol. 73, pp. 784–5.

Balassa, B. (1964) 'Rejoinder', *Economic Journal*, vol. 74, pp. 240–2.

Balassa, B. (1979) 'Export Composition and Export Performance in the Industrial Countries, 1953–1971', *Review of Economics and Statistics*, vol. 61, pp. 604–7.

Barro, R. (1991) 'Economic Growth in a Cross Section of Countries', *Quarterly Journal of Economics*, vol. 106, pp. 407–44.

Barro, R. and X. Sala-i-Martin (1991) 'Convergence across States and Regions', *Brookings Papers on Economic Activity*, pp. 107–82

Beckerman, W. (1962) 'Projecting Europe's Growth', *Economic Journal*, vol. 72, pp. 912–25.

Beckerman, W. (1963) 'Reply', *Economic Journal*, vol. 73, pp. 785–7.

Boltho, A. (1982) 'Economic Growth', in Boltho, A. (ed.), *The European Economy: Growth and Crisis* (Oxford: Oxford University Press).

Broadberry, S. N. (1996) 'Convergence: What the Historical Record Shows', in Crafts and van Ark (eds), *Quantitative Aspects*.

Castels, G. and S. Dowrick (1990) 'The Impact of Government Spending Levels on Medium-Term Economic Growth in the OECD, 1960–85', *Journal of Theoretical Politics*, vol. 2, pp. 173–204.

Chatterji, M. and M. Wickens (1983) 'Verdoorn's Law and Kaldor's Law: A Revisionist Interpretation', *Journal of Post Keynesian Economics*, vol. 5, pp. 397–413.

Cornwall, J. (1968) 'Postwar Economic Growth in Europe: A Re-Evaluation', *Review of Economics and Statistics*, vol. 50, pp. 360–83.

Crafts, N. (1992) 'Institutions and Economic Growth: Recent British Experience in an International Context', *West European Policy*, vol. 15, no. 4, pp. 16–38.

Crafts, N. (1995) 'The Golden Age of Economic Growth in Western Europe, 1950–1973', *Economic History Review*, vol. 48, no. 3, pp. 429–47.

Crafts, N. and T. C. Mills (1996) 'Europe's Golden Age: An Econometric Investigation of Changing Trend Rates of Growth', in Crafts and van Ark (eds), *Quantitative Aspects*.

Crafts, N. and G. Toniolo (1996) 'Overview', in Crafts and Toniolo (eds), *Economic Growth*.

Crafts, N. and G. Toniolo (eds) (1996) *Economic Growth in Postwar Europe* (Cambridge: Cambridge University Press).

Crafts, N. and B. van Ark (eds) (1996) *Quantitative Aspects of Europe's Postwar Growth* (Cambridge: Cambridge University Press).

Cripps, T. F. and R. J. Tarling (1973) *Growth in Advanced Capitalist Economies, 1950–1970* (Cambridge: Cambridge University Press).

David, P. (1994) 'Technological Change, Intangible Investments and Growth in the Knowledge-Based Economy: the US Historical Experience', paper presented at the OECD Conference on *Employment and Growth in the Knowledge-Based Economy*, Copenhagen (November).

Denison, E. F. (1967) *Why Growth Rates Differ. Postwar Experience in Nine Western Countries* (Washington, DC: Brookings Institution).

Eichengreen, B. (1996) 'Institutions and Economic Growth: Europe After World War II', in Crafts and Toniolo (eds), *Economic Growth*.

Fei, J. C. H. and G. Ranis (1964) *Development of the Labor Surplus Economy: Theory and Policy* (Homewood, Ill.: R. D. Irwin).

Feinstein N. C., P. Temin and G. Toniolo (1996), *The European Economy Between the Wars* (Oxford: Oxford University Press).

Gerschenkron A. (1963) *Economic Backwardness in Historical Perspective* (Cambridge, MA: Belknap Press).
Glyn A., A. Hughes, A. Lipietz and A. Singh (1990), 'The Rise and Fall of the Golden Age', in S. Marglin and J. Schor (eds), *The Golden Age of Capitalism. Reinterpreting the Postwar Experience* (Oxford: Clarendon Press), pp. 39–125.
Gomulka, S. (1971) *Inventive Activity, Diffusion and the Stages of Economic Growth*, Institute of Economics, Aarhus University.
Hardach, G. (1987) 'The Marshall Plan in Germany, 1948–1952', *Journal of European Economic History*, vol. 16, pp. 433–85.
Hounshell D. (1984) *From the American System to Mass Production* (Baltimore, MD: Johns Hopkins University Press).
Houthakker, H. S. and S. P. Magee (1969) 'Income and Price Elasticities in World Trade', *Review of Economics and Statistics*, vol. 51, pp. 111–25.
Kaldor, N. (1966) *Causes of the Slow Growth of the United Kingdom* (Cambridge: Cambridge, University Press).
Kindleberger, C. P. (1967) *Europe's Postwar Growth. The Role of Labor Supply* (Cambridge, MA: Harvard University Press).
Kormendi, R. C. and P. C. Meguire (1985) 'Macroeconomic Determinants of Growth', *Journal of Monetary Economics*, vol. 16, pp. 141–63.
Krugman, P. (1989) 'Differences in Income Elasticities and Trends in Real Exchange Rates', *European Economic Review*, vol. 33, pp. 1031–54.
Kuznets, S. (1965), *Economic Growth and Structure* (London: Heinemann).
Lamfalussy, A. (1961) 'Europe's Growth: Due to Common Market?' *Lloyds Bank Review* (October)
Lamfalussy, A. (1963) *The United Kingdom and the Six. An Essay on Economic Growth in Western Europe* (London: Macmillan).
Layard, R., S. Nickell and R. Jackman (1991) *Unemployment* (Oxford: Oxford University Press).
Levine R. and D. Renelt (1992) 'A Sensitivity Analysis of Cross-Country Growth Regressions', *American Economic Review*, vol. 82, pp. 942–63.
Lewchuk, W. (1992) 'Fordist Technology and Britain: The Diffusion of Labour Speed-up', in B. J. Jeremy (ed.) *The Transfer of International Technology. Europe, Japan and the USA in the Twentieth Century* (Aldershot: Edward Elgar), pp. 7–32.
Lewis, A. W. (1954) 'Development with Unlimited Supply of Labor', *The Manchester School*, vol. 22, pp. 139–91
Lucas, R. F., Jr. (1993) 'Making a Miracle', *Econometrica*, vol. 6, pp. 251–72.
Maddison, A. (1959) 'Economic Growth in Western Europe', *Banca Nazionale del Lavoro Quarterly Review* (March).
Maddison, A. (1960) 'The Postwar Business Cycle in Western Europe and the Role of Government Policy', *Banca Nazionale del Lavoro Quarterly Review* (June), pp. 99–148.
Maddison, A. (1964) *Economic Growth in the West* (London: Macmillan).
Maddison, A. (1991) *Dynamic Forces in Capitalist Development* (Oxford: Oxford University Press).
Maddison, A. (1991) *Dynamic Forces in Capitalist Development* (Oxford: Oxford University Press).
Maddison, A. (1995) *Monitoring the World Economy, 1820–1992* (Paris: OECD).
Maier, D. (1987), *In Search of Stability* (Cambridge: Cambridge University Press).

Nonaka, K. (1991) 'The Knowledge Creating Economy', *Harvard Business Review* (November–December).

OECD (1993) *Economic Outlook*, 54 (December).

Ofer, G. (1992) 'Productivity, Competitiveness and the Socialist System', in B. G. Hickman, *International Productivity and Competitivness* (New York: Oxford University Press).

Olson, M. (1982), *The Rise and Decline of Nations* (New Haven: Yale University Press).

Oulton, N. and M. O'Mahony (1994) *Productivity and Growth* (Cambridge. Cambridge University Press).

Paque, H. (1994) 'The Causes of Post-War Slumps and Miracles. An Evaluation of Olsonian Views on German Economic Performance in the 1920s and 1950s', *CEPR Working Paper*, 981 (London: CEPR).

Postan, M. (1967) *An Economic History of Western Europe 1945–1964* (London: Macmillan).

Rossi, N. and G. Toniolo (1996), 'Italy', in Crafts and Toniolo (eds), *Economic Growth.*

Rowthorn, A. P. (1975) 'What Remains of Kaldor's Law?', *Economic Journal*, 85, pp. 10–19.

Sachs, J. D. and A. M. Warner (1995) 'Economic Convergence and Economic Policy', *NBER Working Paper*, 5039 (February).

Temin, P. (1989) *Lessons from the Great Depression* (Cambridge, MA: MIT Press).

Thirlwall, A. P. (1979) 'The Balance of Payments Constraint as an Explanation of International Growth Rate Differences', *Banca Nazionale del Lavoro Quarterly Review*, 128, pp. 44–53.

Toniolo, G. (1971) 'Le cause dello sviluppo europeo del dopoguerra: una riconsiderazione', *Quaderni Storici*, vol. 16, pp. 174–200.

Unger, G. and F. Van Waarden (1994), 'Interest Associations and Economic Growth. A Critique of Mancur Olson's 'Rise and Decline of Nations', *CEPR Discussion Paper*, 894 (London: CEPR)

Verdoorn, P. J. (1949) 'Fattori che regolano lo sviluppo della produttività del lavoro', *L' Industria*, vol. 1, pp. 45–53.

6 Have the Extent and the Impact of Chronic Malnutrition been Underestimated? A Theory of Technophysio Evolution and its Implications for Nutritional Standards*

Robert W. Fogel
UNIVERSITY OF CHICAGO

The debate over the extent of chronic malnutrition in developing countries, which began after the Second World War, has been conducted largely between investigators associated with the FAO, WHO, and the World Bank (FAWOB) on the one hand and critics who believe that their estimates of the extent of malnutrition are too high.

Few investigators have suggested that the FAWOB estimates are too low.[1] One reason for the neglect of this possibility is the tendency of investigators to explicitly or implicitly assume that affluent persons in affluent countries reached genetic potential during the middle decades of the twentieth century and that no further improvements in physiology were possible without some major genetic breakthrough. That proposition, which was widely accepted in biomedical circles during the 1970s, has recently come under scrutiny by investigators concerned with problems of aging.[2]

These new aging studies do not rule out genetic factors but suggest something much less rigid than genetic programming of absolute life spans. An emerging theory of aging combines genetic susceptibility of various organs with cumulative insults as a result of exposure to risk. One important implication of this line of work is that there exists a synergism between technological and physiological improvements that has produced a form of human evolution that is biological but not genetic, rapid, culturally transmitted, and not necessarily stable. I call this process, which still is ongoing in both rich and developing nations, '*technophysio evolution*'.[3]

Unlike the genetic theory of evolution through natural selection, which applies to the whole history of life on earth, technophysio evolution applies only to the last 300 years of *human history*, and particularly to the last century. Despite its limited scope, technophysio evolution appears to be relevant to forecasting likely trends over the next century or so in longevity, the age of onset of chronic diseases, body size, and the efficiency and durability of vital organ systems. The theory also has implications for the measurement of the extent of chronic malnutrition in various countries.

The chapter is divided into three sections. Section 1 reviews the evolution of the debate over the proper way to measure undernutrition (which I also refer to as 'chronic malnutrition'). Section 2 proposes methods of measuring chronic malnutrition consistent with the theory of technophysio evolution. Section 3 reconsiders some aspects of the 'adaptation controversy'.

1 CHANGING VIEWS OF CHRONIC MALNUTRITION AND OF THE METHODS OF MEASURING IT

Nutritional science was still in its infancy during the early twentieth century. It was not until the turn of the century that Wilbur O. Atwater and his collaborators had estimated the energy requirements of basal metabolism.[4] Except for scurvy, specific nutrient deficiencies were not discovered until after the First World War: vitamin D for rickets in 1922, thiamine for beriberi in 1933, and niacin for pellagra in 1937 (Kiple, 1993).[5]

By the end of the Second World War nutritional science had matured to the point that it was possible to ask and provide reasonable answers to the question of the extent of malnutrition in various countries around the world. That task was undertaken by the Food and Agriculture Organization of the United Nations (FAO), which monitored the food supply through a series of surveys, the fifth of which was completed in 1985.[6] These surveys were based on the construction of national food balance sheets that made it possible to estimate in many countries the daily number of calories available for consumption *per capita*.[7] This information was supplemented by household dietary surveys based on reports of the food consumed by all the individuals in the household over periods from one to several days. The food diaries generally revealed a substantially lower level of caloric consumption than did the national balance sheets. The validity of these methods of estimating the consumption of food became central points of controversy.

Equally controversial were efforts to estimate average physiological requirements of energy in countries around the world.[8] In addition to estimating the energy required for basal metabolism, it was necessary to estimate the minimal amount of energy required for maintenance as well as the specific amounts of energy required for different tasks. The work of numerous investigators on these issues was summarized and synthesized in a series of expert consultations. Published in 1957, 1973 and 1985, these consultations yielded somewhat contradictory assessments of all three categories of energy requirements: basal metabolism, maintenance and activities (FAO, 1957; FAO/WHO, 1973; WHO, 1985).

There was an important shift in the conception of nutritional diseases that began in the late 1950s and extended through the mid-1970s. Prior to that period nutritional diseases were limited to those caused by specific nutrient deficiencies, such as pellagra, rickets and beriberi. General undernutrition, so widespread in developing nations, was considered to be a normal, if undesirable, characteristic of these societies. During the 1950s and 1960s physicians, nutritionists, and epidemiologists began to define substantial undernutrition as a disease called '*protein–energy malnutrition*' (PEM). In the *Ninth International Classification of Diseases* (US Department of Health and Human Services, 1980) and in the publications of the World Health Organization (WHO), anthropometric indicators are used to specify the degree of PEM.[9] These anthropometric indicators include low weight-for-age, low weight-for-height, and low height-for-age. Low weight-for-height or for-age is called 'wasting' and low height-for-age is called 'stunting'. A series of studies during the 1970s and 1980s demonstrated that weight at given ages, weight-for-height, and height-for-age were effective predictors of the risk of morbidity and mortality among children under 5.[10]

Perhaps the most important development during this period was the discovery of a synergy between infections and malnutrition. Scrimshaw, Taylor and Gordon (1968) showed that while malnutrition makes infections more severe, infections in turn increase the severity of malnutrition. Mechanisms through which malnutrition reduces resistance to infection include reduced production of humoral antibodies, impaired cell-mediated immunity, and weakened phagocytosis. Conversely, infections, regardless of the etiology of the infectious agent, worsen nutritional status through increased metabolic loss of nutrients, reduced appetite, decreased absorption, and the diversion of nutrients to combat the infection.

The transformation of undernutrition from a normal condition to a disease intensified the criticisms of the FAWOB approach to chronic malnutrition. Three main lines of criticism emerged. It was argued, first, that methods of constructing balance sheets grossly exaggerated the level of nutrient consumption in rich countries (by underestimating losses in distribution and plate waste) and underestimated the nutrients available in poor countries (by omitting non-standard types of foods). Second, the threshold of malnutrition was overestimated by a failure to take adequate account of the extent to which undernourished individuals could successfully adapt to their situation.[11] The third line of criticism focused on the use of the United States and British growth standards as a basis for judging stunting and wasting among individuals in South Asia and other regions in which malnutrition was prevalent.[12] The counter-interpretation was summed up by the aphorism 'small but healthy'.

2 THE IMPLICATIONS OF TECHNOPHYSIO EVOLUTION FOR THE ASSESSMENT OF CHRONIC MALNUTRITION

A difficulty with the FAWOB approach to the measurement of chronic malnutrition is that their standards are based on heights and weights derived either from British body builds of the early 1960s and 1970s or US body builds of the early 1970s. Neither the British nor the United States claim that their body builds are optimal. They claim only that they are representative of the actual distribution of height, weight, and weight-for-height at specific ages in their respective countries. In practice, however, it has been assumed that the fiftieth centile of these distributions is optimal.

Should the fiftieth centile of the British and American height distributions be accepted as the standard for developing nations? Critics of FAWOB have called these standards too high. However, a recent study of growth patterns of Indian children revealed that the age-specific height and weight distributions of affluent Indian children were quite similar to the distributions at corresponding ages obtained from the United States and Great Britain (Agarwal *et al.*, 1991).

That finding, important as it is, does not settle the issue. It merely confirms that the environmental constraints on the growth of affluent Indians are similar to those prevailing in Britain. The finding does not demonstrate that affluent Indian children are not stunted relative to their genetic potential nor does the finding establish that the fiftieth centile of the British and American height distributions is optimal.

2.1 The Problem of Perspective in an Age of Technophysio Evolution

If human physiology was static there would be far less difficulty in establishing anthropometric standards for measuring chronic malnutrition in poor nations. However, as is illustrated by Figure 6.1, there have been enormous changes in British physiology over the past two centuries.[13] Figure 6.1 presents the bottom half of current Dutch growth centiles. The average heights of successive generations of male adolescents in Great Britain between 1748 and 1993 are superimposed on that grid. It can be seen that as one generation succeeded another, the average trajectory of adolescent growth moved up the grid. The upward movement was uneven. The largest increase took place during the twentieth century.

Obviously, a judgement of the severity of malnutrition in India today depends on which of the height profiles shown in Figure 6.1 is chosen as the standard. Suppose we used not the British height profiles of the 1960s as the standard for judging the deficit in current Indian stature, but those of the 1920s which were only at the fifth centile of the current Dutch standard (see Figure 6.1). The switch to the British standard of the 1920s

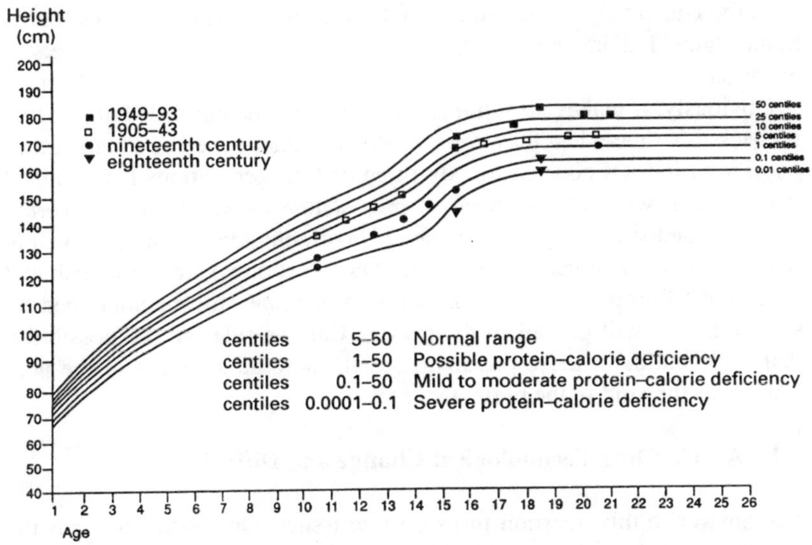

Source: Fogel, Floud *et al.* (in progress).

Figure 6.1 Secular trends in the average heights of male adolescents in Great Britain, 1748–1993

would make Indian malnutrition today seem less severe because the nutritional status of British children 70 years ago was relatively poor by current Dutch standards. Even British children of the early 1960s fall short of the current Dutch standard by about a half a standard deviation.

I have used the Dutch standard to assess British stature because the Dutch are currently the tallest population in the world, with males averaging about 181 cm at maturity, which is about 4 cm greater than the stature of mature males in both Britain and the United States today. In 1860, however, Dutch males were only 164 cm at maturity. British and American males were also shorter at maturity in 1860 than they are today, but in 1860 the British were 4 cm taller than the Dutch while the Americans were 8 cm taller than the Dutch. In other words, heights have grown substantially over the past four generation in all three societies. But the Dutch have grown most rapidly, partly because they were more stunted during the nineteenth century than were either the British or the Americans.[14]

Notice that a height of 164 cm at maturity would put the Dutch of 1860 below the first percentile of the current Dutch height distribution (see Figure 6.1). In other words, if we use the current Dutch standard, we would conclude that the Dutch in 1860 and Indians in the 1980s suffered from similar degrees of chronic malnutrition. On the other hand, if we used the Dutch height distribution of 1860 as the standard for good nutritional status, Indians in the 1980s would be judged to have good levels of nutrition.

Obviously, it makes no sense to use European height distributions that go back to a time when they were severely malnourished as a standard of good nutrition. Of course, nobody three or four generations ago realized that children who were then of average stature or weight were severely malnourished since they had no way of predicting that stature and weight would increase as much as they have. The question is, are the British and other West Europeans as well as North Americans still malnourished by standards that will prevail in the future? Can we rule out the possibility that body builds in these populations will increase as much in the next century as they did in the previous one?

2.2 Accelerating Technological Change and Diffusion

The answer to this question turns on two issues. One issue concerns the past, and the likely future, of technological change. The other is the past, and the likely future, of technologically-induced physiological change. Figure 6.2 provides an insight into the first issue. It shows the growth of the world's population during the last 11 000 years and also indicates

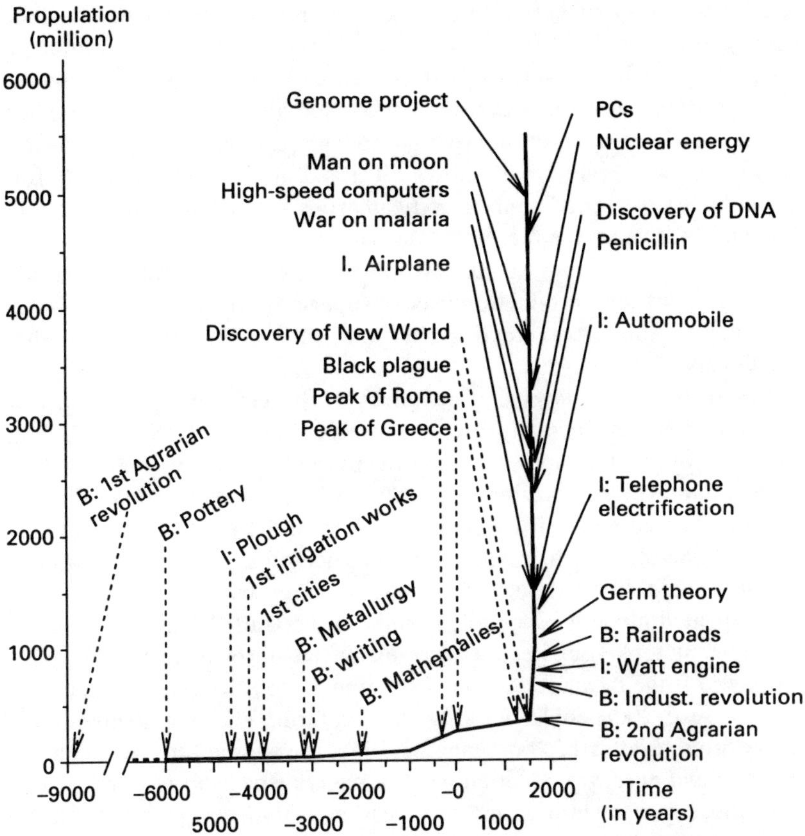

Notes: I = invention; B = beginning. There is usually a lag between the invention of a process or a machine and its general application to production. 'B' is intended to identify the beginning, or the earliest stage, of this diffusion process.

Sources: Cipolla (1974), Clark (1961), Fagan (1977), McNeill (1971), Piggott (1965), and Trewartha (1969); see also Allen (1992, 1994), Slicher van Bath (1963), and Wrigley (1987).

Figure 6.2 The growth of the world population and some major events in the history of technology

some of the major events in the history of technology. During all but the last 11 000 years our species survived on the meager food supply that was possible under a technology of hunting-and-gathering. For nearly 190 000 years we lived in far-flung communities, each of which was quite small and barely able to cope with its environment.[15]

The discovery of agriculture broke the tight constraint on the food supply imposed by the previous hunting-and-gathering technology, making it possible to release between 10 and 20 per cent of the labour force from the direct production of food, and also giving rise to the first cities. However, even these processes developed very slowly by current standards. As Figure 6.2 shows, it took about 4000 years before agriculture superseded hunting and gathering as the main source of food. It took 5000 years for the first cities to emerge, 6000 years to develop writing, and 7000 years to invent mathematics. Nevertheless, the new technology of food production was so superior to the old one that it was possible to support a much higher rate of population increase than previously.

Figure 6.2 also shows that advances in the technology of food production after the Second Agricultural Revolution, which began about 1700, produced far more dramatic demographic changes than the First Agricultural Revolution, since for the first time in human history it became possible to free most of the labour force from the production of food. It was the liberation of humankind from agricultural production that made possible the dramatic rise in the manufacturing and service sectors that accompanied modern economic growth. In the United States in 1800, for example, it took four people working on the farm to feed one person working off the farm. Today, however, one person working on the farm is able to feed 200 people working off the farm. The new technological breakthroughs after 1700 in manufacturing, transportation, trade, communication and energy production were in many respects even more striking than those in agriculture, and they also contributed significantly to the growth of agricultural productivity.[16]

These new technologies and the concomitant changes in the organization of production permitted the world's population to increase at so high a rate that the line of population in Figure 6.2 appears to explode, rising almost vertically. In 1650 the total world population was about half a billion. The 1 billion mark was crossed in 1805, the 2 billion mark in 1927, and the 4 billion mark in 1974. Although the rate of population growth is beginning to slow down, it is forecast that world population will exceed 8 billion by 2020. Technological progress has been so great, and has accelerated so rapidly, that the world's supply of food and commodities has outstripped the pace of population growth during each of the 3 doubling periods since 1650, despite dire predictions that it was impossible to do so.

To my mind nothing dramatizes the incredible rate of acceleration in technological change more than the fact that it was impossible to transport human beings in heavier-than-air vehicles until 1903. But 66 years later there was an astronaut standing on the moon and having a conversation with fellow astronauts on earth that was overheard and observed by hundreds of millions of people around the globe.

Not only has technological change accelerated dramatically but the diffusion of modern technology has also accelerated greatly over the past two centuries. Modern economic growth began first in Great Britain early in the eighteenth century. It did not begin in the United States until the late eighteenth century. France joined them after the Napoleonic era. By the middle of the nineteenth century the circle expanded to include the Netherlands, Germany, Switzerland, Denmark, Norway, Sweden, Canada and Australia. Japan, Russia, and Argentina did not enter onto the path of modern economic growth until the end of the nineteenth century. For Italy and other West European nations, modern economic growth was delayed until the beginning of the twentieth century. Except for Japan, modern economic growth did not extend to Asia until after the Second World War.

Today, however, the most remarkable instances of rapid economic growth are in Asian and Latin American countries, which together represent more than half of the population of the world. Beginning in the early 1950s, first Japan, and then the Asian 'Tigers' (South Korea, Taiwan, Singapore and Hong Kong) and more recently China, Malaysia, Thailand, Indonesia, India and more than a dozen other countries often referred to as 'Emerging Market Economies' began growing in both GDP and in product *per capita* at rates that far exceeded the long-term experience of the early leaders. Japan has set the standard for this pattern. Its GDP increased by nearly 14-fold in just 4 decades, taking Japan from an impoverished land with characteristics typical of countries at low levels of development to the second wealthiest nation in the world. That large a leap took more than a century and a half in the West.[17]

2.3 Secular Trends in Average Food Supplies and BMI

What has the rapidly accelerating pace of technological change meant for the food supply? As a result of recent work by agricultural historians that question can now be answered.

Table 6.1 provides estimates of the daily supply of calories that goes back to the beginning of the eighteenth century. These estimates show that even in Britain, which had the most technically advanced agriculture during the eighteenth century, chronic malnutrition was exceedingly severe in 1700. The average daily caloric supply in Britain in 1700 was at

Table 6.1 Secular trends in the daily caloric supply in France and Great Britain, 1700–1989 (kcal *per capita*)

Year	*France*	*Great Britain*
1700		2095
1705	1657	
1750		2168
1785	1848	
1800		2237
1803–12	1846	
1845–54	2480	
1850		2362
1909–13		2857
1935–9	2975	
1954–5	2783	3231
1961		3170
1965	3355	3304
1989	3465	3149

Source: Fogel, Floud *et al.* (in progress).

the current level of Bangladesh. Although caloric supplies rose over the course of the eighteenth century, the British did not attain the level of the current Indian *per capita* supply until the start of the nineteenth century. As late as the middle of the nineteenth century the British *per capita* caloric supply was at or below the average caloric supply of nations that the World Bank designates as 'low-income economies'. The situation in France during the eighteenth century was even worse. Its *per capita* caloric supply put it at the level of poorest nations today such as Mozambique, Ethiopia and Somalia. It was not until well into the twentieth century that France and Great Britain achieved the type of food abundance that is currently characteristic of OECD nations (3417 kcals *per capita* daily).[18]

Table 6.1 thus confirms the evidence on stature contained in Figure 6.1. Both indicate that Europeans typically suffered from severe malnourishment until the turn of the twentieth century. This conclusion is buttressed by evidence on weight-for-height which indicates that the majority of the French during the eighteenth century were 'wasted', having Body Mass Indexes (BMI = kg/m^2) that were 20 per cent or more below current levels. In the English case, about 40 per cent of males fell into the category of 'wasted'. Thus the escape from severe chronic malnutrition is a recent phenomenon even for the rich countries of the world, belonging mainly to the twentieth century.[19]

2.4 The Relationship Between Body Size, the Risk of Chronic Morbidity and the Risk of Death

A number of recent studies suggest that current mean heights in Western Europe and the United States are suboptimal, when the optimal height is defined as that which minimizes the odds of dying over a specific age interval or the odds of developing chronic diseases over that interval. It is also possible to estimate the BMI or weight, at given heights, that minimize the odds of developing chronic diseases (at given ages). Two recent studies that suggest that current mean heights may be suboptimal are displayed in Figure 6.3. Part A of Figure 6.3 shows that short Norwegian men aged 40–59 at risk between 1963 and 1979 were much more likely to die than tall men. Part B shows that height is also an important predictor of the relative likelihood that men aged 23–49 would be rejected from the Union Army during 1861–5 because of chronic diseases. Despite significant differences in ethnicity, environmental circumstances, the array and severity of diseases and time, the functional relationship between height and relative risk are strikingly similar in the two cases.

Figure 6.4 shows that the same relationship between ill health and stature exists among males covered by the US National Health Interview Survey (NHIS) for 1985–8. Stunting during developmental ages had a long reach and increased the likelihood that people would suffer from chronic diseases at middle and late ages.

Waaler, the pioneer in this work, also studied the relationship in Norway between BMI and the risk of death in a sample of 1.7 million individuals. Curves summarizing his findings are shown in Figure 6.5 for both men and women. Within the range 22–28, the curve is relatively flat, with the relative risk of mortality hovering close to 1.0. However, at BMIs of less than 22 and over 28, the risk of death rises quite sharply as BMI moves away from its mean value.[20]

Figure 6.6 is termed a Waaler surface. It brings height, weight, BMI and the risk of dying into a single diagram. This figure contains three kinds of curves. The elliptical solid lines are iso-mortality curves. Each of these lines shows all the combinations of height and weight that yield a given level of mortality risk. The broken lines are iso-BMI curves. Each of these shows all the combinations of height and weight that yield a given BMI. The heavy solid line running through the minimum point of each iso-mortality curve is the curve giving the weights that minimize risk at each height.

Figure 6.6 shows that even when body weight is maintained at what Figure 6.5 indicates is an 'ideal' level (BMI = 25), short men are at

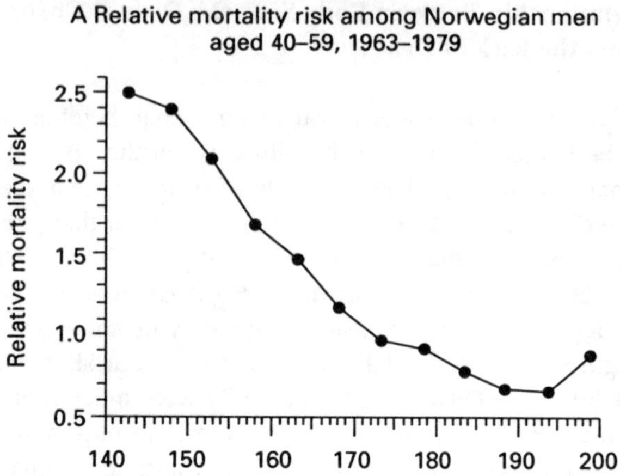

Source: Waaler (1984)

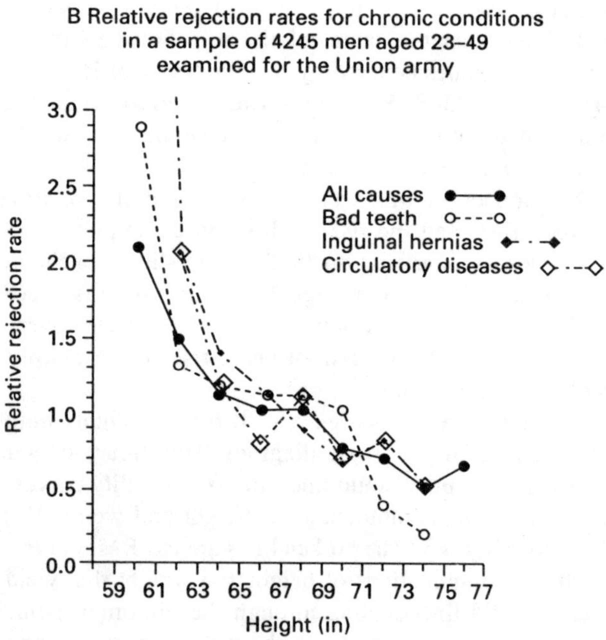

Source: Fogel (1993).

Figure 6.3 Comparison of the relationship between body height and relative risk in two populations

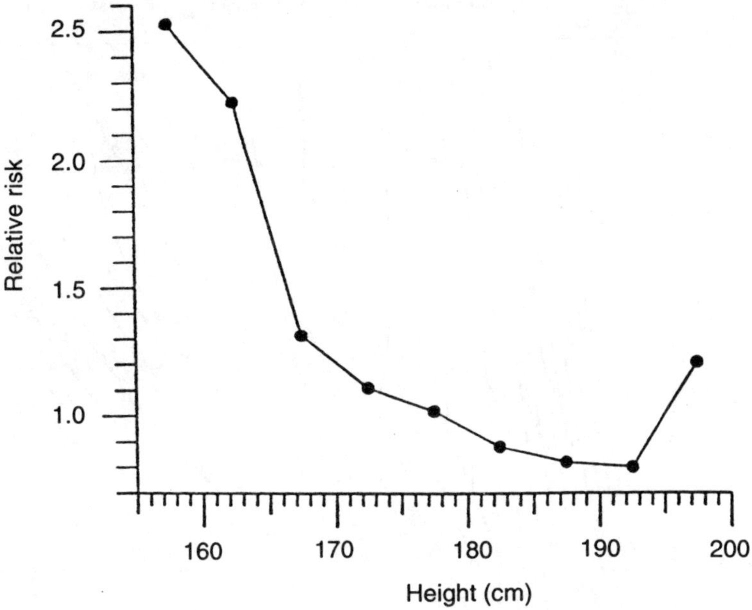

Source: Fogel, Costa and Kim (1993).

Figure 6.4 The relationship between body height and the risk of ill health in NHIS veterans aged 40–49

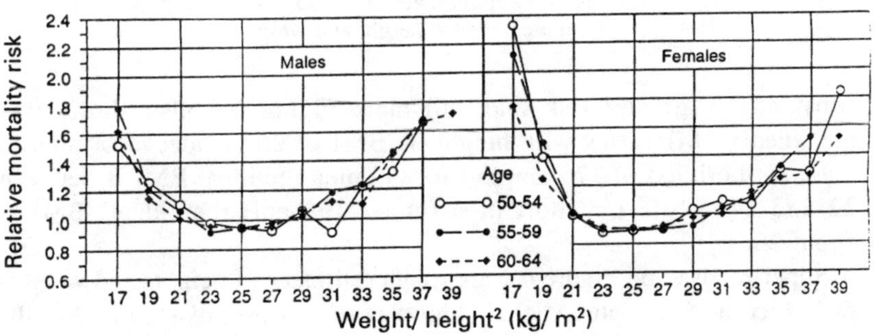

Source: Waaler (1984).

Figure 6.5 Relationship between BMI and prospective risk among Norwegian adults aged 50–64 at risk, 1963–79

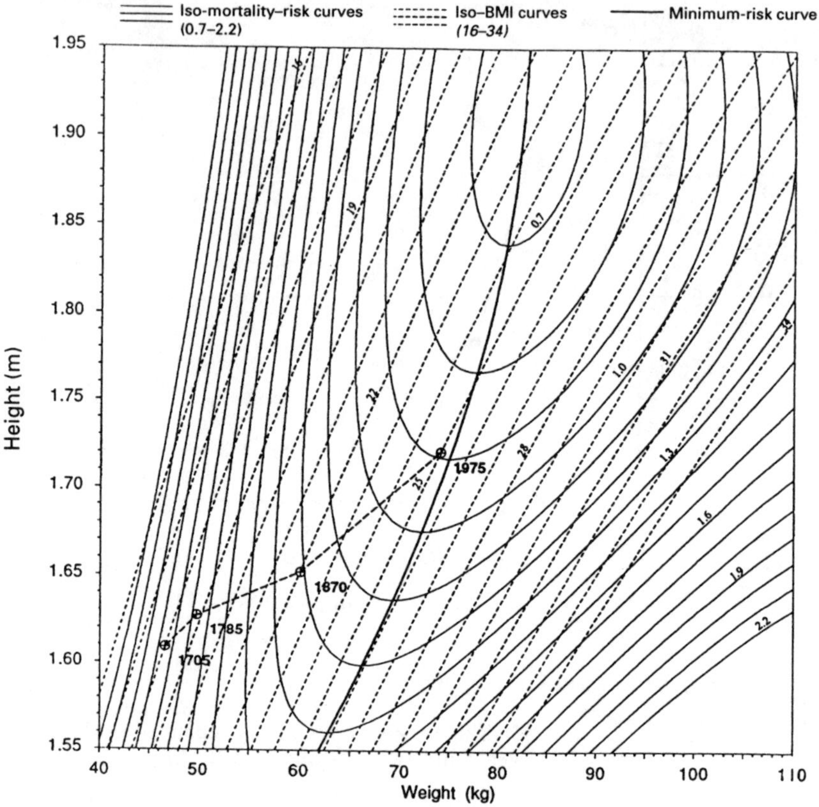

Figure 6.6 Iso-mortality curves of relative risk for height and weight among Norwegian males aged 50–64, with a plot of the estimated French height and weight at four dates

substantially greater risk than tall men. Figure 6.6 also shows that the 'ideal' BMI varies with height. A BMI of 25 is 'ideal' for men in the neighborhood of 176 cm, but for tall men the ideal BMI is between 22 and 24, while for short men (under 168 cm) the 'ideal' BMI is about 26.

Superimposed on Figure 6.6 are rough estimates of heights and weights in France at four dates (Fogel, Floud *et al.*, in progress). In 1705 the French probably achieved equilibrium with their food supply at an average height of about 161 cm and BMI of about 18. Over the next 270 years the food supply expanded with sufficient rapidity to permit both the height and the weight of adult males to increase. Figure 6.6 implies that while factors associated with height and weight jointly explain about 90 per cent of the estimated decline in French mortality rates over the period between c. 1785 and c. 1870, they explain only about 50 per cent of the decline in mortality rates during the past century.

Poor body builds increased vulnerability to diseases, not just contagious diseases, but chronic diseases as well. American males born during the second quarter of the nineteenth century were the first generation to reach age 65 in the twentieth century. They were not only stunted by today's standards, but their BMIs at adult ages were about 15 per cent lower than current US levels. The implication of combined stunting and low BMI is brought out by Figure 6.7 which presents a Waaler surface for morbidity based on NHIS data for 1985–8 that is similar to the Norwegian surface for mortality.

Figure 6.7 also presents the coordinates in height and BMI of Union Army veterans who were 65 or over in 1910 and of veterans (mainly of the Second World War) who were the same ages during 1985–8. These coordinates predict a decline of about 35 per cent in the prevalence of chronic disease among the two cohorts, which is quite close to what actually occurred. Table 6.2 compares the prevalence of chronic diseases among Union Army men aged 65 and over in 1910 with two surveys of veterans of the same ages in the 1980s. That table indicates that among the elderly heart disease was 2.9 times as prevalent, musculoskeletal and respiratory diseases were 1.6 times as prevalent, and digestive diseases were 4.7 times as prevalent among veterans aged 65 or over in 1910 as in 1985–8.[21]

Have Waaler curves and surfaces been shifting over time? It is too soon to answer that question with any confidence. Work is currently underway to construct Waaler curves and surfaces from morbidity and mortality data obtained from a large sample of data from the Union Army veterans covering the period between 1890 and 1930. Preliminary analysis based on a small subsample suggests that the Waaler curve in BMI for mortality for these men is quite similar to that shown for Norwegian males in Figure 6.5 (Costa and Steckel, forthcoming). This finding, incidently, contradicts the contention that the left-hand part of the Waaler curves in BMIs is attributable primarily to smoking, since smoking was relatively rare in the 1890s.

On the other hand, Kim (1995) has recently examined a succession of NHIS surveys between 1982 and 1992. These surveys indicate that the optimal weight at each height has been slowly shifting to the right. At a mean height of 175 cm for males, the optimal BMI has increased from about 25.9 to about 26.5 during this decade.

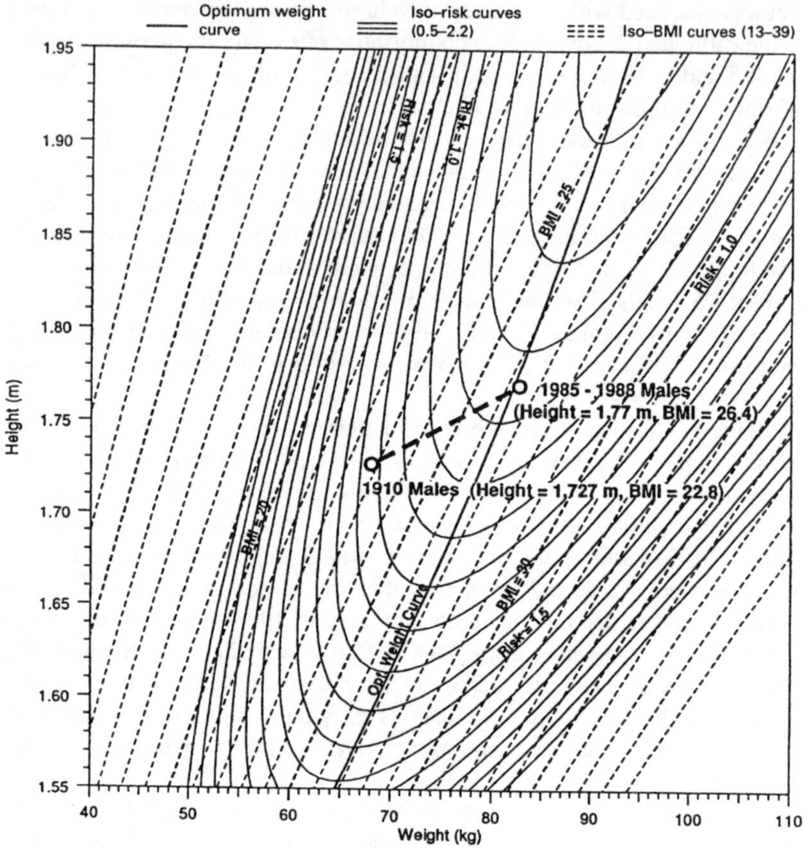

All risks are measured relative to the average risk of morbidity (calculated over all heights and weights among NHIS 1985–8 white males aged 45–64).

Source: Kim (1993).

Figure 6.7 Health improvements predicted by NHIS, 1985–8 health surface

2.5 Physiological Foundations for Waaler Surfaces and Curves

What is the basis for the predictive capacity of Waaler surfaces and curves? Part of the answer resides in the realm of human physiology. Variations in height and weight appear to be associated with variations in the chemical composition of the tissues that make up these organs, in the quality of the electrical transmission across membranes, and in the functioning of the endocrine system and other vital systems.

Table 6.2 Comparison of the prevalence of chronic conditions among Union army veterans in 1910, veterans in 1983 (reporting whether they ever had specific chronic conditions), veterans in NHIS 1985–8 (reporting whether they had specific chronic conditions during the preceding 12 months), aged 65 and above (%)

Disorder	*Union army veterans*	*1983 veterans*	*Age-adjusted 1983 veterans*	*NHIS 1985–8 veterans*
Skin or musculoskeletal	68.4	48.1	47.5	45.8
Musculoskeletal	67.7	47.9	47.2	42.5
Digestive	84.0	49.0	48.9	18.0
Hernia	34.5	27.3	26.7	6.6
Diarrhoea	31.9	3.7	4.2	1.4
Genito–urinary	27.3	36.3	32.2	8.9
Central nervous, endocrine, metabolic, or blood	24.2	29.9	29.1	12.6
Circulatory	90.1	42.9	39.9	40.0
Heart	76.0	38.5	39.9	26.6
Varicose veins	38.5	8.7	8.3	5.3
Hemorrhoids	44.4			7.2
Respiratory	42.2	29.8	28.1	26.5
Neoplasms	2.2	13.1	11.5	9.2

Source: Fogel (1993).

Research in this area is developing rapidly and some of the new findings are yet to be confirmed. The exact mechanisms by which malnutrition and trauma in utero or early childhood are transformed into organ dysfunctions are still unclear. What is agreed upon is that the basic structure of most organs is laid down early, and it is reasonable to infer that poorly developed organs may break down earlier than well developed ones (Tanner, 1990, 1993).

Recent research bearing on the connection between malnutrition and body size and the later onset of chronic diseases can conveniently be divided into three categories. The first category involves forms of malnutrition (including the ingestion of toxic substances) that cause permanent, promptly visible physiological damage, as is seen in the impairment of the nervous systems of foetuses due to excess consumption of alcohol or of smoking by pregnant women. It appears that protein–energy malnutrition

(PEM) in infancy and early childhood can lead to a permanent impairment of central nervous system function. Iodine deficiency in utero and moderate-to-severe iron deficiency during infancy also appear to cause permanent neurological damage.

Not all damage due to retarded development in utero or infancy caused by malnutrition shows up immediately. In a recent series of studies David Barker and his colleagues have reported that such conditions as coronary heart disease, hypertension, stroke, non-insulin-dependent diabetes and autoimmune thyroiditis begin in utero or in infancy, but do not become apparent until mid-adult or later ages.[22] In these cases, individuals appear to be in good health, and function well in the interim. However, early onset of the degenerative diseases of old age appears to be linked to inadequate cellular development early in life.

Certain physiological dysfunctions incurred by persons suffering from malnutrition can become irreversible or fatal if the malnutrition persists long enough. This category of dysfunctions includes the degradation of tissue structure, especially in such vital organs as the lungs, the heart and the gastrointestinal tract. In the case of the respiratory system, for example, there is not only decreased muscle mass and strength but also impaired ventilatory drive, biochemical changes in connective tissue, and electrolyte abnormalities.[23]

2.6 The Instability of Technophysio Evolution

Available data on stature and mortality from a number of countries indicate that during the eighteenth and nineteenth centuries technophysio evolution did not proceed steadily in either Europe or the United States. Figure 6.8 summarizes the available data on US secular trends in both stature and mortality since 1720. Both the series on stature and on life expectancy contain striking cycles. Both series rise during most of the eighteenth century, attaining substantially greater heights and life expectations than prevailed in England during the same period. Life expectancy began to decline during the 1790s and continued to do so for about half a century. There may have been a slight decline in the height of cohorts born between 1785 and 1820, but the sharp decline, which probably lasted about half a century, began with cohorts born around 1830. A new rise in heights, the one with which we have long been familiar, probably began with cohorts born during the last decade of the nineteenth century and continued for about 60 years. Similar cycles in height occurred in Hungary, Sweden and Britain.[24]

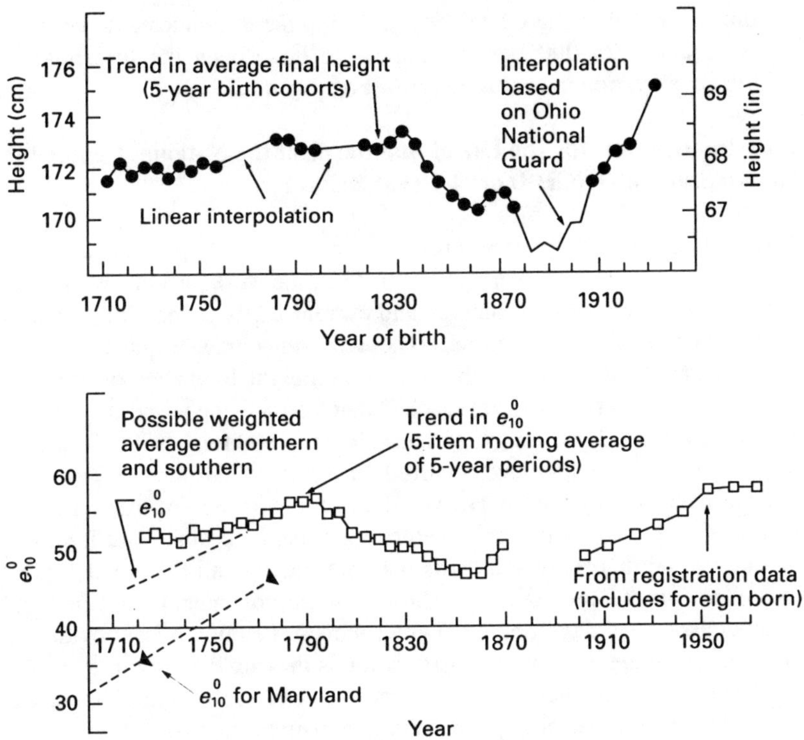

Figure 6.8 The trend in the mean final weight of native-born white American males and the trend in their life expectancy at age 10 (e_{10}) (height by birth cohort; e_{10} by period)

Although the mix of factors tending to retard improvements in nutritional status and health varied from one country to another, one factor stands out more than any other: rapid urbanization. In both Europe and America the urban population during the nineteenth century grew far more rapidly than at any other time in history, exceeding the capacity of the cities to supply clean water, remove waste, and contain the spread of infection (Bairoch, 1988; de Vries 1984). The mortality rate appears to have been influenced both by the size of the city and by the rapidity of its rate of growth. In the case of the United States around 1830, cities with 50 000 or more persons had more than twice the death rates of rural areas, and similar patterns have been observed for Europe. The exact threshold at which city size began to affect mortality rates varied with time, place, and circumstance, but in the United States during the mid-nineteenth century, cities of about 25 000 persons appear to have been the threshold of significant elevation in mortality rates (Fogel *et al.*, 1978).

2.7 Implications for the Use of Standards of the National Center for Health Statistics (NCHS) or of Great Britain

Although US and British children and adults live longer and have less disease than their counterparts in South Asia, the work on Waaler surfaces indicates that current final heights and current BMIs in the United States and Britain may be suboptimal. There is, of course, a question as to whether any society can reach an average height for males of 190 cm. Although no society has as yet reached that average, the possibility cannot now be ruled out. Few, if any, persons alive in 1800 forecast the increases in European stature that have occurred during the subsequent 195 years.[25]

Continued use of the NCHS standards for purposes of assessing the extent of malnutrition in less developed nations is feasible. But it should be understood that these standards may not indicate all the physiological improvements that are obtainable through an improvement in nutrition and in other aspects of developmental environment. Pending further evidence, an interim change worthy of consideration is making the growth curves of the Netherlands the international standard, since it is the nation that has so far achieved the greatest improvement in nutritional status.[26]

3 SOME ASPECTS OF THE ADAPTATION CONTROVERSY FROM THE PERSPECTIVE OF TECHNOPHYSIO EVOLUTION

Figure 6.6 and Table 6.1 make it clear that the limitation of body size has been one of the principal ways of adapting to low levels of energy. The point is not merely that height and BMI increased as the *per capita* supply of food increased. It is also that the traditional agricultural technology was too inefficient to have sustained a large average body size. If Frenchmen in 1800 were as large on average as they are today, there would not have been enough energy to produce the food supply, since all of the available energy would have been required for basal metabolism (see Fogel, Floud *et al.*, in progress).

Viewed historically, it makes little sense to talk about whether stunting (or wasting) is a desirable form of adaptation since there was no alternative. Indeed, it is only when the technology of food production became much more efficient than it had been during the eighteenth century, that it was possible to sustain large people. It was only after that juncture that individuals generally could have chosen between more energy and more industrial goods or other non-food commodities.

Figures 6.3, 6.4, 6.6 and 6.7 show that the cost of adaptation among stunted individuals cannot be measured merely by using cross-sectional data to determine whether productivity is positively correlated with stature. That procedure does not take into account the rate of decline in human capital over the life-cycle. Since stunting accelerates the rate of depreciation in human capital, the discounted present value of output is, on average, lower (cf. Dasgupta, 1993). Even if, at a given age, a short person who is still in the labour force is as productive as a tall one, more short than tall persons of that age have left the labour force because of disability or death (see Costa, 1995; Lee, 1995). Hence, there is sample selection bias in econometric studies that omit from consideration those members of a cohort who are no longer in the labour force. Even studies that show a positive effect of stature or BMI on output have biased the effect downward unless they have taken account of the omitted observations.

Figure 6.6 and 6.7 also point to another problem that is often overlooked. To equalize the rate of depreciation in human capital, stunted individuals require higher BMIs than tall individuals. For example, to equalize the odds of retaining good health in middle ages, a person of 165 cm needs a BMI that is 25 per cent higher than a person of 181 cm. However, when risks are equalized, the basal metabolic rate (BMR) of the stunted individual is higher than that of tall individuals. Figures 6.6 and 6.7 imply, therefore, that saving on the energy for basal metabolism requires an increased rate of depreciation in human capital. Hence, the essence of adaptation via body size to an inadequate food supply is a tradeoff of current metabolic needs for increased life-cycle risk of morbidity and mortality (see Fogel, Floud *et al.*, in progress).

Notes

* Research on this paper was supported by NIH Grant AG10120, NSF Grant SES-9114981, and the Charles R. Walgreen Foundation.

1. Recent overviews of the debate are contained in Payne (1990), Waterlow (1992), Beaton (1992), Osmani (1992a) and Dasgupta (1993).
2. The question of whether there is an upper limit to life in the neighborhood of 85 ± 7 years has been central to many recent aging studies. Some investigators have linked measures of biomedical and socioeconomic stress early in life to the odds of getting specific chronic diseases or of dying from

specific causes at middle and late ages. Other studies have used animal models to demonstrate that the $_nq_x$ schedule (the age-specific odds of dying over a specified interval) can be improved by changing environmental conditions, with life expectation increased several-fold. Still other studies have shown that age-specific mortality rates of individuals at very late ages have been declining continously for half a century in some 28 nations for which reliable data are available. Studies of Danish twins revealed that genetic factors accounted for about 30 per cent of the variation in mortality rates and environmental factors for about 70 per cent. See Fries (1980, 1989); Vaupel (1991a, 1991b); Thatcher (1992); Vaupel and Lundström (1994); Kannisto (1994); Kannisto *et al.* (1994); Carey *et al.* (1992); Curtsinger *et al.* (1992).

3. See Fogel (1997).
4. The Atwater factors which established the energy available per gram of protein, carbohydrates, and fat were also developed at this time (Carpenter, 1994; Atwater and Bryant, 1900).
5. It was not until 1943 that a committee set up by the National Academy of Sciences issued the first recommended dietary allowances of essential nutrients (National Research Council, 1943). Rough estimates of the energy required for different levels of work also go back to Atwater. However, the estimation of caloric requirements for specific activities was not worked out until after the Second World War (cf. Atwater, 1902).
6. The work of the FAO was spurred by the world-wide crisis in the supply of food precipitated by the disorganization of agriculture in war-torn countries. Estimates of the supply of food in 1946–47 revealed that the food production *per capita* was 15 per cent lower than in pre-war years. A variety of means were undertaken to increase the food supply rapidly. Government-organized relief efforts led by the United Nations included large direct shipments of food from the United States. The most important factor relieving the shortage, however, was the development of new scientific methods that revolutionized food production. These included the spread of commercial fertilizers to countries in the Third World that had never previously used them or had used them only to a very limited degree. Synthetic insecticides and pesticides also came into wide use in both developed and less developed regions, greatly reducing crop losses. Even more significant was the increasing use of such high-yield seeds as hybrid corn and new varieties of rice. The output of meat was increased through the use of animal vaccines, antibiotics, and hormones (FAO 1946, 1952, 1964, 1977, 1987).
7. The first survey provided balance sheets for countries initially covering about half the world's population. In addition to estimating the energy available in that food supply, estimates were made of the composition of the diet including protein, vitamins and trace elements (FAO 1946, 1952, 1964, 1977, 1987; cf. Fogel, 1993).
8. Equations were worked out relating the energy requirement for basal metabolism to specific climatic conditions and to the height, weight, and surface areas of individuals. See, for example, Quenouille *et al.* (1951).
9. The extreme manifestations of PEM are kwashiorkor and marasmus. Both diseases involve severe wasting of body tissue and, in the case of kwashiorkor, is combined with edema (Waterlow, 1992).

10. Sommer and Lowenstein (1975); Chen, Chowdhury, and Huffman (1980); Billewicz and MacGregor (1982); Kielmann *et al.* (1983); Martorell (1985).
11. A number of statistical criticisms were also raised with respect to methods used to establish the caloric threshold of malnutrition as well as to the use of household diaries to relate the prevalence of malnutrition to income levels. See Osmani (1992a); Srinivasan (1992); Dasgupta (1993).
12. See Gopalan, Payne, Osmani, and Srinivasan, among others, in Osmani (1992b); see also Sukhatme (1982). It was argued that even if Western standards did not exaggerate the extent of stunting and wasting in Asia, the FAWOB analysis did not address the costs of being small. The evidence showing that small individuals were more likely to suffer illness was challenged, as was the evidence on the nexus to the severity of illness. The claim that large people were more productive than small ones was also contested.
13. The Dutch growth centiles are computed from 1985 data analyzed by Roede and van Wieringen (1985) and also reported in Eveleth and Tanner (1990). The observations of adolescent English boys are collected from a variety of sources identified in Fogel, Floud *et al.* (in progress, Figure 6.6).
14. On the British see Floud, Wachter and Gregory (1990); on the Americans see Costa and Steckel (forthcoming); on the Dutch see van Wieringen in Falkner and Tanner (1986).
15. Life expectation at birth was just 25 years and the minority of persons who survived childhood often died violently at relatively young ages. As late as 9000 years Before the Common Era (BCE), at the beginning of the agricultural era, the total population of the world was only about 7 million people, less than one-quarter of the population of Tokyo today (United Nations, 1973).
16. In 1800, 80 per cent of the US labour force worked in agriculture (Lebergott 1966). Today, less than 2 per cent of the US labour force works in agriculture and about 40 per cent of the food supply (measured in calories) is exported (US Bureau of the Census, 1995; US Department of Agriculture, 1993).
17. Life expectation at birth increased from 29 years in 1930 to 60 years in 1990. An increase of that magnitude required two-and-a-half centuries in England and France. The sharp drop in the death rates of developing nations led to an enormous surge in the growth of population which in turn led to widespread fears that the food supply could not keep up with population growth and that industrialization would be thwarted. However, none of these forecasts turned out to be true (Carr-Saunders, 1964; World Bank, 1992, 1993; Wrigley and Schofield, 1981; Keyfitz and Flieger, 1968, 1990; Weir, 1989; Dublin and Lotka, 1936; Kuznets, 1971).
18. The data on the secular trend of British calories available for consumption are from Fogel, Floud *et al.* (in progress). Data on current calories available for consumption are from the World Bank (1992).
19. The initial concepts of good stature and good BMI were those prevailing in the OECD nations during the early decades of the twentieth century. BMI in the range of 20–24 were thought to be best, because the average BMI during the late nineteenth and early twentieth century was relatively low by current experience. Recent evidence suggests that the stature and BMI prevailing

during the early decades of the twentieth century still reflected both continuing and residual effects of malnutrition on physiology (see Fogel, Floud *et al.*, in progress).

20. For studies of the relationship between BMI and mortality rates for mature adults in other countries see Allebeck and Bergh (1992) and Peck and Vågerö (1989) for Sweden; Marmot, Shipley and Rose (1984) for Britain.
21. Young adults born between 1822 and 1845 who survived the deadly infectious diseases of childhood and adolescence were not freer of degenerative diseases than persons of the same ages today, as some have suggested, but more afflicted. Hernia rates at ages 35–39, for example, were more than three times as prevalent in the 1860s as in the 1980s. Of special note is the much higher incidence of clubfoot in the 1860s – a birth anomaly which suggests that the uterus was far less safe for those awaiting birth than it is today (see Fogel, Costa and Kim 1993).
22. Many of these studies are republished in Barker (1992) and are synthesized, interpreted, and applied to a wide range of issues in medicine and public health in Barker (1994).
23. Malnutrition also has been related to the atrophy of the mucosal cells of the gut, the inhibition of wound healing, increased likelihood of traumatic shock and of sepsis, impaired functioning of the endocrine system, increased tendency to oedema, electrical instability that can provoke acute arrhythmias, and degenerative joint diseases (Saba, Dillon and Lanser, 1993; Idiaquez, 1988; Hill, 1990; McMahon and Bistrian, 1990; Fisler, 1992) (cf. Manton, 1993).
24. Komlos (1989); Sandberg and Steckel (1980, 1987, 1988); Floud, Wachter and Gregory (1990); cf. Komlos (1994).
25. The slowdown in the increase in height in the Netherlands, the United States and some other countries does not necessarily mean that the secular increase has come to an end, since, as Figure 6.8 illustrates, such slow-downs, or even reversals, have occurred in the past without marking the end of secular increase.
26. There is no compelling evidence to contradict the assumption that the difference between current Dutch and US stature is due primarily to techno-physio rather than genetic factors. In 1860 the average height of Dutch males at maturity was 8 cm less than that of the United States and the Dutch did not exceed average US heights until after the Second World War.

References

Agarwal, K. N., D. K. Agarwal, D. G. Benakappa, S. M. Gupta, P. C. Khanduja, S. P. Khatua, K. Ramachandran, P. M. Udani and C. Gopalan (1991) *Growth Performance of Affluent Indian Children (Under-Fives), Scientific Report*, vol. 11 (New Delhi: Nutrition Foundation of India).

Allebeck, P. and C. Bergh (1992) 'Height, Body Mass Index and Mortality: Do Social Factors Explain the Association', *Public Health*, vol. 106, no. 5, pp. 375–82.

Allen, R. C. (1992) *Enclosure and the Yeoman: The Agricultural Development of the South Midlands, 1450–1850* (Oxford: Clarendon Press).

Allen, R. C. (1994) 'Agriculture during the Industrial Revolution,' in R. Floud and D. McCloskey eds, *The Economic History of Britain since 1700*, 2d edn (Cambridge University Press), vol. 1, pp. 96–122.

Atwater, W. O. (1902) *Principles of Nutrition and Nutritive Value of Food, US Department of Agriculture Farmers' Bulletin*, 48.

Atwater, W. O. and A. P. Bryant (1900) 'Availability and Fuel Value of Food Materials', Storrs Agricultural Experiment Station, 12th annual report for 1899, pp. 73–110.

Bairoch, P. (1988) *Cities and Economic Development: From the Dawn of History to the Present*, trans. C. Braider (Chicago: University of Chicago Press).

Barker, D. J. P. (1994) *Mothers, Babies, and Disease in Later Life* (London: BMJ Publishing Group).

Barker, D. J. P. (ed.) (1992) *Foetal and Infant Origins of Adult Disease* (London: *British Medical Journal*).

Beaton, G. H. (1992) 'The Raymond Pearl Memorial Lecture, 1990: Nutrition Research in Human Biology: Changing Perspectives and Interpretations', *American Journal of Human Biology*, vol. 4, no. 2, pp. 159–77.

Billewicz, W. Z. and I. A. MacGregor (1982) 'A Birth to Maturity Longitudinal Study of Heights and Weights in Two West African (Gambian) Villages, 1951–1975', *Annals of Human Biology*, vol. 9, no. 4, pp. 309–20.

Carey, J. R., P. Liedo, D. Orozco and J. W. Vaupel (1992) 'Slowing of Mortality Rates at Older Ages in Large Medfly Cohorts', *Science*, vol. 258, no. 5081, pp. 457–61.

Carpenter, K. J. (1994) 'The Life and Times of W. O. Atwater (1844–1907)', *Journal of Nutrition*, vol. 124, suppl. 9, pp. 1708S–14S.

Carr-Saunders, A. M. (1964) *World Population: Past Growth and Present Trends* (Oxford: Oxford University Press, 1936; reprint, London: Frank Cass & Co.)

Chen, L. C., A. K. M. A. Chowdhury and S. L. Huffman (1980) 'Anthropometric Assessment of Energy–Protein Malnutrition and Subsequent Risk of Mortality among Pre-school Aged Children', *American Journal of Clinical Nutrition*, vol. 33, no. 8, pp. 1836–45.

Cipolla, C. M. (1974) *The Economic History of World Population*, 6th edn (Harmondsworth: Penguin Books).

Clark, J. G. D. (1961) *World Prehistory: An Outline* (Cambridge: Cambridge University Press).

Costa, D. L. (1995) 'Health and Labor Force Participation of Older Men, 1900–1991' (Cambridge, MA: MIT), mimeo.

Costa, D. L. and R. H. Steckel (forthcoming) 'Long-Term Trends in Health, Welfare, and Economic Growth in the United States', in R. H. Steckel and R. Floud (eds), *Health and Welfare during Industrialization* (Chicago: University of Chicago Press).

Curtsinger, J. W., H. H. Fukui, D. R. Townsend and J. W. Vaupel (1992) 'Demography of Genotypes: Failure of the Limited Life-Span Paradigm in *Drosphila melanogaster*', *Science*, vol. 258, no. 5081, pp. 461–3.

Dasgupta, P. (1993) *An Inquiry into Well-Being and Destitution* (Oxford: Oxford University Press).

Dublin, L. I. and A. J. Lotka (1936) *Length of Life: A Study of the Life Table* (New York: Ronald).

Eveleth, P. B. and J. M. Tanner (1990) *Worldwide Variation in Human Growth*, 2nd edn (Cambridge: Cambridge University Press).

Fagan, B. M. (1977) *People of the Earth*, 2d edn (Boston: Little, Brown & Co.)

Falkner, F. and J. M. Tanner (eds) (1986) Human Growth, vol. 3, *Methodology*, 2nd edn (New York: Plenum Press).

FAO (1946) *World Food Survey* (Rome: FAO).

FAO (1952) *Second World Food Survey* (Rome: FAO).

FAO (1957) *Calorie Requirements: Report of the Committee on Calorie Requirements. FAO Nutritional Studies*, 15 (Rome: FAO).

FAO (1964) *Third World Food Survey* (Rome: FAO).

FAO (1977) *Fourth World Food Survey* (Rome: FAO).

FAO (1987) *The Fifth World Food Survey* (Rome: FAO).

FAO/WHO (1973) *Energy and Protein Requirements: Report of a Joint FAO/WHO Ad Hoc Expert Committee, WHO Technical Report Series*, 522 (Rome: FAO and WHO).

Fisler, J. S. (1992) 'Cardiac Effects of Starvation and Semistarvation Diets: Safety and Mechanisms of Action', *American Journal of Clinical Nutrition*, 56, suppl. 1, pp. 230S–34S.

Floud, R., K. W. Wachter and A. Gregory (1990) *Height, Health, and History: Nutritional Status in the United Kingdom, 1750–1980* (Cambridge: Cambridge University Press).

Fogel, R. W. (1993) 'New Sources and New Techniques for the Study of Secular Trends in Nutritional Status, Health, Mortality, and the Process of Aging', *Historical Methods*, vol. 26, no. 1, pp. 5–43.

Fogel, R. W. (1997) 'A Theory of Technophysio Evolution, with Some Implications for Forecasting Population, Health Care Costs and Pension Costs', *Demography*, vol. 33, no. 1, pp. 49–66.

Fogel, R. W., D. L. Costa and J. M. Kim (1993) 'Secular Trends in the Distribution of Chronic Conditions and Disabilities at Young Adult and Late Ages, 1860–1988: Some Preliminary Findings', paper presented at the NBER Summer Institute, Economics of Aging Program (26–28 July).

Fogel, R. W., R. Floud, D. L. Costa and J. M. Kim (in progress) 'A Theory of Multiple Equilibria between Populations and Food Supplies: Nutrition, Mortality and Economic Growth in France, Britain and the United States, 1700–1980' (Chicago: University of Chicago), mimeo.

Fogel, R. W., S. L. Engerman, J. Trussell, R. Floud, C. L. Pope and L. T. Wimmer (1978) 'The Economics of Mortality in North America, 1650–1910: A Description of a Research Project', *Historical Methods*, vol. 11, no. 2, pp. 75–108.

Fries, J. F. (1980) 'Aging, Natural Death and the Compression of Morbidity', *New England Journal of Medicine*, vol. 303, no. 3, pp. 130–6.

Fries, J. F. (1989) 'The Compression of Morbidity: Near or Far?' *Milbank Quarterly*, vol. 67, no. 2, pp. 208–32.

Hill, G. L. (1990) 'Some Implications of Body Composition Research for Modern Clinical Management', *Infusionstherapie*, vol. 17, suppl. 3, pp. 79–80.

Idiaquez, J. (1988) 'Nutritional Status and Autonomic Nervous System Function', *Functional Neurology*, vol. 3, no. 2, pp. 205–9.

Kannisto, V. J. (1994) *Development of Oldest-Old Mortality, 1950–1990: Evidence from 28 Developed Countries* (Odense: Odense University Press).

Kannisto, V., J. Lauritsen, A. R. Thatcher and J. W. Vaupel (1994) 'Reductions in Mortality at Advanced Ages: Several Decades of Evidence from 27 Countries', *Population and Development Review*, vol. 20, no. 4, pp. 793–810.

Keyfitz, N. and W. Flieger (1968) *World Population: An Analysis of Vital Data* (Chicago: University of Chicago Press).

Keyfitz, N. and W. Flieger (1990) *World Population Growth and Aging: Demographic Trends in the Late Twentieth Century* (Chicago: University of Chicago Press).

Kielmann, A. A., C. DeSweemer, D. Chernichovsky, I. S. Uberoi, N. Masih, C. E. Taylor, R. L. Parker, W. A. Reinke, N. Kakar and R. S. S. Sarma (1983) *Child and Maternal Health in India: The Narangwal Experiment*, vol. 1, *Integrated Nutrition and Health* (Baltimore, MD: Johns Hopkins University Press).

Kim, J. M. (1993) 'Economic and Biomedical Implications of Waaler Surfaces: A New Perspective on Height, Weight, Morbidity, and Mortality' (Chicago: University of Chicago), mimeo.

Kim, J. M. (1995) 'The Health of the Elderly, 1990–2035: An Alternative Forecasting Approach Based on Changes in Human Physiology, with Implications for Health Care Costs and Policy' (Chicago: University of Chicago), mimeo.

Kiple, K. F. (ed.) (1993) *The Cambridge World History of Human Disease* (Cambridge: Cambridge University Press).

Komlos, J. (1989) *Nutrition and Economic Development in the Eighteenth Century Habsburg Monarchy: An Anthropometric History* (Princeton: Princeton University Press).

Komlos, J. (ed.) (1994) *Stature, Living Standards, and Economic Development: Essays in Anthropometric History* (Chicago: University of Chicago Press).

Kuznets, S. (1971) *Economic Growth of Nations: Total Output and Production Structure* (Cambridge, MA: Harvard University Press, Belknap Press).

Lebergott, S. (1966) 'Labor Force and Employment, 1800', in D. S. Brady with R. A. Easterlin, W. N. Parker and A. Fishlow (eds), *Output, Employment, and Productivity in the United States after 1800, National Bureau of Economic Research Studies in Income and Wealth*, 30 (New York: National Bureau of Economic Research), pp. 117–204.

Lee, C. (1995) 'Secular Trends in LFPR of Older Males, 1890–1930' (Chicago: University of Chicago), mimeo.

Manton, K. G. (1993) 'Biomedical Research and Changing Concepts of Disease and Aging: Implications for Long-Term Forecasts for Elderly Populations', in K. G. Manton, B. H. Singer and R. M. Suzman (eds), *Forecasting the Health of Elderly Populations* (New York: Springer–Verlag), pp. 319–65.

Marmot, M. G., M. J. Shipley and G. Rose (1984) 'Inequalities in Death–Specific Explanations of a General Pattern?' *Lancet*, vol. 8384 (5 May), pp. 1003–6.

Martorell, R. (1985) 'Child Growth Retardation: A Discussion of its Causes and Its Relationship to Health', in K. Blaxter and J. C. Waterlow (eds), *Nutritional Adaptation in Man* (London: Libby), pp. 13–29.

McMahon, M. M. and B. R. Bistrian (1990) 'The Physiology of Nutritional Assessment and Therapy in Protein–Calorie Malnutrition', *Disease-a-Month*, vol. 36, no. 7, pp. 373–417.

McNeill, W. (1971) *A World History*, 2nd edn (New York: Oxford University Press).

National Research Council, Food and Nutrition Board (1943) *Recommended Dietary Allowances* (Washington, DC: National Academy of Sciences).

Osmani, S. R. (1992a) 'On Some Controversies in the Measurement of Undernutrition', in S. R. Osmani (ed.), *Nutrition and Poverty* (Oxford: Clarendon Press), pp. 121–64.

Osmani, S. R. (ed.) (1992b) *Nutrition and Poverty* (Oxford: Clarendon Press).

Payne, P. R. (1990) 'Measuring Malnutrition', *IDS Bulletin*, vol. 21, no. 3, pp. 14–30.

Peck, A. M. N. and D. H. Vågerö (1989) 'Adult Body Height, Self Perceived Health and Mortality in the Swedish Population', *Journal of Epidemiology and Community Health*, vol. 43, no. 4, pp. 380–4.

Piggott, S. (1965) *Ancient Europe: From the Beginnings of Agriculture to Classical Antiquity* (Chicago: Aldine).

Quenouille, M. H., A. W. Boyne, W. B. Fisher and I. Leitch (1951) *Statistical Studies of Recorded Energy Expenditure in Man, Technical Communication*, 17 (Aberdeen: Commonwealth Bureau of Animal Nutrition).

Roede, M. J. and J. C. van Wieringen (1985) 'Growth Diagrams, 1980', *Tijdshrift voor Sociale Gezondheidszorg*, vol. 63, suppl., pp. 1–34.

Saba, T. M., B. C. Dillon and M. E. Lanser (1953) 'Fibronectin and Phagocytic Host Defense: Relationship to Nutritional Support', *Journal of Parenteral and Enteral Nutrition*, vol. 7, no. 1, pp. 62–8.

Sandberg, L. G. and R. H. Steckel (1980) 'Soldier, Soldier, What Made You Grow So Tall? A Study of Height, Health, and Nutrition in Sweden, 1720–1881', *Economy and History*, vol. 23, no. 2, pp. 91–105.

Sandberg, L. G. and R. H. Steckel (1987) 'Heights and Economic History: The Swedish Case', *Annals of Human Biology*, vol. 14, no. 2, pp. 101–10.

Sandberg, L. G. and R. H. Steckel (1988) 'Overpopulation and Malnutrition Rediscovered: Hard Times in Nineteenth-Century Sweden', *Explorations in Economic History*, vol. 25, no. 1, pp. 1–19.

Scrimshaw, N. S., C. E. Taylor and J. E. Gordon (1968) *Interactions of Nutrition and Infection* (Geneva: World Health Organization).

Slicher van Bath, B. H. (1963) *The Agrarian History of Western Europe A D 500–1850* (London: Edward Arnold).

Sommer, A. and M. S. Lowenstein (1975) 'Nutritional Status and Mortality: A Prospective Validation of the QUAC Stick', *American Journal of Clinical Nutrition*, vol. 28, no. 3, pp. 287–92.

Srinivasan, T. N. (1992) 'Undernutrition: Concepts, Measurement, and Policy Implications', in S. R. Osmani (ed.), *Nutrition and Poverty* (Oxford: Clarendon Press), pp. 97–120.

Sukhatme, P. V. (ed.) (1982) *Newer Concepts in Nutrition and Their Implications for Policy* (Pune: Maharashtra Association for the Cultivation of Science Research Institute).

Tanner, J. M. (1990). *Foetus into Man: Physical Growth from Conception to Maturity*, rev. edn (Cambridge, MA: Harvard University Press).

Tanner, J. M. (1993) 'Review of D. J. P. Barker's *Fetal and Infant Origins of Adult Disease*', *Annals of Human Biology*, vol. 20, no. 5, pp. 508–9.

Thatcher, A. R. (1992) 'Trends in Numbers and Mortality at High Ages in England and Wales', *Population Studies*, vol. 46, no. 3, pp. 411–26.

Trewartha, G. T. (1969) *A Geography of Populations: World Patterns* (New York: John Wiley).

United Nations (1973) *The Determinants and Consequences of Population Trends*, vol. 1 (New York: United Nations).

US Bureau of the Census (1995) *Statistical Abstract of the United States: 1995*, 115th edn (Washington, DC: GPO).

US Department of Agriculture, National Agricultural Statistics Service (1993) *Agricultural Statistics, 1993* (Washington, DC: GPO).

US Department of Health and Human Services (1980) *The International Classification of Diseases, 9th Revision, Clinical Modification*, 3 vols (Washington, DC: GPO).

van Wieringen, J. C. (1986) 'Secular Growth Changes', in F. Falkner and J. M. Tanner (eds), *Human Growth*, vol. 3, *Methodology*, 2nd edn (New York: Plenum Press), pp. 307–31.

Vaupel, J. W. (1991a) 'The Impact of Population Aging on Health and Health Care Costs: Uncertainties and New Evidence about Life Expectancy' (Odense: Center for Health and Social Policy, Odense University), mimeo.

Vaupel, J. W. (1991b) 'Prospects for a Longer Life Expectancy', paper presented at the Annual Meeting of the Population Association of America, Washington DC (21–23 March).

Vaupel, J. W. and H. Lundström (1994) 'Prospects for a Longer Life Expectancy', in D. Wise (ed.) *Studies in the Economics of Aging* (Chicago: University of Chicago Press).

Vries, J. de (1984) *European Urbanization 1500–1800* (London: Methuen).

Waaler, H. T. (1984) 'Height, Weight, and Mortality: The Norwegian Experience', *Acta Medica Scandinavica*, suppl. 679 (Stockholm), pp. 1–51.

Waterlow, J. C. (with A. M. Tomkins and S. M. Grantham-McGregor) (1992) *Protein Energy Malnutrition* (Sevenoaks: Edward Arnold).

Weir, D. R. (1989) 'Markets and Mortality in France, 1600–1789', in J. Walter and D. Schofield (eds), *Famine, Disease and The Social Order in Early Modern Society* (Cambridge: Cambridge University Press), pp. 201–34.

Weir, D. R. (1993) 'Parental Consumption Decisions and Child Health during the Early French Fertility Decline, 1790–1914', *Journal of Economic History*, vol. 53, no. 2, pp. 259–74.

WHO (1985) *Energy and Protein Requirements. Report of a Joint FAO/WHO/UNU Expert Consultation, WHO Technical Report Series*, 724 (Geneva: WHO).

World Bank (1992) *World Development Report 1992* (New York: Oxford University Press).

World Bank (1993) *The East Asian Miracle: Economic Growth and Public Policy* (New York: Oxford University Press).

Wrigley, E. A. (1987) 'Urban Growth and Agricultural Change: England and the Continent in the Early Modern Period,' in E. A. Wrigley (ed.), *People, Cities and Wealth: The Transformation of Traditional Society* (Oxford: Basil Blackwell), pp. 157–93.

Wrigley, E. A. and R. S. Schofield (1981) *The Population History of England, 1541–1871: A Reconstruction* (Cambridge, MA: Harvard University Press).

7 On the Optimal Duration of Migration

Marianne Røed
INSTITUTE FOR SOCIAL RESEARCH, OSLO

and

Oded Stark
UNIVERSITY OF OSLO AND UNIVERSITY OF VIENNA

1 INTRODUCTION AND MOTIVATION

The notion that labour migration will take place in the presence of a wage differential and that in the absence of a wage differential migration will not take place lies at the heart of research on labour migration. However, this notion does not capture the soul of labour migration. There is a strong implicit assumption that the wage differential is exogenous to the individual migrant. Yet migration, as a form of investment in human capital, can change the differential substantially. Furthermore, other variables also impinge on labour migration, indeed migration can well take place in the absence of a wage differential. Return migration is subject to similar considerations. When some of the returns to migration are realized upon return migration, return may take place in spite of the wage differential between abroad and home being positive. An example of this is a higher purchasing power of savings accruing from work abroad at home than abroad. Since consumption requires time, it is not possible to leave abroad for home an instant prior to the termination of life in order to enjoy a very large consumption in a very short time spell. Hence the optimal duration of stay abroad can be shown to be shorter than the duration of working life (Stark, Helmenstein and Yegorov, 1997).

The central idea of the present chapter is that work abroad could enhance skills for work at home in a manner which work at home cannot. This skill amplification, which entails a higher home wage, can elicit migration even if the wage differential between abroad and home is negative, and attract return even if the (narrowed) wage differential between abroad and home remains positive – given that living at home, as such, confers utility which living abroad does not. When income at home increases with time spent abroad the migrant weighs an additional increase in the home-country wage against a shorter home spell during which the increase can be enjoyed. In comparison to a situation in which the home income enhancement is absent, it may be optimal to return home earlier.

Prior to presenting the model and delineating its key implications we provide a rationale for the skill and earning enhancement arising from work abroad. Consider a large country. Rich experience relevant to the performance of tasks associated with assignment A can be gained by rotation to assignments A', A'', and so on – say the managing of other production plants. However, a small country may not have A', A'', and so on available to it, with the result that useful experience can only be gained abroad. Moreover, a small open country may be characterized by a high ratio of tradeables to non-tradeables which renders an international exposure of managers and workers alike highly useful. In the fields of management, technology, markets for goods and services, as well as in the spheres of language and culture, knowledge about other countries may be of considerable value to the export- and import-oriented sectors. The demand for skills acquired through work abroad may be greater in small countries than in large countries. As long as additional experience in A is less useful than additional experience of the same duration in A', A'', and so on, the sequence migration – return migration will be an effective means for enhancing earnings.

Empirical studies of recent migration patterns indicate that the duration of migration is shorter than the duration of working life – indeed, the probability of return migration within a few years of migration is quite high. A study of migration from and within Scandinavia reveals that nearly 80 per cent of the Danes and the Norwegians who moved from their country of origin in 1981 returned within 9 years. For Sweden, the corresponding percentage was between 50 and 60 (Schröder, 1996). The high incidence of temporary migration suggests that presumably migrants consider how working abroad may affect their wage at home upon their return. In the presence of an income enhancement, the very purpose of migration might indeed be a lifting of the home country's earning schedule. Hence, the economic incentives of international migration may be underestimated when only the income differences between countries are considered. The incidence of temporary migration further suggests preference of home country residence. Living abroad entails a sacrifice, a price akin to the shadow price of labour in the theory of labour supply (Heckman, 1974).

Empirical studies also indicate that the propensity to migrate varies considerably. For example, during the 1980s Scandinavians with higher education had a migration propensity approximately three times higher than that of Scandinavians with only basic education. The average migration propensity of Norwegian economists and business administrators was approximately 60 per cent higher than the average migration propensity of Norwegian civil engineers. The corresponding figure for Swedes was approximately 50 per cent (Schröder, 1996; Larsen and Røed, 1992). It is reasonable to assume that the skill composition of a migration flow reflects variation across groups with respect to the expected returns from migration. This variation may be partly a consequence of differences in the rate of human capital accumulation conferred by working abroad.

We study the effect on migration of a positive relationship between the duration of work abroad and the subsequent expected income in the home country. Migratory behaviour is captured by two variables: the individual's migration probability, that is, the probability that an individual migrates during a specific time period, and the number of periods the individual works abroad, in particular, the variance of this number for a group of individuals (defined, for example, by educational background) to which the individual belongs. We investigate the relationship between these dependent variables and a set of variables that commonly and not so commonly feature in the received literature. We construct a wage function that relates the number of periods spent working abroad to the subsequent earning possibilities in the home country, and we introduce heterogeneity of the population with respect to the preference for home-country residence. The key results of the analysis are pooled together in the concluding Section 5.

2 THE MODEL

The individuals of interest are all the potential migrants within a country – the 'population at risk'. In principle, this population may consist of the entire work-force. In each period, every potential migrant chooses whether to work in the home country or whether to work abroad.[1] The individual displays a preference for home-country residence, that is, the momentary utility is always higher when living at home, given a fixed consumption of goods and services. Capital markets are assumed to be perfect. It is thus possible to separate the decision regarding location from the decision regarding the time distribution of consumption, and we may consider a potential migrant's life-time utility as depending upon the aggregate time spent in the home country and on the total consumption of goods and services. Preferences result in indifference curves that are convex to the origin in the time abroad – home consumption plane. The financial constraint can be expressed as an equality between the present discounted value of the consumption of goods and services, and the present discounted value of net income. To simplify, we assume a zero rate of interest. The wage rate at home is a positive function of the number of periods spent working abroad.[2] With these assumptions in mind, the migration behaviour of an individual follows from:

$$\text{Max } U(C, H) \text{ where } U_C > 0, U_{CC} < 0, U_H > 0, U_{HH} < 0, U_{CH} > 0 \quad (1)$$

subject to:

$$C_i = (T - H)W^f + HW^h \quad (2)$$

$$W^h = w(T - H) \qquad \text{where } w' \geq 0, \text{ and } w'' < 0. \quad (3)$$

$$\text{If } w' = 0,\ W^h = W^o \text{ for every } H;$$
$$\text{if } w' > 0,\ W^h = W^o \text{ when } H = T.$$

U is the life-time utility function of an individual; C is the (discounted) value of life-time consumption; H is the total time spent in the home country; and T is the length of the time horizon. Hence $H \in (1, T)$.[3] W^h is the home-country wage while W^o is the wage rate which prevails at home when the individual chooses not to go abroad at all ($H = T$), or if working abroad has no effect on the home-country wage rate ($w' = 0$). W^f is the wage rate abroad. To simplify, we assume that W^o and W^f are constant. The individual cannot choose the number of hours of work per day; we assume that the utility function incorporates variations in the given length of the working day between countries.

The *income premium of migration* is defined as the difference between the home-country wage the individual attains after working abroad and the home-country wage prior to working abroad: $W^h - W^o$.

Maximization of (1) subject to (2) and (3) gives the first-order conditions for an optimal allocation between life-time consumption and time spent in the home country.[4] The marginal rate of substitution between H and C, given by U_H/U_C, is *the shadow price of home-country residence*. This shadow price is the utility of a marginal unit of time living in the home country expressed in terms of the consumption goods (or money value). It follows from the first-order conditions that when an interior maximum is reached,[5] this rate is equal to the marginal 'revenue' from an additional period of work abroad:

$$U_H/U_C = W^f - W^h + w'H. \quad (4)$$

The marginal revenue is the opportunity cost of home-country residence, that is, the consumption forgone by the last period the individual chooses to stay at home. In addition to a wage differential between abroad and home ($W^f - W^h$), this revenue includes the marginal increase in the income premium of an additional period abroad (w') multiplied by the number of periods the individual is able to enjoy this increase (H). Thus, when the first derivative of the wage function is positive, an acceptable wage offer from abroad may be even lower than the home wage.

When the marginal revenue exceeds the shadow price at $H \approx T$, the individual will migrate, that is:

$$\text{If } W^f - W^o + w'T > U_H/U_C \qquad \text{when } H \approx T, \text{ then } H < T. \tag{5}$$

The adjustment of H and C is determined by (1) – (4). When the shadow price exceeds the marginal revenue at $H \approx T$ the individual will not migrate thus leading to a corner solution:

$$\text{If } U_H/U_C > W^f - W^o + w'T \qquad \text{when } H \approx T, \text{ then } H = T. \tag{6}$$

Since our objective is to analyze how the existence and the size of the income premium influence migratory behaviour, we have to place some restrictions on the wage and utility functions. We thus assume that the individual's preferences are represented by a Cobb–Douglas utility function:

$$U = AC^a H^{1-a} \qquad 0 < a < 1. \tag{7}$$

Equation (7) implies that the elasticity of C with respect to H is constant along the indifference curves, that is, $e_{C,H} = -\left(\frac{1-a}{a}\right)\Big|_{dU=0}$. The expression $-\left(\frac{1-a}{a}\right)\Big|_{dU=0}$ is the percentage reduction in C that results from a one per cent increase in H, given the restriction of a constant utility level. Note that $1 - a$ expresses the strength of the preference for home-country residence: a higher value of $1 - a$ (and accordingly a lower value of a) arises from a greater appreciation of living at home relative to the consumption of goods.

We assume that the 'population at risk' is continuously distributed along the interval [0,1] with respect to the value of a. Thus, $f(a)$ and $F(a)$ are, respectively, the density and the cumulative distribution functions.

The home-country wage function is given a double log-linear representation:

$$W^h = W^o e^{\beta \ln(1+T-H)}. \tag{8}$$

Upon differentiation with respect to $1 + T - H$ it is easy to show that when $\beta > 0$, then $W^{h'} > 0$, and that when $0 < \beta < 1$, then $W^{h''} < 0$.

By (8) we place a restriction of constant elasticity with respect to time spent working abroad on the wage function, that is, $e_{W^h,\,1+T-H} = \beta$. Equation (8) further implies that given $T - H$, $W^h - W^o$ increases with β. Hence β measures the size of the income premium.

Equation (4) can now be rewritten as:[6]

$$\frac{1-a}{a}\frac{C}{H} = W^f - W^h + \frac{\beta}{1+T-H} W^h H \tag{9}$$

where, as in (4), the left-hand side denotes the shadow price of home-country residence, and the right-hand side denotes the marginal revenue from staying abroad another period.

3 THE MIGRATION PROBABILITY: ANALYSIS OF THE CORNER SOLUTION

We have established that an individual will work abroad when the marginal revenue exceeds the shadow price at $H \approx T$. Given the restrictions on the utility and wage functions, this applies when:

$$W^f - W^o + \beta W^o T > (1-a)W^o/a. \tag{10}$$

By (10), the wage differential at which migration takes place between abroad and home ($W^f - W^o$) decreases with the value of the income premium.

Having assumed that with regard to the value of a the population of potential migrants is continuously distributed along the interval [0,1], we may find, given fixed values of W^o, W^f, β and T, a critical value of a, $a = a^*$, which brings about equality in (10):

$$a^* = \frac{1}{\left(\dfrac{W^f}{W^o} + \beta T\right)}. \tag{11}$$

Those individuals whose $a \approx a^*$, are about indifferent when it comes to choosing migration since their level of utility stays approximately the same whether or not they migrate. We refer to these individuals as *marginal migrants*. Those individuals whose $a < a^*$ do not migrate, while those individuals whose $a > a^*$ migrate. This distinction draws on the simple idea that, everything else being equal, those whose preference for home-country residence is relatively weak migrate, while those whose home-country preference is relatively strong do not. Looking at the entire work-force it is reasonable to consider the strength of this preference to be distributed continuously.

The migration probability (P) may now be defined as the probability that an individual who is randomly selected from a given population group[7] has a value of a greater than a^*:

$$P(H<T) = P(a>a^*) = P\left(a > \frac{1}{\frac{W^f}{W^o} + \beta T} \right) \tag{12}$$

$$= 1 - F(a^*) = 1 - \int_0^{a^*} f(a)da$$

Equation (12) provides a functional relationship between the migration probability and the exogenous variables β, W^o, W^f, T, and the parameters which shape the distribution of the population with respect to a.

Differentiating the migration probability with respect to the exogenous variables gives the following results:

$$\frac{dP}{d\beta} = f(a^*)\frac{T}{\left(\frac{W^f}{W^o} + \beta T\right)^2} = f(a^*)Ta^{*2} > 0, \tag{13}$$

$$\frac{dP}{dW^f} = f(a^*)\frac{1}{W^o}a^{*2} > 0, \tag{14}$$

$$\frac{dP}{dW^o} = -f(a^*)\frac{W^f}{W^{o2}}a^{*2} < 0, \tag{15}$$

$$\frac{dP}{dT} = f(a^*)\beta a^{*2} > 0. \tag{16}$$

The derivatives of the migration probability with respect to β, W^f, W^o in (13), (14) and (15), respectively, have the expected signs. Equation (16) shows that T has a positive influence on the migration probability when β is greater than zero, but none when β is equal to zero. A prolongation of the time horizon ($dT > 0$) raises total income; given the number of periods abroad, the marginal revenue of migration is increased, when $\beta > 0$, as a given income premium can be enjoyed over a longer period of time.[8] Thus, when $\beta = 0$, the demand for time in the home country is affected only by the positive income effect which increases the demand for both types of goods (when neither good is inferior). As to the marginal migrants (those whose $a \approx a^*$), it can be shown that the increased demand for time at home, which is due to the income effect, is equal to the extra time available.[9] Due to the increase in the marginal revenue of migration, which arises when $\beta > 0$, the adjustment of the demand for time in the home country is affected by a positive income effect and by a negative substitution effect. Thus, when $\beta > 0$, the marginal migrant increases the demand for time in the home country by less than the extra time available, and the migration probability increases.[10]

Given the number of years in school, it may be reasonable to assume that there is a strong negative correlation between the length of the planning horizon, T, and age. Thus, $\beta > 0$ may further explain the widely observed empirical negative relationship between age and the probability of migration, be it temporary or permanent. An interesting question is how the value of β affects the relationship between the migration probability and the other exogenous variables in the model, that is, how this value influences dP/dW^f, dP/dW^o and dP/dT. Equations (13) – (16) show that the change in the migration probability arising from a change in one of the exogenous variables is a product of the value of a^* and the value of the density function at a^*. Thus, without making specific assumptions about the distribution function of the population with respect to a this question cannot be addressed.

A prediction offered by the preceding analysis is that the migration probability increases with the value of the income premium. In addition, the migration probability decreases faster with age when the income premium is positive.

4 THE DURATION OF STAY ABROAD: ANALYSIS OF THE INTERIOR SOLUTION

How will the value of β affect the optimal duration of migration and the variance of the optimal duration of migration for a given population group? Indirect derivation of the budget constraint (2) and the first-order conditions in note 6 with respect to β and a gives:

$$\frac{dH}{d\beta}=\frac{-H^2W^h\left[\ln(1+T-H)\left(\frac{\beta}{1+T-H}-\frac{1}{aH}\right)+\frac{1}{1+T-H}\right]}{D} \tag{17}$$

where

$$D=\frac{1}{a}\left[W^f-W^h+\frac{\beta}{1+T-H}W^hH\right]+\frac{H\beta}{1+T-H}W^h\left[\frac{H(1-\beta)}{1+T-H}+2\right]>0;$$

$$\text{when}\quad H\approx T:\frac{dH}{d\beta}=\frac{-W^0T^2}{D_{(H\approx T)}}<0,$$

$$\text{when}\quad H=1:\frac{dH}{d\beta}=\frac{\frac{W^h}{T}\left[\ln T\left(\frac{T}{a}-\beta\right)-1\right]}{D_{(H=1)}}>0,\ \text{provided that } T>T_0$$

where T_0 is defined by $\ln T_0\left(\frac{T_0}{a}-\beta\right)-1=0$,

and

$$\frac{dH}{da}=\frac{-\frac{1}{a^2}(W^f(T-H)+W^hH)}{D}<0. \tag{18}$$

We find that $\frac{dH}{d\beta}<0$ when $H\approx T$ (and thus when $a\approx a*$), and that $\frac{dH}{d\beta}>0$ when $H=1$.[11] We also find that $\frac{dH}{da}<0$ for all values of $H<T$. An increase in β encourages those whose a is relatively low to increase their time abroad. These individuals value highly staying at home.

Because with a higher β they are better compensated for their absence away from home in terms of extra consumption upon their return home, they are willing to incur migration or prolong their absence. On the other hand, those who value consumption relatively highly (and home-stay a little – these are the high a_i type) have allocated much of their time to staying abroad. They now find, when β is higher, that staying home pays better in terms of extra consumption. Therefore they will shorten their stay abroad. Hence, we predict an inverse relationship between β and the variance of $T-H$:

$$\frac{d\,\mathrm{Var}(T-H)}{d\beta}<0. \tag{19}$$

Consequently, when comparing two groups of individuals with different values of β, we would expect to find a lower variance of H in the group with the higher β. Figures 7.1 and 7.2 illustrate this. When β increases, the demand for time at home is affected by a positive income effect and by a negative substitution effect. Given a fixed value of $T-H$, the marginal revenue of migration increases with β at a rate which decreases with $T-H$. For the higher values of $T-H$, the marginal revenue of migration might

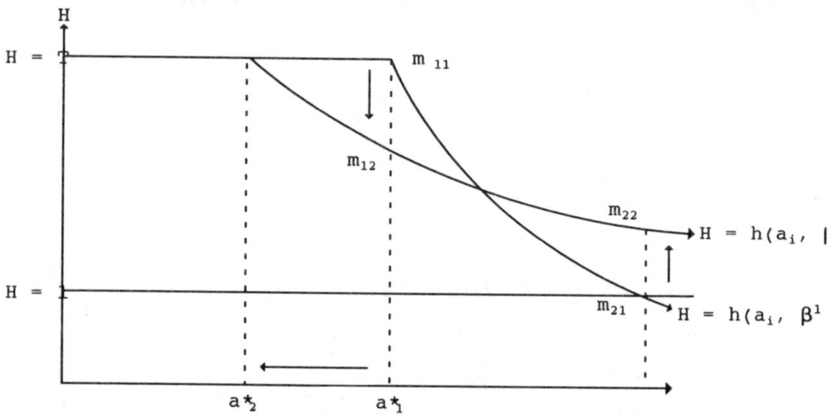

Figure 7.1 Time spent in the home country (H) as a function of a_i, displayed for two different values of β, $\beta^1<\beta^2$. Upon an increase of β from β^1 to β^2, a^* decreases from a_1^* to a_2^* and the demand for time at home adjusts downwards (from m_{11} to m_{12} at a_1^*) for relatively low values of a_i, and upwards (from m_{21} to m_{22} at $H\approx 1$) for relatively high values of a_i.

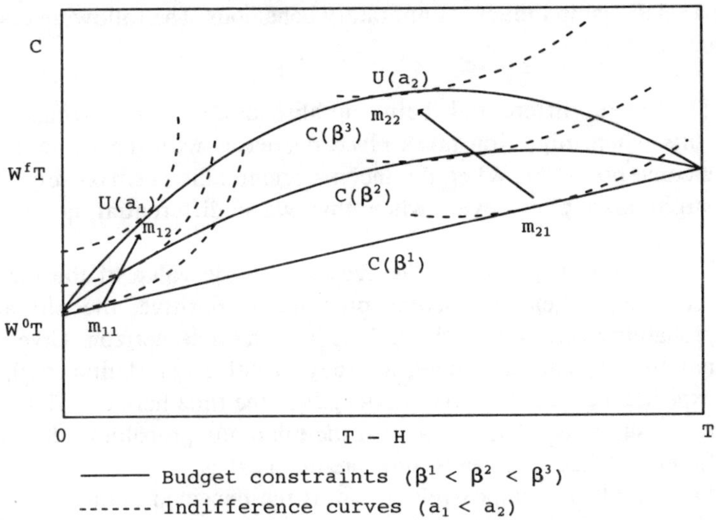

Figure 7.2 The optimal allocation between time spent away from home ($T - H$) and consumption of goods and services (C) for different values of a and β.

even become negative when β increases. Thus, the negative substitution effect on the demand for time at home also decreases with $T - H$. On the other hand, the positive income effect increases with the value of $T - H$ (up to the point where the marginal revenue becomes negative). Accordingly, when low values of $T - H$ (and a) prevail, the negative substitution effect dominates and an increase in β is followed by a decrease in the demand for home-country residence. This case is illustrated by a move from m_{11} to m_{12} in Figures 7.1 and 7.2. However, beyond a certain value of $T - H$ (and thus a), the sum of these effects becomes positive, that is, the positive income effect of an increase in β dominates. This case is illustrated by a move from m_{21} to m_{22} in Figures 7.1 and 7.2.

5 CONCLUSIONS

The key idea of this chapter is that work abroad can amplify skills for working at home in a manner which working at home cannot. We refer to a positive relationship between the home wage and the time spent working abroad as the income premium of migration. We investigate how such a relationship influences migratory behaviour. The following results obtain:

1. The wage differential between abroad and home which prevails when migration takes place decreases with the value of the income premium. When the income premium is positive, migration might take place even when this wage differential is zero or negative.
2. The migration probability increases with the value of the income premium. When the income premium is positive, the migration probability increases with the length of the time horizon. Given the number of years in school, a strong negative correlation might be expected between age and the length of the time horizon. Thus, this result supports a hypothesis that the migration probability decreases faster with age when an income premium exists.
3. In general, it is impossible to say if the expected duration of stay abroad increases or decreases with the income premium. This duration depends on the relative strength of the preference for home-country residence as opposed to the preference for consumption. We did find, though, that the variance of the duration of stay abroad decreases in the size of the income premium.

We can tie in these analytical results with the general observations made at the outset. We suggested that on average the income premium of migration decreases with the size of the country and increases with the ratio of tradeables to non-tradeables. Thus, we should expect that the results listed above will apply particularly to the migration behaviour of individuals from small open economies.

Notes

1. This choice is fully free within the Nordic region, for example, though not in other contexts.
2. For the sake of concentrating on essentials we ignore other individual traits that impinge on wage determination in the home country.
3. Since our interest is in temporary migration, the possibility of a corner solution at $H = 0$ is ignored.
4. The first-order conditions are $U_C = \lambda$ and $U_H = \lambda(W^f - W^h + w'H)$, where λ is the Lagrange multiplier.

5. Given our assumptions about the utility function and the wage function, the second-order conditions for a maximum are fulfilled.
6. Given (7) and (8), the first-order conditions for optimal allocation between life-time consumption and time spent in the home country are now

$$AaC^{a-1}H^{1-a} = \lambda \text{ and } AC^{a}(1-a)H^{-a} = 1\left(W^{f} - W^{h} + \frac{b}{1+T-H}W^{h}H\right),$$

where λ is the Lagrange multiplier.
7. A population group is defined by the members' common values of the exogenous variables β, W^{o}, W^{f} and T. With respect to a, the group is continuously distributed on the interval [0,1].
8. Recall that the right-hand side of (9) is the marginal revenue from migration. Given a fixed value of $T-H$, the marginal revenue increases with T:

$$\left[\frac{d\left(W^{f} - W^{h} + \dfrac{\beta}{1+T-H}W^{h}H\right)}{dT}\right]\Bigg|_{d(T-H)=0} = \frac{\beta}{1+T-H}W^{h} > 0.$$

9. When $\beta = 0$, substitution of C from (2) into (9) and differentiation of (9) with respect to T give

$$\left(\frac{dH}{dT}\right)\Bigg|_{\beta=0} = \frac{(1-a)W^{f}}{W^{f}-W^{0}}.$$ Since, from (11), $a^{*}\Big|_{\beta=0} = \dfrac{W^{o}}{W^{f}}$ it follows

that $\left(\dfrac{dH}{dT}\right)\Bigg|_{\beta=0,a=a^{*}} = \dfrac{(1-a^{*})W^{f}}{W^{f}-W^{o}} = 1.$ This result draws on the restrictions placed on the utility function in (5), that is, a constant elasticity along the indifference curves.
10. If the assumption of a constant elasticity along the indifference curves does not apply, the increased demand for time at home, which is due to the income effect, may be less than the extra time available. Thus, the migration probability may increase even when $\beta = 0$. However, due to the negative substitution effect, the migration probability will increase more when $\beta > 0$.
11. It turns out that these results do not depend on the utility function being of the Cobb-Douglas type. They hold upon usage of the general formulation (1).

References

Heckman, J. (1974) 'Shadow Prices, Market Wage, and Labour Supply', *Econometrica*, vol. 42, pp. 679–94.

Larsen, K. A. and M. Røed (1992) 'Norwegian Professions in the European Labour Market', Institute for Social Research, Oslo, *Report*, 92: 3.

Stark, O., C. Helmenstein and Y. Yegorov (1997) 'Migrants' Savings, Purchasing Power Parity, and the Optimal Duration of Migration', *International Tax and Public Finance*, vol. 4, pp. 307–24.

Schröder, L. (1996) 'Scandinavian Skill Migration in the 1980s', in P. J. Pedersen (ed.), *Scandinavia without Borders – Skill Migration and the European Integration Process* (Amsterdam: North-Holland).

Part III
Agriculture

8 Agricultural Development: Issues, Evidence and Consequences[1]

Yair Mundlak
UNIVERSITY OF CHICAGO

Donald Larson
THE WORLD BANK

and

Al Crego
THE WORLD BANK

1 THE ISSUES

Many roads lead to the interest in agricultural development, and it is only natural that we find differences among economists in their analyses and more so in perspectives, emphasis and conclusions about the process and its outcome. To provide a perspective for our discussion, it is useful to list the central issues related to agricultural growth:

- Agriculture as a supplier of food
- The welfare of farmers and more generally, the rural population
- The role of agriculture in economic development
- The impact of government intervention on the performance of the agricultural sector as a subject of political economy.

Traditionally agriculture has been studied with the purpose of checking the validity of general economic propositions, and this also applies to the study of various aspects of growth.

Keeping this diversity of interests in mind, it is instructive to conduct the discussion against the background of the evidence. To do so, we present results from a comprehensive examination of a data base of a large number of countries for the period 1960–90 or thereabouts.[2] The chapter highlights important empirical propositions – mostly known but often ignored – and provides a quantitative dimension of the cross-country variability of levels and rates of change over time. It is then followed by a short overview of the consequence for policy and analysis. Given space limitations, no attempt is made here to document all the assertions. This will be done elsewhere (Mundlak, forthcoming).

2 THE EVIDENCE

2.1 Supply and Demand

The Global Food Experience – An Overview

There is a keen interest in future market developments related to food supply. This interest is more intense than in other sectors because of the unique role of food and the nature of its demand. Much of the concern with food supply can be explained by the fear of supply shortages and hunger at some point in the near or remote future. In the dialogue on this issue, reference is sometimes made to the experiences of countries that suffered food shortages for extended periods of time or to episodes of hunger in affluent economies. Although traumatic, such episodes do not generalize to give a correct global picture. It is here where the empirical perspective is essential.

A summary of the growth experience of countries is given in Figure 8.1, which presents a frequency distribution of total agricultural production growth rates for the period 1967–92 for 130 countries.[3] The curve to the left is drawn with equal weight for each country. At any point on the graph, the reading on the vertical axis shows the proportion of countries whose growth rate did not exceed the corresponding value on the horizontal axis. There is a wide spread in country performances, but most countries had positive growth, and the median rate is 1.92 per cent per year. As some of the low-growth countries are small in terms of their agricultural production, this curve does not provide a good view of the changes in global supply. A better view is obtained when the relative size of country is taken into account. This is done in the curve to the right, where the countries are weighted by their relative importance in world agricultural production. Countries with negative growth rates carry very little weight in terms of their contribution to overall food production. The median average growth rate of the weighted distribution is 2.25 per cent. This

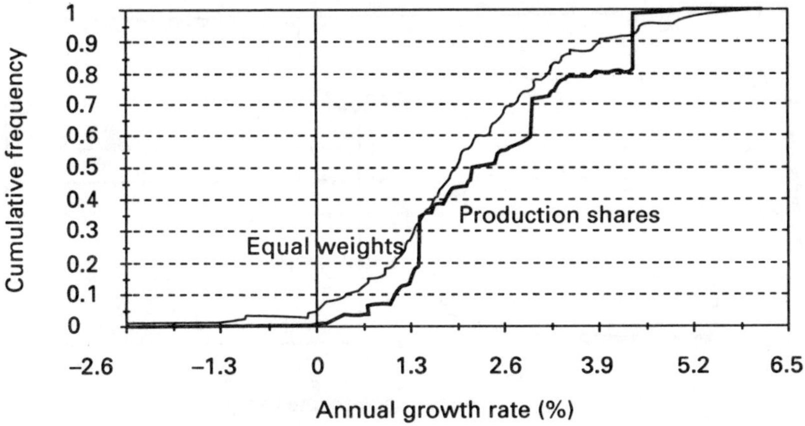

Figure 8.1 Total agriculture production, 1967–92, 130 countries

means that 50 per cent of the food production is produced in countries whose growth rates exceeded 2.25 per cent, and the remaining is produced by countries with lower but usually positive rates. Put another way, growth rates have been somewhat higher in countries with large agricultural production.

Has supply lagged demand? If this were the case, agricultural prices would have risen, but this has not happened. This is seen in Figure 8.2, which presents the distribution of the rates of change of agricultural prices over the same time period.[4] Domestic farm prices are deflated by domestic consumer price indices. The median of the unweighted distribution is –0.45 per cent per year and when we weigh the countries by their importance in world production, the median changes to –0.61 per cent per year. Note that the vertical line at zero growth rate cuts the graph of the weighted distribution at 0.71, indicating that 71 per cent of world production in the period 1967–92 was produced in countries where real prices fell.

Because the prices in Figure 8.2 are of aggregate output, their rates of change tend to be biased upward. As income increases, there is a shift in consumption and production to higher-value products, and this change in composition causes the aggregate price to increase. Thus, the fact that we observe a decline in prices even despite an upward bias suggests that supply grew faster than demand. This result is consistent with the finding reported in Binswanger *et al.* (1987) that over the period 1900–84, world prices of important agricultural commodities, such as the major cereals, deflated by US wholesale prices, declined at average annual rates of 0.5 to

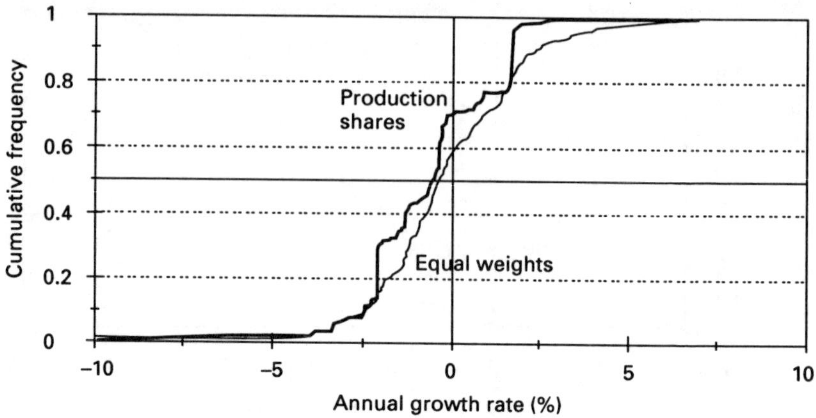

Figure 8.2 Agricultural prices, 112 countries

0.7 per cent. This overview indicates that recent experience, which generalizes well to the entire post-war period, is of faster growth of supply compared to demand.

Demand and Agricultural Growth

What are the sources of the spread in growth rates? This is of course the main question in the study of growth in general, and of agricultural growth in particular. The search for answers naturally focuses on the supply side. However, before examining factors related to supply, it is instructive to examine the role of demand.

On the whole, agricultural products are tradeable, and therefore there is no need for each country to increase its production to meet domestic demand changes. Some countries can benefit from comparative advantage and reduce their production in an environment of growth and of reduction of trade restrictions. Such behaviour may explain some of the observed spread in growth rates. For instance, Singapore's agricultural production more than doubled between 1967 and 1979, but declined thereafter to such an extent that 1992 production was below that of 1967. Other countries do not fully utilize their potential in agricultural production in order to protect farm income and are engaged in policies that involve a reduction of their domestic production and restrictions on imports. Together these restrictions indicate that there have been excess supplies. Further, import barriers further restrict the expansion of production in exporting countries as potentially importing countries attempt to use their own markets for the development of their farm sector.

An indirect view of the role of demand can be obtained by comparing the distribution of growth rates of *per capita* output, presented in Figure 8.3, with *total* output, in Figure 8.1. The median rate of change of *per capita* production of the equal weight distribution is –0.03 per cent although in about 51 per cent of the countries output exceeded population growth. Taking into account the production weights, the median growth rate is 0.7 per cent, and output growth exceeded population growth in countries that accounted for 81 per cent of world production. Such a pronounced difference between the two distributions underlines the importance of distinguishing between country problems and global problems, and the pitfall of generalizing from country performance to world performance.

We also note that the graphs in Figure 8.3 are more steep than the corresponding graphs in Figure 8.1.[5] This implies a higher concentration of countries around the median growth rate, that is, the variance of *total* growth rates is larger than that of *per capita* rates. This concentration in the centre indicates that many countries met a large part of growth in demand through home production. In fact, on the whole, production growth exceeded population growth somewhat because of the increase in demand due to the rise in income as well as the decline in prices. Clearly, this development is consistent with demand derived from production growth.

A more direct view of the role of demand is obtained by comparing the rate of growth of agricultural *per capita* output with that of *per capita* total output, taken as a measure of income. Ignoring trade for a moment, we

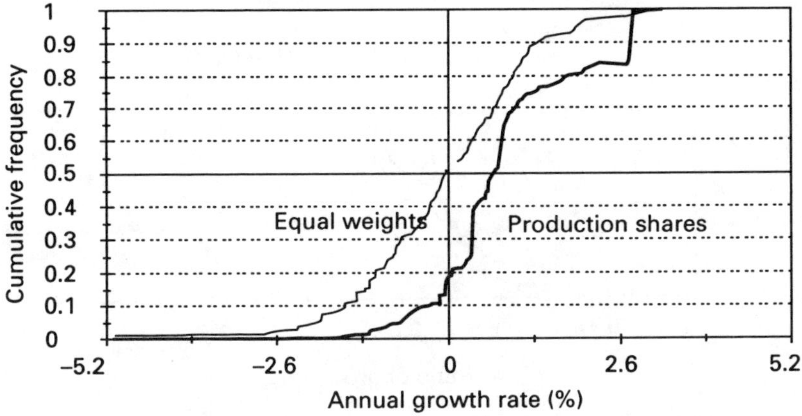

Figure 8.3 Per capita agricultural production, 1967–92, 130 countries

note that for the closed economy under constant prices this ratio is roughly the income elasticity for food. We say 'roughly', because agriculture is not identical with food and it includes industrial crops whose demand is not the same as that of food. However, in most countries, food dominates agricultural production.

Figure 8.4 presents the distribution of such a ratio for growth in real *value* for 91 countries during 1960–92.[6] The median values are 0.82 and 0.86 for the weighted and unweighted distributions, respectively. Since prices were not constant and rather declined, this result serves as an upper bound for the income elasticity.

We emphasize the role of demand because most discussions of economic growth deal with a single-good economy where there are no prices, except for the discount rate. However, the single-good economy is an aggregate of many sectors, and therefore the discussion of growth at the sectoral level adds a dimension missing from aggregate models. Indeed, when it comes to agriculture, it is demand which has an enormous impact on the dynamics of the sector.

Trade

Agriculture produces a tradeable product, but the foregoing review indicates a tendency toward self-sufficiency. This is reflected in the fact that trade accounts for only 10–12 per cent of total world production. This

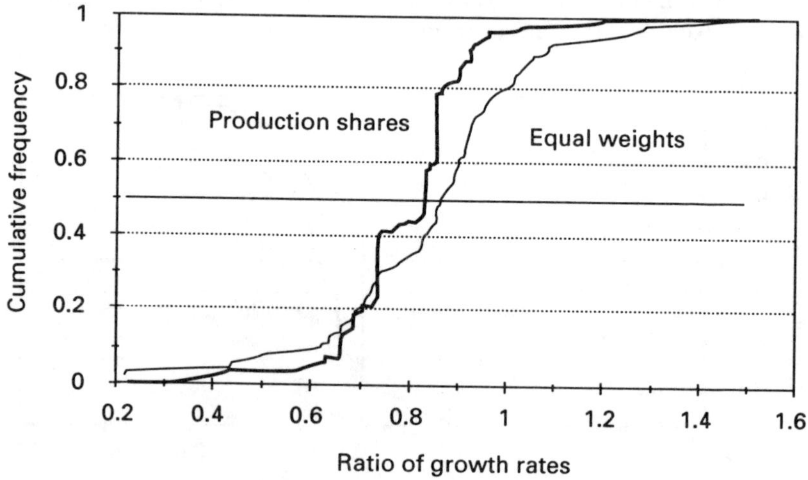

Figure 8.4 Per capita GDP growth ratio, agriculture to total, 1960–92, 91 countries

tendency toward self-sufficiency is in part due to policies as indicated above, but is also due to objective market conditions. The margin between import and export prices may be wide, distribution costs within the country, both for the exporter and the importer, can be high, especially in countries with inadequate infrastructure.

2.2 Inputs and Productivity Changes

Turning to the supply side, the joint event of output growth and declining prices indicates that productivity growth more than offsets the effect of the declining prices on profitability. To evaluate the sources of growth we examine changes in land and labour, the two inputs that together account for a large proportion of output.

Land

It is often thought that agricultural land is a fixed quantity. This view is true for countries' total physical areas whereas cultivated land (hereafter 'land,') is an economic quantity and, as seen in Figure 8.5, it was subject to changes. In 65 per cent of the countries the cultivated area increased during 1967–92, with a median average annual growth rate of 0.4 per cent. For the world as a whole, the average annual growth rate was 0.58 per cent, which amounts to about 15.7 per cent growth for the period as a whole. Land growth was faster in tree crops, 1.48, than in annual crops,

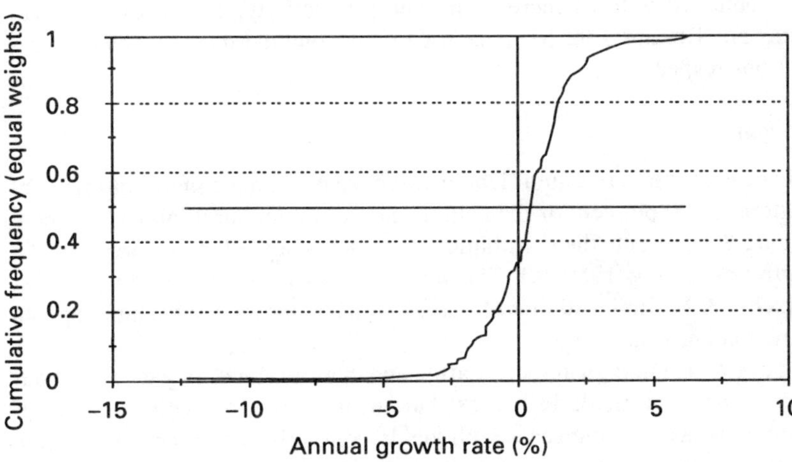

Figure 8.5 Harvested land, 1967–92, 131 countries

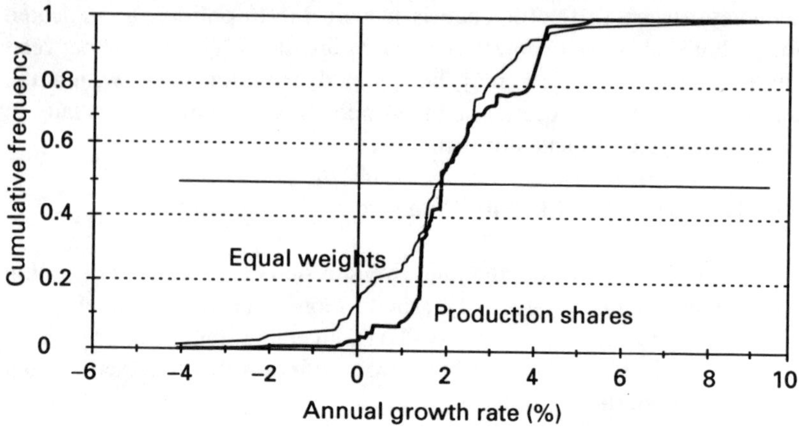

Figure 8.6 Land productivity, 1960–92, 87 countries

0.52, per cent per year. Thus, in spite of the lower prices for agriculture, it was still profitable to expand the area of agricultural land.

The growth rate of land is much smaller than that of output and this reflects an increase in land productivity. Figure 8.6 presents the distribution of growth rates in average land productivity for 87 countries. In 11 countries (13 per cent of the countries) the average productivity declined, but these countries carry small production weights (less than 2 per cent of production) and the weighted distribution shows a concentration in the positive growth rates. Thus, the bulk of world production was obtained with an increase in land productivity. The median growth rates are 1.8 and 1.92 per cent for the unweighted and weighted distributions respectively.

Labour

Changes in the agricultural labour force have taken a somewhat different pattern. In 40 per cent of the countries, *total* agricultural labour declined. Figure 8.7 presents the distribution of changes in the labour force for 148 countries during 1950–90. The median growth rate was 0.56 per cent which, while similar to that of harvested land, shows a substantial spread across countries.

Several technological factors affected labour demand. In part, the labour requirement, particularly harvest labour, is increasing with the level of output and as such increases with yields. Similarly, when the composition of output changes from cereals to fruits and vegetables, labour requirements increase as well. Also, an increase in livestock production

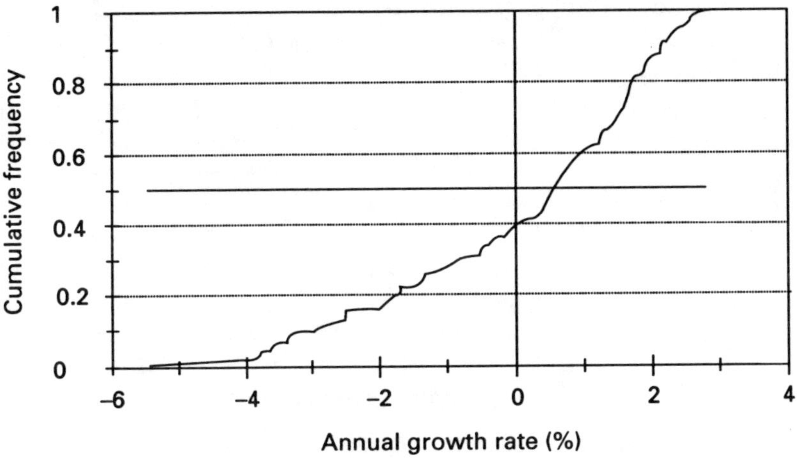

Figure 8.7 Agricultural labour, 1950–90, 148 countries

frequently increases labour requirements for agricultural labour. Finally, the increase in cultivated land adds to the labour demand. On the other hand, mechanization of agriculture reduces the labour requirements. All of this concerns demand for labour input, but the data report a different variable: the labour force in agriculture. This measure includes workers not fully employed in agriculture, and many of them eventually leave agriculture, but the timing and the degree of such migration depends on the off-farm work and income opportunities.

With all these qualifications, the net effect of mechanization on agricultural labour input is detected in the labour – land ratios which are presented in Figure 8.8. In about half of the countries this ratio declined, and the rate of decline was stronger than the rate of increase in the other half of countries. This uneven effect is attributed to the dependence of the degree of mechanization on the economic environment, which determines the profitability of mechanization. It is the poorer countries, with lower wage–rental ratios, that rely more heavily on labour than on machines. In those countries, the off-farm migration was not sufficient for the data to show a decline in the actual labour input in agriculture.

When output per unit of land increases while the labour per unit of land is constant, there is an increase in productivity. The distribution of the growth rates of average labour productivity in 87 countries is drawn in Figure 8.9. The growth rates of average labour productivity are somewhat higher than that of average land productivity. The median rates are 2.0 and 2.6 per cent for the unweighted and weighted distributions, respectively. A

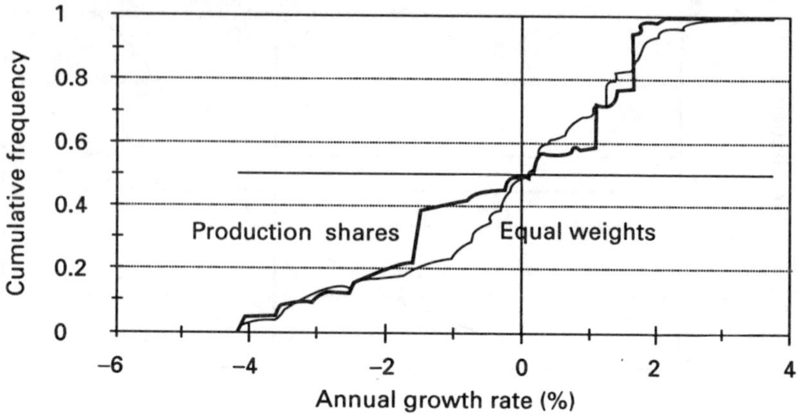

Figure 8.8 Labour to land ratio, 1960–92, 87 countries

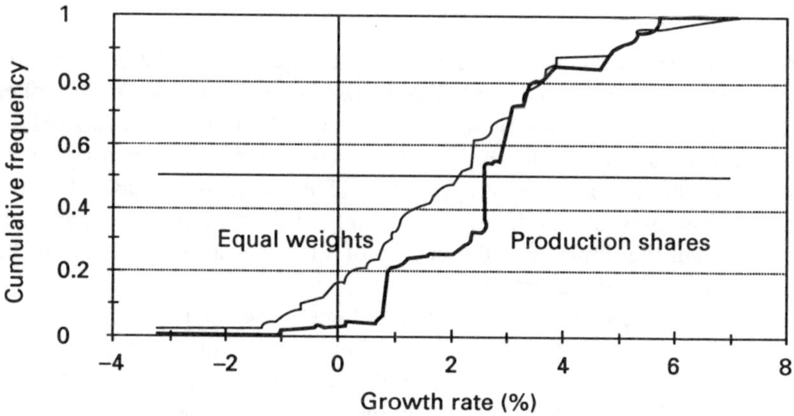

Figure 8.9 Average labour productivity, 1960–92, 87 countries

comparison of the weighted distributions of average labour and land productivity for 87 countries is presented in Figure 8.10.[7]

Changes of these partial-productivity measures reflect changes in the agricultural labour force, cultivated land, other inputs and technology. The major input that is missing from the discussion so far is capital. Data on this variable is limited but preliminary estimates indicate that it grew faster than output. However, its factor share in total output can be quite high and hence it can have a strong direct effect on productivity. In any case, it is important to emphasize that perceived productivity changes are outcomes of decisions on inputs and implemented

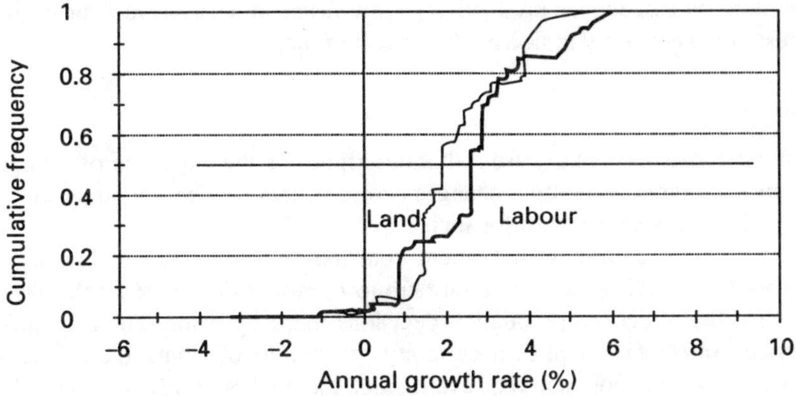

Figure 8.10 Labour and land productivity, 1960–92, 87 countries

technology. These decisions are endogenous and have to be studied in conjunction with, and as a part of, the productivity analysis. We return to this subject below.

How does the productivity performance in agriculture compare with that in non-agriculture? Figure 8.11 presents the distribution of the differences in the growth rates of average labour productivity in non-agriculture and agriculture. The median values are –1.58 and –1.1 for the unweighted and weighted distributions, respectively, which implies a higher growth rate in average labour productivity in agriculture. However, what is

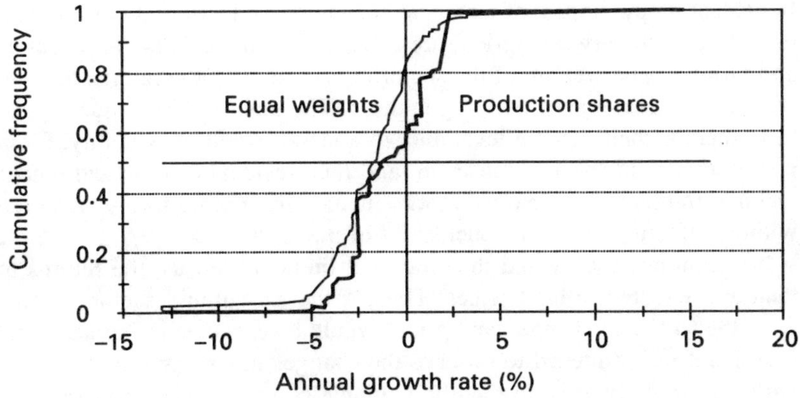

Figure 8.11 Differential growth of labour productivity, non-agriculture minus agriculture, 1960–92, 88 countries

striking is that labour productivity grew faster in agriculture than in the rest of the economy in nearly 80 per cent of the countries.

Summary

What comes out clearly from this description is the existence of a large spread in input and output changes across countries. The important question here is what accounts for such a spread and, more specifically, to what extent the economic environment contributes to this spread. The term 'economic environment' is used here to represent the set of all the variables that affect the production decisions made by firms. These include prices, interest rates, price uncertainty, availability of inputs, the competitiveness of the input markets, availability and quality of infrastructure, the access to new information, the legal and organizational infrastructure needed to conduct business activity, the stability of the economic variables, tax structure and the like. Not all of these variables changed to a degree that affects production in a given country in any given period, and the strategy of research is to concentrate on isolating the effects of the important variables that did change. The list of pertinent variables may vary from country to country and the purpose of a country analysis is to identify them and thereby supplement the results obtained in a cross-country analysis.

3 AGRICULTURE AND FARMERS

In evaluating the impact of technical change on agriculture it is important to differentiate between agriculture as an economic activity (or a sector) and farmers. The welfare of the sector is measured by the returns to land, which is the factor specific to agriculture. The main welfare issue related to farmers is their income level and, to a lesser extent, its stability. Farm operators benefit from increases in land rent, residual income and labour income. In this discussion, we ignore income from other forms of capital without affecting the main conclusions of the discussion.

As economic theory and the empirical literature tell us, the returns to land are reflected in land prices. Thus, if the agricultural sector benefits from the technical change, land prices would be expected to increase, and it is therefore of interest to observe the changes in land prices over time. Unfortunately, there is no readily available comprehensive data set with time series of land prices for various countries. In view of the importance of this variable, we are assembling data by an intensive library search (together with Rita Butzer). At this point we review some of the data assembled thus far.

A cross-country comparison of land prices is a difficult task because of quality differences, notwithstanding the difficulty of quantifying the importance of the economic environment that affects such prices. Nevertheless, the time path of land prices in the various countries is telling. There are two ways, pertinent to our discussion, to look at land prices. The first is to deflate land prices by the price of the agricultural product, and the second is to deflate them by the price of the consumption good as measured by the 'CPI'. The first, referred to as the output measure, provides the price of land reflecting its productivity, whereas the second, referred to as the consumption measure, indicates the value of land in terms of the purchasing power it has over an aggregate consumption good, whose price is measured by the CPI.

Figure 8.12 shows the pattern of real agricultural land prices for the United States, Canada, South Africa and Japan, countries for which extended time series are currently available. In Figure 8.12, land prices are reported as indices with 1986 = 1. Panel A shows the output measure of land prices whereas panel B shows its consumption measure. By both measures, land prices declined in the pre-war period. They were gradually increasing in the immediate post-war period, this rise gained impetus during the inflationary period of the 1970s and came to an end in the early 1980s, when the economies started to deflate.

Comparing land prices at the beginning and end of each series, we see that by the output measure prices are considerably higher, but by the consumption measure there is little change. In the United States, the consumption–land price index was 0.84 in 1992, compared to 0.73 in 1910. For Canada the values for 1990 and 1914 are 0.87 and 0.76, respectively. The series for South Africa begins in 1940 at a level of 0.88, whereas the 1993 value is 0.65. Data for other countries show the same trend. On the whole, prices in the 1990s are historically relatively low, and it is remarkable that land prices today are not much different from those at the beginning of the century. Moreover, land prices reflect subsidies to agriculture. If account were taken for subsidies (which are relatively new), then land prices would exhibit even less growth over their historic levels.

Another striking observation is the high correlation between the price movements for the four countries plotted in Figure 8.12, as well as for most countries. The correlation is stronger for the output than for the consumption measure. This correlation indicates that much of the impact of the dramatic changes in agricultural technology was transmitted to the various countries (or at least to those observed here). However, the

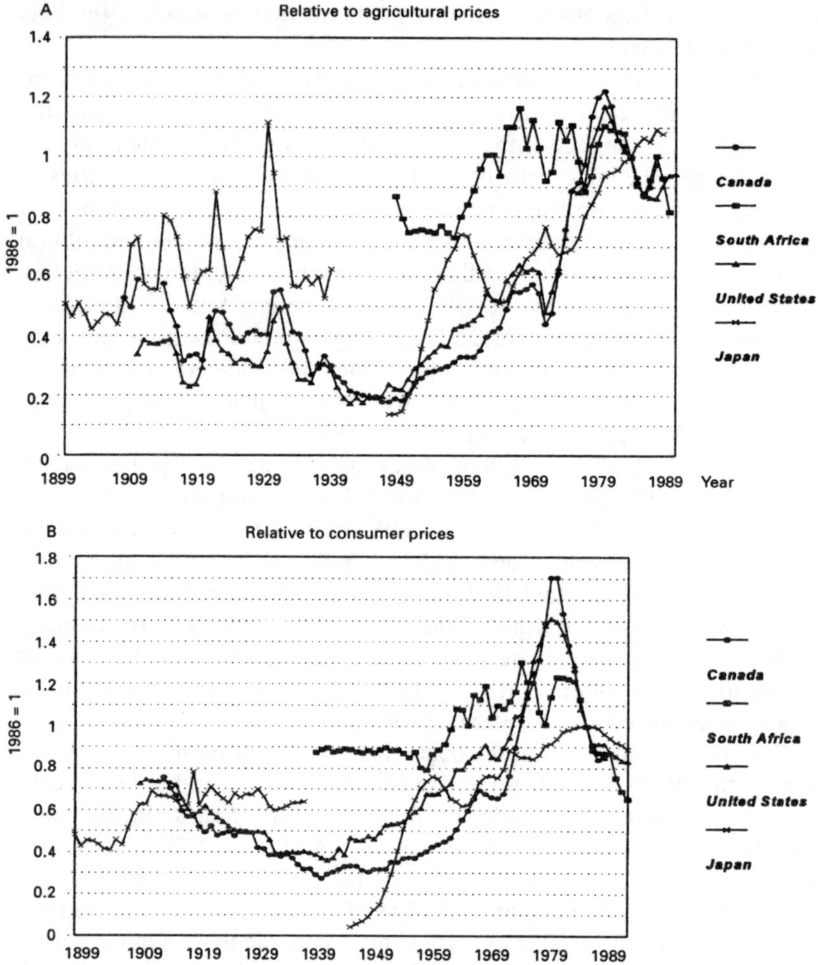

Figure 8.12 The price of land in agriculture

benefits were not captured by agriculture and eventually were distributed to the consumers. This was done through a decline in agricultural prices relative to prices of the other consumption goods.

The changes in the welfare of people in agriculture is a different, and far more complex, story. The income of farmers is the return to their labour and factors in their possession. Aside from the returns to land discussed above, which applies mainly to land owners, labour income is the main income source for farm operators and primarily the only source for landless labour.[8] Data on returns to labour are deficient. Therefore, we will examine changes in the structural composition of the labour force and infer the impact of the changes in technology on labour.

Even though in most countries there was an increase in the agricultural labour force, this increase lagged behind the increase in the total labour force due to off-farm migration. This is seen by comparing the growth rates of agricultural labour with that of the population. Under the assumption of equal fertility rates in agriculture and non-agriculture, the growth rate of agricultural labour *less* that of the population gives the rate of labour migration from agriculture to non-agriculture, expressed as a percentage of the agricultural labour force.[9] The distribution of this difference in growth rates for 148 countries is plotted in Figure 8.13, which shows that such migration took place in practically all countries. The median average annual migration rate for the period 1950–90 is 1.97 per cent. That is, at the median the agricultural labour force declined at an annual average rate of about 2 per cent.

In interpreting this result, it should be noted that off-farm migration is determined not only by changes in agricultural profitability but also by changes in labour demand in non-agriculture as well as sectoral differences in the level of standard of living. A detailed study of off-farm migration based on the cross-country data for the period 1950–90 appears in Larson and Mundlak (1995). Naturally, when labour income in agriculture is low, people will migrate to other sectors. Thus, off-farm migration is probably the most important single process that contributes to the alleviation of rural poverty. This result should be kept in mind in judging not only economic processes but also institutional and legal

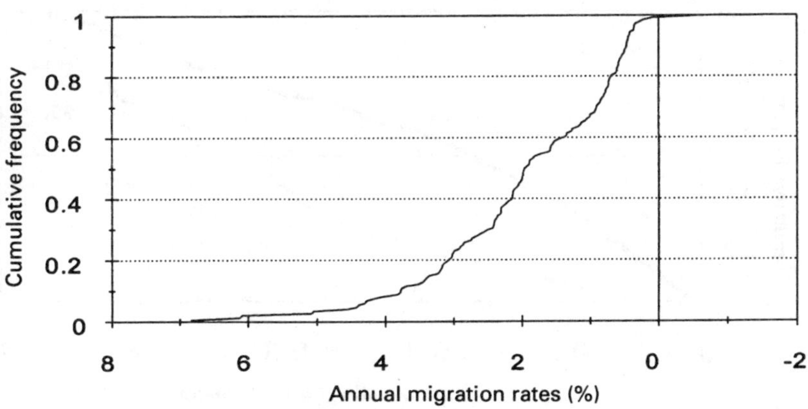

Figure 8.13 Off-farm migration rates, 1950–90, 148 countries

reforms. There is nothing more effective in improving people's welfare than allowing them to choose freely between opportunities and thus escape areas of hardship. The traditional exploitation of agricultural labour may have taken place because migration opportunities for such labour were restricted by institutional arrangement, by lack of infrastructure, or by lack of opportunities outside of agriculture. For migration to take place, opportunities in non-agriculture are required. This is where economic growth comes in as a factor in the alleviation of agricultural-based poverty.

4 AGRICULTURE AND DEVELOPMENT

The technological change in agriculture had two important effects on the economy as a whole. First, it improved the overall food supply while prices declined and thus improved consumer welfare. Second, it made it possible to produce more output with relatively less labour and thus facilitated the development of non-agriculture. As a result of the migration, the share of agriculture in the total labour force has declined. This is seen in Figure 8.14, in which the share is plotted for 148 countries for the years 1950 and 1990. The share varies considerably among countries. It is high in less-developed economies and declines with the level of development. Even so, it has declined in all countries. The median share was 70 per cent in 1950, but only 33 per cent in 1990. The proportion of countries with a share below 10 per cent increased from 1.3 per cent in 1950 to 15 per cent in 1990. Few indicators are better able to tell the story of the role of

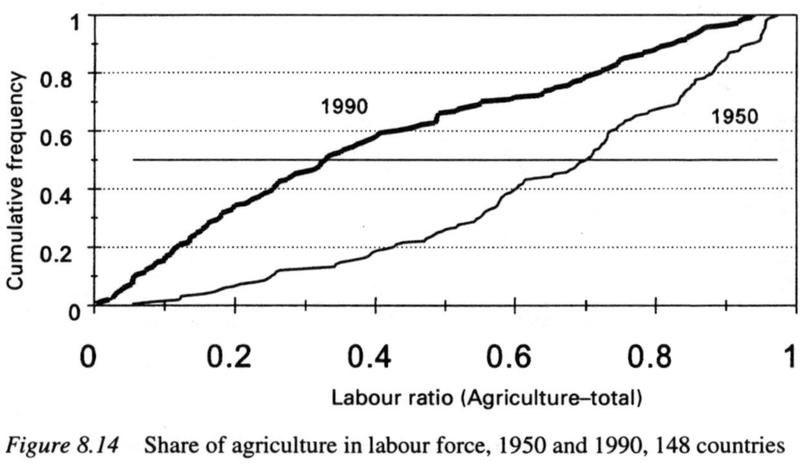

Figure 8.14 Share of agriculture in labour force, 1950 and 1990, 148 countries

agriculture in economic development: the freeing of labour that is a necessary condition for development. Therefore, understanding of the process of off-farm migration, and the determinants of its rate, contributes to our understanding of the process of development.

The net outcome of the processes reviewed above is a decline in the relative importance of agriculture in total output. The change in the distribution of this share in the 40-year period between 1950 and 1990, as seen from Figure 8.15, is indeed noteworthy: the median for this group of 67 countries declined from 30 to 8 per cent over this period.[11]

In summary, technological change in agriculture serves the rest of the economy by increasing supplies at lower prices and contributing labour to the development of non-agriculture. At the same time, in the longer run, none of the benefits are captured in agriculture. Who would stand to benefit from further increases in agricultural productivity in the future? There is no reason to think that the future will be any different from the past.

This welfare conclusion has an important policy implication for the finance of agricultural research. Historically, much agricultural research was publicly financed because the fruits of the research cannot be internalized by the researcher. The foregoing discussion indicates that it is indeed in the interest of the public at large to promote research that will produce technological change in agriculture. Therefore, the burden of this research should be carried by the public at large and not by agriculture, which does not seem to capture and maintain the benefit from it. Furthermore, because

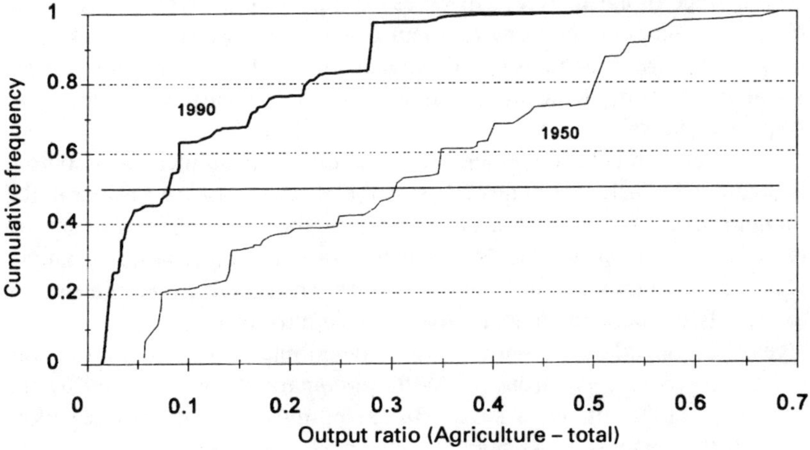

Figure 8.15 Share of agriculture in GDP, 1950 and 1990, 67 countries

the fruits of the research are eventually spread to all countries, a strong case can be made for financing research internationally. But countries can take lead in advancing technology and benefit from it until the new technology spreads to other countries. Also, for countries to take advantage of global developments, they must have an ongoing active research programme. Thus, there is a strong case for country finance of its own research as well.

5 RESEARCH IMPLICATIONS

An important conclusion to be drawn from the foregoing review is that the underlying process of agricultural growth is universal but its pace varies over time and across countries. The basic question is how to account for this variability. There is no simple answer to this question because there is no single factor that can provide the answer. This is also true when it comes to the evaluation of the consequences of policies. Much research on agricultural policy concentrates on the implications of sector-specific policies, which are pertinent but by themselves insufficient to unfold the whole story.

The process of development is a process of continuous adjustments made by households and firms. These adjustments and their consequences are spread over time and as such are dynamic in their nature. They are carried out in response to changes in the economic environment subject to the prevailing constraints. Thus the key to understanding the economic performance of agriculture, as well as other sectors, is in the study of the impact of the economic environment on such decisions. The task is to formulate a framework that will channel the net effect of the various variables forming the economic environment into measures conducive to empirical analysis.

The approach is based on the simple premise that an increase in output is obtained by a change in resources, in the efficiency of their use or in the implemented technology. For most countries, the limiting factor to growth is not the available technology as determined by the frontier of knowledge, because they are far from the frontier. The pressing research issue is to identify the constraints that prevent the country from taking full advantage of the available technology, and the determinants that control the pace of convergence to the frontier. As these constraints are affected by the economic environment, a successful mapping of the economic environment to variables considered by producers in making their production decisions can form the framework for the analysis.

There are several important blocks in this formulation. First is the mapping of the economic environment to sectoral incentives. Second is the impact that sectoral incentives have on factor demand and factor supply. Third is the dependence of the implemented technology on incentives and on resource and other constraints. In this, an explicit account should be taken of the fact that decisions have consequences in more than one period. The dependence of factor demand on incentives is obvious. A good illustration of the dependence of factor supply on incentives is that of labour, where off-farm migration is affected by the intersectoral income differentials. A good illustration of the dependence on constraints is that of the choice of techniques. Different techniques have different resource requirements, where on the whole, the more advanced techniques are more capital (human and physical)-intensive. Hence, capital scarcity determines the pace of implementation of new techniques. As decisions on the implemented technology are made jointly with the decisions on input demand, that demand also depends on the same constraints that affect the implemented technology. The research and policy implications of this point cannot be overemphasized.

Underlying the process of implementation of new techniques is the flow of new techniques, or changes in the available technology. Such a flow is correlated with investment in research and development (R&D) but, more profoundly, it depends on the advancement in basic knowledge which, by its very nature, follows a random walk. The voluminous literature that aims to explain this flow, for which agriculture is a good example, provides plenty of anecdotal evidence but no structural model, and therefore little predictive power.

The empirical knowledge of the various blocks makes it possible to simulate the economy and to evaluate the consequences of various policies. This is the approach taken in Mundlak *et al.* (1989) for Argentina and Coeymans and Mundlak (1993) for Chile. These studies construct simulation models along the lines indicated above which are fitted to the historical data. Thereafter, the model is simulated to evaluate the consequences of alternative policies of interest within a historical context in order to understand the dynamic, quantitative effect of various policies and to infer from them desirable courses of action for future development.

6 THE PRODUCTION STRUCTURE OF AGRICULTURE

Technology and competitive conditions play a role in the determination of supply. Almost any of the foregoing discussion involves attributes of technology. Technical change is the key factor for growth and affects income distribution. Factor shares determine the relationships between factor prices and product prices and the competitive position of a sector. Returns to scale affect the size distribution of firms. Elasticities of substitution affect the functional distribution of income due to capital accumulation. Not independent of any of the above is the question of supply response and factor demand. Hence, the empirical analysis of technology, and its changes, is of cardinal importance.

The literature on production functions and related topics deals with various aspects of the subject but falls short of providing an integrated framework which is readily applicable in the evaluation of the dynamics of agriculture. To provide an insight into this literature we summarize some key findings on the central issues pertinent to the construction of such a framework based on a recent literature review (Mundlak, 1997). There are two fairly distinct periods in the study of agricultural production functions, before and after duality. The changing of the guards was in the early 1970s. Duality is a powerful theory to analyze supply issues using primal or dual functions. However, its empirical use is more limited. As a result, the appearance of duality changed not only the method of estimation but also the questions asked to the extent that there is little continuity in the subjects of interest. This is illustrated below.

The empirical work on agricultural production functions originated in a methodological paper by Tintner (1944) and an application by Tintner and Brownlee (1944). This work was influenced by the work of Paul Douglas and it thus took 15 years to adopt the work of Douglas in agricultural economics application. The primal estimation of the Cobb–Douglas function was the centrepiece in the pre-duality work. The approach does not impose competitive conditions on the estimation but instead submits them to empirical testing. Such testing often shows a difference between observed factor shares and the estimated production elasticities. This result is not an absolute rejection of the prevalence of the competitive conditions but rather a conditional result, based on the model and the statistical procedure used. Still, it is indicative of the existence of deviations from such conditions.

Empirical results maintain that the elasticity of labour never exceeds 0.5, and in most cases it varies in the range of 0.25–0.45. This value is less than the elasticity of labour in non-agriculture. If all non-labour income is considered to be capital income, then the result supports the position that agriculture is cost-capital-intensive and therefore less susceptible to increases in the wage rate than non-agriculture. Also, the factor share of labour in agriculture has declined with time, indicating that technical change was labour-saving.

The elasticity of land varies between zero, in some cases, and about one-third. We interpret this elasticity to be a measure of the competitive position of agriculture. From the perspective of farm income it is meaningful to look at the sum of labour and land elasticities, and this sum often fluctuates around 0.5.

One motivation for estimating production functions is to provide weights for the computation of technical change. However, this approach has not provided any substantive advantage compared to the use of factor shares, even though they may not be the same as the production elasticities. The reason is that specification errors and interpretation of statistical studies are often greater than the discrepancies between the factor shares and the true production elasticities. An example is the error involved in finding increasing returns to scale and its subsequent incorporation in the computation of total factor productivity (TFP). This leads to the elimination of residuals in comparisons of growth over time or productivity differences across countries. Such a procedure was motivated by the belief that all growth can be accounted for and therefore there should be no residual (Griliches, 1963). However, this belief has no foundation, and it is inconsistent with theory.

An important feature common to many studies is a lack of robustness in the estimates and their dependence on the selected variables and sample coverage. This result is consistent with the interpretation that the implemented technology is sensitive to variations in the economic environment.

What distinguishes the dual from the primal approach is the appearance of prices in the empirical equation. Hence, in evaluating the performance of this approach we address the following questions:

- What has been the contribution of prices to the empirical equation?
- What additional information is obtained from the dual equations and how can they be interpreted?
- Are the underlying assumptions of duality met?
- What are the statistical benefits of this approach?

The dual estimates are obtained by regressing factor shares on prices, a time trend and sometimes output. When the change in use of inputs is decomposed to price, technology (more correctly, time) and output effects, trend and output account for most of the changes whereas the role of prices is the least important. Thus the apparent direct contribution of prices to the explanation of inputs or output variations is rather limited. There is an indirect contribution that works through the impact on the quasi-fixed inputs, not captured in the usual dual estimates, but this is not discussed here.

On the whole, the own-price elasticities reported in the literature are less than one. There is no uniformity in the signs of the cross-elasticities but, in general, most inputs appear to be substitutes. The price elasticities of factor demand and product supply are usually obtained under the assumption that factor supplies are perfectly elastic. In practice, this is not the case. Consequently, the magnitude of the estimated elasticities are affected and the results need not represent demand-driven substitution. This is particularly relevant to elasticities related to labour, land and capital.

Interestingly, on the whole, the studies based on duality do not show increasing returns to scale. Moreover, technical change, obtained by including a time trend in regressions of factor shares is largely labour-saving, capital-using, and fertilizer-using. The results on land are somewhat ambiguous. However, this is reflective of the data. Therefore, the effect of including prices was not sufficient to change conclusions that could be drawn from the raw data. This does not give a strong mark to the analysis in that the results are obvious without it.

Duality between technology and prices holds under well defined conditions that can be tested empirically. In most studies, these underlying conditions are not fully met, particularly concavity of the cost function and convexity of the profit function. Therefore, the estimated technology is inconsistent with the basic premises of the model. In a way, this is the most disappointing result because duality is a very powerful theory. An important question, then, is why the theoretical results are inconsistent with the empirical analysis. There is more than one reason, but probably the most important one is the improper treatment of technology.

One of the expected virtues of duality has been its apparent solution of the simultaneous equation bias realized in some primal estimators. However, a closer examination of this issue indicates that in general dual estimators are inferior to primal estimators (Mundlak, 1996).

In summary, a close examination of the literature suggests that various anomalies and apparent inconsistencies in empirical results can be interpreted within the framework of the choice of techniques which views the implemented technology to be sensitive to the economic environment. This provides an appropriate framework for empirical analysis and provides the necessary insight for the evaluation of changes in policies.

Notes

1. This chapter was originally a paper prepared for the IEA congress in Tunis (December 1995). In part it is based on Mundlak (forthcoming). We have benefited from research assistance by Rita Butzer and Nanae Yabuki.
2. This research has been conducted at the World Bank under a research grant (RPO 679–03). The data were assembled from known international sources such as FAO, ILO, the World Bank, and the IMF as well as from country publications. The results are presented in terms of empirical distributions. The number of countries and the period covered in the figures vary according to data availability.
3. Unless indicated otherwise, all growth rates are computed from a semi-logarithmic regression of the variable in question on time.
4. The number of countries varies across figures because of incomplete data sets.
5. In making such a statement, we note that the vertical axis in the two figures is the same and that the units of the horizontal axis are also the same.
6. Based on national accounts data, converted to dollars and deflated by the US GDP deflator.
7. The variance of the average land productivity is lower than that of the average labour productivity. This is due to bigger variance in the rates of change of the labour force than of land. The pattern of changes in land and labour productivity is discussed by Hayami and Ruttan (1985).
8. Part of the rent (residual income) may also be shared by tenants, depending on the nature of the contract.
9. The assumption of equal fertility rates is made here for purpose of illustration. The migration rates could be estimated under the assumption of different fertility rates.
10. The median in 1990 for a larger set of countries is 9 per cent. Figure 8.15 contains fewer countries, being limited to those on which we have data also for 1950.

References

Binswanger, H. P, Y. Mundlak, C. Young, and A. Bowers (1987) 'On the Determinants of Cross-country Aggregate Agricultural Supply', *Journal of Econometrics*, vol. 36, pp. 111–31.

Coeymans, J. E. and Y. Mundlak (1993) 'Sectoral Growth in Chile: 1962–82', *International Food Policy Research Institute, Research Report*, vol. 95.

Griliches, Z. (1963) 'Estimates of the Aggregate Agricultural Production Function from Cross-Sectional Data', *Journal of Farm Economics*, vol. 45, pp. 419–28.

Hayami, Y. and V. Ruttan (1985) *Agricultural Development – An International Perspective* (Washington, DC: Johns Hopkins University Press).

Larson, D. and Y. Mundlak (1995) 'On the Intersectoral Migration of Agricultural Labour', *Working Paper*, 1425 (Washington, DC: The World Bank, International Economics Department); a shorter version is *Economic Development and Cultural Change*, vol. 45 (2), 1997, pp. 295–319.

Mundlak, Y., D. Cavallo and R. Domenech (1989) 'Agriculture and Economic Growth, Argentina 1913–1984', *Research Report*, vol. 76 (Washington, DC: International Food Policy Research Institute).

Mundlak, Y. (1997) 'Agricultural Production Functions – A Critical Review', *Working Paper* No. 9702 (Rehovot: The Center for Agricultural Economic Research).

Mundlak, Y. (1996) 'Production Function Estimation: a Revival of the Primal', *Econometrica*, vol. 64, no. 2, pp. 431–8.

Mundlak, Y. (forthcoming) *Agriculture and Economic Growth* (Cambridge, MA: Harvard University Press).

Tintner, G. (1944) 'A Note on the Derivation of Production Functions from Farm Records', *Econometrica*, vol. 12, pp. 26–34.

Tintner, G. and O. H. Brownlee (1944) 'Production Functions Derived from Farm Records', *Journal of Farm Economics*, vol. 26 (August), pp. 566–71 (a correction is in *Journal of Farm Economics* February 1953, p. 123).

9 Incentive Distortions in Developing Agriculture in South Africa and Implications for Tenure Reform

W. Lieb Nieuwoudt, Graham Moor and Rupert Baber
UNIVERSITY OF NATAL, SOUTH AFRICA

1 INTRODUCTION

The political transformation in South Africa is a political marvel. One reason why this was accomplished is that potential conflict areas were diffused by pre-emptive steps taken before democratic elections. In terms of land distribution, mechanisms were set in place allowing for land transfers from state and predominantly white-owned commercial farms to small-scale black farmers. These steps are required to alleviate the extreme skewedness of land access, reflected by the fact that the white minority owns about 87 per cent of South Africa's agricultural land. The new government has proposed various resettlement models to achieve land transfers to previously disenfranchised black farmers, ranging from private ownership to group resettlement (LAPC, 1993).

However, land reforms which attempt to address broad issues of redistribution and restitution at national level, while ignoring the resultant impact on economic incentives at the individual level, may be counterproductive. In this regard, there is concern that group ownership will reduce economic incentives to invest in land improvements, and that land use will not be sustainable (Lyne and Roth, 1994).

This chapter examines how the existing structure of property rights has impacted on agricultural incentives in South Africa. In South Africa, 87 per cent of agricultural land is privately owned by commercial farmers. These farmers have received significant state support (R&D and financing) in the past. The sector is characterized by moderate increasing efficiency and levels of land conservation. By contrast, the communal sector, comprising 13 per cent of agricultural land, is characterized by stagnation and widespread resource degradation. One reason for the latter is that this sector has received little technical and state support to date. The likely change in focus of state research and extension to the small-grower sector under the new government should alleviate this problem. A second reason for the underdevelopment of the communal sector is the lack of incentives to invest under communal ownership. This problem will remain into the future and is the focus of this chapter.

Communal land ownership is common in the developing agricultural sectors of Southern African countries (South Africa, Lesotho, Botswana, Namibia, Zimbabwe and others). The further north one progresses up the continent, the more individualized property rights become. A possible reason for this phenomenon is that colonial governments entrenched the position of traditional chiefs in Southern Africa. In turn, the chiefs promote communal tenure as they derive power from their role of allocating land under customary law. To study the effect of incentive distortions under communal land ownership in South Africa, the likely impact of a group ownership resettlement model on economic incentives is explored. Survey data from small-scale farmers in Zimbabwe are analyzed to investigate the interaction between land tenure security and economic incentives under a wide range of geographically adjacent tenure institutions, including government resettlement programmes. These tenure options are unique to the Zimbabwean small-scale agricultural sector and are likely to be instructive for the proposed resettlement in South Africa.

2 ECONOMIC INCENTIVES

Property rights are an endogenous response to the need for economic coordination in the face of interdependence and serve to reduce the real resource losses faced by individuals as a result of imperfect information. These losses are grouped under the term ‘transaction costs’, and include the search, advertising, inspection, and negotiating costs surrounding voluntary exchange, as well as the risks associated with such exchange. The level of transaction costs determines: (1) the extent to which individual economic agents are able to profitably exchange property rights for mutual benefit, and (2) the occurrence of situations where the cost of bringing the associated harmful or beneficial effects to bear on the decisions of one or more of the interacting agents is too high to make it worthwhile.

While economic efficiency is most often described by the concept of Pareto-optimality, the only way in which the outcome of the exchange process can be evaluated is through the revealed choice behaviour of individuals to potential exchanges. Different agents will hold different perceptions of the harm and benefit relationships attached to any potential exchange of rights, and there is consequently no means whereby an external observer can determine whether or not the observed level of exchanges stops short of some idealized norms (Buchanan, 1986, p. 94). This means that attention should rather be focused on the incentive structures within different institutional settings.

3 PROPERTY RIGHTS IN THE SUBSISTENCE AREAS OF SOUTH AFRICA

Land tenures in South Africa fall into (a) traditional communal (b) Trust, and (c) individualized tenure. Within these categories an unknown number of local variants exist in response to local–specific economic, social and demographic factors. Individually-held freehold land supports tenancy in the great majority of cases, and given the need for urban use this land has become increasingly residential. Due to its importance only communal tenure will be further discussed.

Traditional communal tenure exists predominantly in the subsistence areas of KwaZulu-Natal and the former Transkei on the eastern seaboard. Property rights are conferred on individuals in terms of customary law. Land is legally held in trust by the chief for the benefit of members of that tribe, while the underlying title rests with the state. Individuals, acting on behalf of the family or agnate group, are granted rights of exclusion to allocated parcels of land. The bundle of rights includes the right to occupy the land, the right to use it, the right to modify it, and the right to transfer land usage through renting or share-cropping. Property rights are said to be 'communal' for the following reasons: first, each married man has the right to be awarded enough building and arable land for his family's needs; secondly, individual agents do not possess the right to permanently alienate the land; and thirdly, the community is able to revoke land allocations following non-use over a designated period of time (Cross, 1990a, p. 11). The individual use and transfer rights found in traditional communal tenure are therefore different from the rights accorded by Western property systems, because they are conditioned by group or secondary rights (Atwood, 1990, p. 662).

Although individuals possess rights of exclusion to their allocated land, and can enforce these rights under customary law, land which is not used for residential purposes, cultivated, or physically 'privatized' (for example, fenced) is treated as a common resource on which all members of the community have the right to graze their animals (Stewart, 1990). Cultivated land can also be made available for grazing during the winter months.

3.1 The Incentive Structure on Grazing Land

Available evidence indicates that grazing land in the subsistence areas is overutilized, leading to continued degradation of the natural resource base, comparatively low yields from animal production, and unacceptably high levels of topsoil erosion (Bembridge, 1986, p. 24; Huntley *et al.*, 1989, p. 56). Evidence of overstocking is highlighted by a study indicating that stocking rates in communal areas of KwaZulu-Natal are 40 to 100 per cent higher than those on land of similar agro-climatic potential on commercial farms in KwaZulu-Natal (McKenzie *et al.*, 1989, p. 5). Herd mortality rates in communal areas are nearly double those recorded on privately-owned farms in KwaZulu-Natal (Lyne, 1989, p. 143), while calving percentages in these two areas are 32 and 80 per cent respectively (Nieuwoudt, 1990, p. 5). Low levels of production efficiency can be attributed to low levels of nutrition.

Community members theoretically possess rights of inclusion to common grazing areas under all the tenure systems of the developing agricultural sector, with the possible exception of freehold tenure. The individual right to be included loses its meaning, however, if these rights to inclusion are not restricted to a distinct and finite group or community of individuals (Ciriacy-Wantrup and Bishop, 1975, p. 715). Individual rights of inclusion are therefore dependent upon group or community rights of exclusion and a necessary condition for the existence of a common property institution is, by definition, restricted access. A sufficient condition for the existence of a common property institution is restrictive rules which are subscribed to by individuals using the resource. The potential for cooperation under restricted access has been analyzed in terms of assurance or security of expectation (see Runge, 1981). There always remains an economic incentive to defect and graze more animals, however, as the marginal private returns to grazing are greater than marginal private costs.

Available evidence indicates that binding restrictions on individual use of the commons are not in effect (Cross, 1990a, p. 10). This also applies to other subsistence areas and leads to the conclusion that property rights to common grazing land can most accurately be described as 'open access.' Isolated instances of privatized grazing do exist.

Open access implies that the number of cattle is not restricted. This leads to pervasive positive and negative externalities. A positive externality exists because individual reductions in the use of open access grazing land confer benefits on every stock-owner, and not just on the individual making the reduction. This is also true of individual investments in time and capital that improve the quality of the resource, such as the planting of pastures. Negative externalities exist in that grazing land may be exploited at a level of negative marginal productivity, if private marginal costs of owning livestock are sufficiently small. These costs consist of the 'opportunity cost' of investing in, and the variable cost of rearing and managing, livestock. Where over-exploitation does take place, the full costs of resource degradation are borne by the entire society, including members of future generations. It is also true that no individual stock-owner has the incentive on his own to acquire sufficient information about the environmental implications of open access grazing (Dasgupta, 1982, p. 17). Lawry *et al.* (1984, pp. 249–52) note that the breakdown of traditional institutions controlling common grazing land is symptomatic of the reorientation of household economic interests away from subsistence production and toward greater integration in the market economy.

3.2 The Incentive Structure on Arable Land

A large and growing volume of literature is emphasizing the stagnation of arable production in the subsistence areas. Lenta (1981, p. 65) estimates, for example, that cereal production *per capita* in subsistence areas of KwaZulu-Natal decreased at an average rate of 1.16 per cent per annum between the periods 1867–72 and 1972–7. Yields are far below those attained on comparable land in the commercial areas (Lyne, 1989; Bembridge, 1986, p. 29).

The degree of cultivation of arable land in the subsistence areas ranges between 20 and 80 per cent of area available (Lenta, 1981; Lyne, 1989). These estimates may provide insufficient indication that available arable land is underutilized, but must be seen together with low yields achieved. This is borne out by a study of arable production in the Transkei which estimated that up to 35 per cent of land ploughed produced no yield whatsoever, leading to the conclusion that at least some of this land was intentionally left unplanted (Jordan, 1983, p. 6). Low yields where crops have been planted are indicative of the failure to adopt suitable planting times, cultivars, and tillage, and inadequate soil fertility and insect or weed control practices. The implication is that economic agents who possess rights of exclusion to arable land are not investing the time and capital necessary for intensive crop production. At the same time the right of stock-owners to use land not cultivated as an open access resource creates an incentive for households to plough marginal and non-arable land, such as steep slopes: under open access the individual derives little benefit from the land, even if he owns livestock, as the economic rent which the resource is capable of yielding is mostly dissipated. Individuals would have a greater incentive to graze non-arable land if the benefits from grazing were internalized.

Agricultural stagnation and low yields in the subsistence areas relate both to discriminatory policies with respect to land distribution and public support, and to the way in which the property institutions in the subsistence areas influence economic incentives. The economic impact of these factors has been well documented. The first constraint to agricultural production is a shortage of suitable labour. The decreasing area of arable land available to households in the subsistence areas has meant that the fixed costs associated with management, labour and information inputs are spread over small volumes of output. Simultaneously increasing expected off-farm wage rates have increased the opportunity cost of household labour in agricultural production.

Households, in attempting to maximize their joint utility consequently find it increasingly worthwhile to substitute purchased food, paid for out of wage remittances, for agricultural production (Low, 1986, pp. 50–3). The second constraint is a shortage of capital (Lenta, 1982, pp. 318–22), which manifests itself as an inability to finance the purchase of intermediate inputs or the purchase/hire of draught animals or tractors where available.

These constraints would be reduced if land could move to those households who had the incentive and ability to invest the requisite time and capital in agriculture. The reason that such transactions do not take place in the subsistence areas is the high level of transaction costs surrounding land transfers under tenure systems. The high level of transaction costs has driven a wedge between the land's value of marginal product in the owner's use, and what this could be if used by a more productive alternative user.

Although the renting and loaning of land is theoretically permitted under traditional communal tenure, there are a number of reasons why transaction costs surrounding such transfers are large. First, these transactions, being of a private nature, are not formally registered and can therefore not be legally enforced. Secondly, the fact that renting or loaning land may entail withdrawing this land from open access grazing means that stockowners have an incentive to discourage such transactions. Finally, the right of the community to retain unutilized land after a number of years creates great uncertainty: there is a perception that leasing or loaning arable land may, by openly demonstrating what may be interpreted as an indifferent attitude towards land use, jeopardize existing property rights (Lyne, 1989, p. 14).

4 IMPLEMENTING FORMAL PRIVATE TENURE

Formal private tenure is fully consistent with the use and transfer rights found in traditional communal tenure, apart from secondary or group rights which condition individual rights. The implementation of formal private tenure in communal areas would therefore entail taking the property rights already recognized informally by the local community out of the realm of informal lineage and community ownership, and making them fully legal (Atwood, 1990, p. 659).

A formally registered title would be unimpeachable, relatively easy to define, and would release land from group or secondary rights. In theory land titling would consequently reduce the transaction costs, including risk, accompanying land transfers. The expected returns to potential buyers and renters of land would be increased, leading to an aggregate outward shift in the demand for land, and the emergence of an active land or rental market: as the market value of land increased, so too would the current owner's opportunity cost of underutilizing land. This would facilitate the movement of land to more productive farmers and those who value it most highly. Furthermore, as individual arable holdings became aggregated, unit production costs would fall as fixed costs associated with management, labour and information inputs were spread over a greater production.

4.1 The Need for Efficient Property Institutions

In order to explore whether or not formal private tenure would be an appropriate tenure system in South Africa, an understanding of the market for different property rights structures is necessary. It is postulated that in this market for predictable behaviour, the forces of supply and demand establish both the optimal combination of attenuated rights of inclusion and exclusion, and the optimal level of definition and enforcement of rights.

The demand for specific property rights is determined by three factors: (1) the demand for the benefit streams emanating directly from the resource; (2) the community's cultural and ideological attitudes towards the fairness of the way in which these benefit streams are partitioned amongst economic agents (see Runge, 1981); and (3) the demand for the indirect benefits provided by traditional community structures which owe their continued existence to the non-economic role of land as a means of ordering society (Cross, 1990a, p. 3).

Factors which determine the potential magnitude of benefit streams emanating from a resource impact upon the demand for property rights in the following way: as the potential magnitude of benefit streams increases, so too does both the significance of externalities and the potential gains from economic interaction and coordination. This implies that the value of information increases, creating a greater demand for property institutions which reduce transaction costs and enhance both the extent to which agents interact to their mutual benefit, and the extent to which the consequences of decisions are brought to bear on the interacting parties.

The supply of property institutions is a function of the relative community or state costs incurred in supporting specific property rights. Once a set of property rights has been legally instituted, the individual claims which they encapsulate must be enforceable. It is also vital that legitimate property rights are administered impartially.

Taking the ethical and social position of a society as given, the optimal choice of property rights, as well as the optimal level of definition and enforcement, will occur at the point where the marginal costs of providing and supporting these property rights equal the marginal benefits from assurance and coordination. This represents an objective criterion whereby the relative efficiency of different property institutions may be measured. 'Efficiency' in this sense is concerned with the extent to which the institutions of a society are responsive to the values and choices of individual citizens (Buchanan, 1986, p. 99). Property institutions should therefore be well adapted to the particular needs and resource constraints facing specific communities.

4.2 The Market for Formal Private Tenure in the Subsistence Areas

The low potential returns to agricultural production in subsistence areas indicate that potential gains from economic interaction may not be sufficiently high to engender a very large demand for the information provided by formal private tenure. Although the disincentive to engage in agricultural production is compounded by the high level of transaction costs under the existing land tenure systems, the agrarian economy in the subsistence areas can be expected to remain weak in the future due to the pervasive structural imbalances which have built up over years, together with the fundamental reorientation of household labour away from agricultural production and towards off-farm employment.

The poor state of animal production is also likely to militate against a great demand for formal private property. The pastoral ecosystems in most of the subsistence areas, such as the humid grasslands of KwaZulu-Natal, require strict control in the interactions between plants and animals in order to optimize productivity. This necessitates the use of sophisticated range management techniques which are most suited to private property rights. The widespread land degradation which has accompanied the absence of grazing controls in the former areas indicates that the presence of grazing externalities are economically significant. Existing circumstances in the subsistence areas virtually dictate, however, that some form of communal grazing will continue to exist. The number of livestock owned by individual households is typically small, the vast majority comprise less than 10 animals. Individual producers consequently lack the incentive to provide the capital for investments such as fencing and watering facilities, as these fixed costs are spread over a small production. This indicates that the demand for formal private tenure with respect to grazing land is not large.

On the other hand, although not enough is systematically known about what rural developing communities in South Africa want from their land system, current endogenous changes to, and developments within, traditional communal tenure indicate that in regions within the subsistence areas an outward shift in the demand for property rights which reduce the level of transaction costs is noticeable. For example, the number of informal sales and leases in these areas has increased (Cohan, cited by Cross, 1990a, p. 6). This concurs with economic theory since an increasing person–land ratio increases the real value of land, relative to other factors of production. Economic theory is further corroborated by empirical evidence from Kenya indicating that customary tenure in that country underwent an endogenous process of individualization in the face of increasing population pressure, overuse and soil erosion (Barrows and Roth, 1990, p. 270).

The move towards greater individual autonomy takes place, however, at the expense of the land ethic. There is a basic conviction in communities that access to land is universal and free to all households (Cross, 1990a, p. 25). The land ethic acts as both a protection against the excessive accumulation of land by individual households and a security to young or incoming households seeking land rights. Without this safeguard, it is often argued, many households would become landless and, in an economy suffering from structural unemployment, this would have severely negative equity implications (Cross, 1990b, p. 545). In this regard, the fact that secondary rights would be eliminated by the implementation of formal private tenure is extremely significant. It is important to note, however, that landlessness is already endemic to the subsistence areas of South Africa, with up to 50 per cent of households not possessing property rights to land, other than for residential purposes. Endogenous innovations to existing land tenure systems will critically depend, however, upon the power balance among vested interest groups at the community level. The group which presently holds political power in these areas, namely the tribal chiefs, headmen and *indunas*, have a vested interest in retaining the existing structure of property rights: they gain economic and social benefits from controlling land transfers (Cross, 1990b, p. 543) and, being stockowners, are currently free to utilize, at no extra cost, the grazing resources and watering points situated on the land of non-stock-owners.

4.3 The Dangers of Implementing Formal Private Tenure in a Suboptimal Situation

The dangers of instituting land registration in a situation where the property rights market indicates that this would not be the optimal tenure system are essentially three-fold. First, if centrally imposed on an unwilling populace it would be both resisted and circumvented. This occurred to some extent in Kenya, where customary controls and procedures have simply continued to govern the transfer and inheritance of land for large numbers of rural people. A similar situation exists on freehold land in South Africa, where heirs often see the registration of transfer as a burdensome and unnecessary process, given their hereditary right (Cross, 1990b, p. 546).

Secondly, the level of transaction costs under formal private tenure may be increased for certain groups of poor households (Atwood, 1990, p. 663) who may have little appreciation of the implications of land registration. At the same time those who appreciate the system, and are in a position to use it, usually consist of a small minority with social or economic advantages. In Wilson's sample of land transactions in Kenya (cited by Barrows and Roth, 1990, p. 277), 55 per cent of buyers of land were self-employed traders or civil servants, while 95 per cent of sellers were farmers with no off-farm work, and land was often sold because of financial hardship, particularly by widows.

Finally, the state may be unable to supply the level of public support needed for the impartial implementation and administration of these rights. Hitchcock (1980) shows that in Botswana a political élite have continued to hold substantial interests in cattle, and have used their influence in being granted formal private rights to land which formerly supported both small stock-owners, with private rights to boreholes, and hunter-gatherer communities. Behnke (1984) indicates that a similar picture emerges from an examination of private ranch development in both Uganda and Kenya. While using their formal rights of exclusion to secure their holdings, these individuals do not have the incentive either to adopt modern farming methods or to invest in capital improvements to their land, in the absence of an active land market. In South Africa, betterment planning consolidated land into residential, arable and grazing areas by breaking up the contiguous land holdings to which individual households had rights of exclusion, and reassigning property rights according to land planning specifications.

5 AN EMPIRICAL ANALYSIS OF THE INTERACTION BETWEEN LAND TENURE SECURITY AND ON-FARM INVESTMENTS

Tenure institutions establish expectations about the rights to resource use in economic activity and about the partitioning of the income stream resulting from economic activity by defining and upholding property rights. Different property institutions can thus be expected to provide different economic incentives to individuals within society. Analysis of survey data collected over a wide range of tenure alternatives in the small-scale agricultural sector of Zimbabwe allows the investigation of economic incentives under different tenure institutions following widespread land reform after Zimbabwe's independence in 1980.

Data for the analysis were gathered by means of a survey interview of small-scale farmers in Manicaland Province, Zimbabwe, during April 1995. The study area was stratified according to different tenure characteristics. Three strata were identified, namely the Small-Scale Commercial Sector (SSCS), the Model A Resettlement Area (RA) and the Communal Area (CA). Within each stratum, a simple random sample of the sampling unit (the household) was drawn and the household head interviewed. A sample of 119 respondents was recorded, 40 from the SSCS, 39 from the RA and 40 from the CA. Among the variables measured were household characteristics, household head characteristics, farm characteristics (including measures of tenure security) and production characteristics. For each individual, data were gathered on both arable and grazing allotments.

In the SSCS, land is initially held under a long-term lease from the government with an option to purchase. Once this option has been exercised, individuals can register freehold title to the land and are free to enter into land transactions. Unlike land in the SSCS, title to land in the RA and the CA is vested in the state. Land in these regions cannot be sold, and no rental market activity was recorded in the survey. Under Model A resettlement, settlers are issued an annual (and conditional) permit to cultivate 5 hectares of arable land, plus access to common grazing. In the CA, communal ownership confers individual rights to plots for houses and arable land, and provides unlimited access to communal grazing held by the community, provided the family remains resident in the area. In both regions, cultivated arable land reverts to communal grazing in the winter months.

5.1 Specification of the Empirical Model

Information on the incidence of six types of land improvements made since acquisition were collected from each household interviewed. These data were combined into investments on arable land (soil liming, fencing arable lands and conservation measures) and investments on grazing land (fencing grazing lands, establishing tree crops and establishing pastures) (Table 9.1). The expected theoretical relationship was found to be strong. Households with more exclusive property rights (SSCS farmers) invested more in all land improvements than those with less exclusive rights (CA and RA farmers).

Table 9.1 Land improvements in the SSCS, RA and CA, Zimbabwe, 1995

	SSCS (40)	*RA (39)*	*CA (40)*
Grazing investment (%):			
Fencing	90	0	0
Pastures	58	3	0
Tree crops	90	8	50
Arable investments (%):			
Fencing	90	41	28
Liming	15	5	5
Conservation	93	53	58

Investments in livestock production are greatest in areas having exclusive grazing rights. Over 90 per cent of SSCS farmers erected cattle fences in their grazing lands, and 58.5 per cent had established pastures or hay crops. Due to the unrestricted access to the communal grazing in the RA and CA, less than 3 per cent of RA and no CA farmers planted pastures. Even on arable land, RA and CA households do not have the incentive to establish pastures for livestock, as arable land reverts to communal grazing in winter. It is striking that 44 per cent of the cattle herd in the CA and 30 per cent of the herd in the RA died as a result of fodder shortages in the 1992 drought, compared to only 22 per cent in the SSCS.

An empirical analysis of the data was undertaken to test the hypothesis that land tenure security positively affects on-farm investments in agriculture. For each household, a measure of investment adoption (*INVEST*) was estimated on both arable and grazing land. 'Investment adoption' is associated with the number of different investments undertaken by the current household head and does not correspond to the effectiveness or extensiveness of their implementation. It is defined as the ratio of the number of different investments made on the farm to the maximum number of investments considered in the survey. Investments in fencing and long-term soil fertility (liming) were considered on arable land, while investments in pastures and tree crops were considered on grazing lands. Consequently, the measure of investment (*INVEST*) could take the value of 0, 0.5 or 1. The adoption of soil conservation measures and the incidence of fencing on grazing land were excluded from the analysis. Conservation measures are required by law in all the strata, and fencing of grazing land is prohibited in the CA and RA, so they do not reflect individual choices.

The equation to be estimated is given in (1):

$$INVEST_{ij} = f(X_{ij}^{t}, X_{ij}^{h}, X_{ij}^{f}) \qquad (1)$$

where investments in agriculture on plot i for household j are a function of X^t, a measure of tenure security, X^h, a vector measuring household characteristics and X^f, a vector measuring farm characteristics.

5.2 Tenure Security in the Empirical Model

Tenure security was estimated by an index (*TENURE*) measuring an individual's perceived breadth and assurance of property rights over specific land parcels (both arable and grazing land). The index was constructed out of the following variables:

A dummy variable (*D*1) scoring 1 if the respondent perceived that he had the right to sell the land without the permission of others, and 0 if otherwise. A dummy variable (*D*2) scoring 1 if the respondent was able to specify an heir to the land, and 0 if otherwise. A dummy variable (*D*3) scoring 1 if the respondent had exclusive use rights to land for the full duration of each year, and 0 if otherwise. Respondents who had continuous use rights, but shared the farm with other farmers, scored 0 for this variable. A dummy variable (*D*4) scoring 1 if the respondent's recorded property rights were enforceable (assured), and 0 if otherwise.

The index measures tenure security on a scale of 0 (least secure) to 4 (most secure). Each farmer received a score for tenure security on both arable and grazing land. Cross-tabulations indicate that farmers in the SSCS score highest on the *TENURE* index (3.15), compared to 0.91 in the RA and 1.06 in the CA. Perceived tenure security was expected to impact positively on investment in on-farm improvements.

Critical to the empirical model is the assumption that tenure security (*TENURE*) is an exogenous variable. Failing this, the tenure variable may be correlated to the error term in the equation leading to biased and inconsistent estimators of the dependant variable. In order to treat land rights as predetermined, it must be shown that farmers cannot alter specific land rights at will (Place *et al.*, 1994, p. 30). Examination of the relationship between tenure security and the time since acquisition shows little correlation, suggesting that farmers were unable to alter their land rights since the time of acquisition ($\rho = 0.095$ in the SSCS, $\rho = -0.092$ in the RA and $\rho = -0.016$ in the CA). The assumption is thus accepted for the empirical analysis, and is consistent with studies by Feder and Onchan (1987) and Place and Hazell (1993).

This assumption does not disregard the endogenous evolution of tenure institutions. However, endogenous institutional change on agricultural land appears constrained in communal areas of Southern Africa. First, problems associated with collective action in large groups (Olson, 1971, p. 48) and resistance from those who stand to lose from an institutional change may prohibit endogenous shifts towards exclusive land rights. Studies in KwaZulu-Natal report forceable resistance by stock-owners at attempts to enclose arable lands (Thomson and Lyne, 1995). Traditional chiefs also resist changes to the status quo. Secondly, competition from the successful large-scale commercial sector dominant in Southern African agriculture has resulted in the increasing marginalization of agriculture as a source of income in communal areas, reducing the demand for exclusive rights to agricultural land.

5.3 Estimation and Results

Owing to the ordinal nature of the dependant variable (*INVEST*), the model was estimated as a logit function using ordinal logistic regression. Results from the regression are presented in Table 9.2.

The variable measuring the farmers' experience (*EXP*) was omitted from the model because it was strongly correlated to the number of years the current household head had been on the land (*FARM*) ($p = 0.604^{**}$). In (1), Table 9.2, the negative and significant coefficient for agricultural potential (*NR*) is inconsistent with economic theory. Farmers in areas of high potential are expected to have a greater incentive to invest in on-farm improvements, as returns to investments are likely to be greater than returns in areas of low potential. The variable was dropped from the model in (2). The variable measuring human capital (measured as the household head's agricultural training (*MF*)) was also not included in (2) as it had a *t*-value smaller than 1 ($t = 0.9$).

The model was stable and the signs of the remaining coefficients were all consistent with *a priori* expectations. The results show that the probability of investing in on-farm improvements is increased significantly (at

Table 9.2 Estimated coefficients for the ordinal logit model of on-farm investments

Explanatory variables	*(1)*		*(2)*	
	Coefficients	*t-value*	*Coefficients*	*t-value*
TENURE	0.549	4.47^{**}	0.600	5.03^{*}
FARM	0.027	2.22^{*}	0.033	2.87^{**}
MF	0.390	1.20	–	–
LOD	0.371	1.75	0.459	2.22^{*}
GFI	0.387	1.96^{*}	0.391	2.18^{*}
NR	–0.596	-2.17^{*}	–	–
Degrees of freedom	228		230	

Notes:
** Denotes statistical significance at the 1 per cent level.
* Denotes statistical significance at the 5 per cent level.

the 99 per cent confidence level) as tenure security (*TENURE*) the time since the plot was acquired (*FARM*) increases. As improvements are accomplished over time, the longer the time spent on the land the greater the probability of investments occurring. The households gross farm income (*GFI*) and liquidity (*LQD*) also exert a positive (and significant) influence on the probability of investment adoption. This is expected given the predominance of dryland maize production (70 per cent of cultivated land area) and the small farm size (2.2 hectares) in the CA and RA, and the importance of off-farm liquidity sources in rural areas (McKenzie and Coetzee, 1988).

5.4 The Influence of Land Titles on Tenure Security and Agricultural Investment

Within the SSCS, 85 per cent of households were eligible for registered title deeds. However, only 50 per cent of these households were in the possession of title deeds registered in the current household head's name. Although households with registered title deeds had greater breadth of property rights and reported a lower incidence of stray cattle and crop losses compared to those without registered title deeds (Moor and Nieuwoudt, 1995), the data suggest that the costs associated with title registration outweigh the benefits. Of the remaining households eligible for registered title, 18 per cent had yet to apply for title deeds, while 32 per cent failed to register a change of ownership upon inheritance. Results from a second ordinal regression analysis, using the possession or otherwise of a registered title deed as a measure of tenure security, indicate that registered title does not significantly increase the likelihood of investment adoption in the SSCS.

6 IMPLICATIONS FOR REFORM NEEDS IN SOUTH AFRICA

Available evidence indicates that the structure of property rights characteristic on both grazing and arable land in subsistence areas of South Africa are a constraint on agricultural productivity and investment. Regression results from Zimbabwean data indicate that increased tenure security (breadth and assurance) contributes significantly to the adoption of on-farm investments in agriculture. Given the similarities between communal tenure in Zimbabwe and South Africa, this lends further support to the notion that indigenous tenure institutions in South Africa are indeed a constraint on agricultural productivity. The data also suggest that land redistribution without cautious consideration of individual incentives reduces the likelihood of on-farm investments and sustained agricultural production.

Low potential returns to agricultural production in subsistence areas, together with resistance from those who stand to lose from an institutional change, are likely to constrain any endogenous shift towards more exclusive property rights. This is compounded by the existence of pervasive structural imbalances which have built up over the past years through discriminatory legislation. However, this does not suggest that formal private tenure should be centrally imposed on communities. In the presence of institutional constraints, land titling is not sufficient to ensure increased economic incentives. The implication is that while secure and enforceable property rights engender significantly higher levels of investment on agricultural land, increased privatization of property rights should follow a process of widespread consultation at community level. On resettled land, groups of farmers on freehold land should be informed of the proven options to individual title and communal ownership. Pro-active state assistance is urged. It is recommended that government facilitate the evolution of private institutions by vigorously disseminating information about alternative business organisations (trusts and companies) and facilitating collective action by reducing transaction costs.

References

Atwood, D. A. (1990) 'Land Registration in Africa: The Impact on Agricultural Production', *World Development*, vol. 18, pp. 659–71.

Barrows, R. and M. Roth (1990) 'Land Tenure and Investment in African Agriculture: Theory and Evidence', *Journal of Modern African Studies*, vol. 28, pp. 265–97.

Behnke, R. H. Jr (1984) 'Fenced and Open-range Ranching: The Commercialization of Pastoral Land and Livestock in Africa', in J. R. Simpson and P. Evangelou (eds), *Livestock Development in Sub-Saharan Africa: Constraints, Prospects, Policy* (Boulder: Westview Press), pp. 261–84.

Bembridge, T. J. (1986) 'An Overview of Agricultural and Rural Development Problems in Less Developed Areas of Southern Africa', *Development Southern Africa*, 3(1), pp. 20–36.

Buchanan, J. M. (1986) *Liberty, Market and State: Political Economy in the 1980s* (Brighton: Wheatsheaf).

Ciriacy-Wantrup, S. V. and R. C. Bishop (1975) 'Common Property as a Concept in Natural Resources Policy', *Natural Resources Journal*, vol. 15, pp. 713–27.

Cross, C. R. (1990a) 'Land Tenure in Black Rural Areas: Social and Political Underpinnings', unpublished paper, Department of Development Administration and Politics, University of South Africa.

Cross, C. R. (1990b) 'Mythology and Mystery Tours in Land Reform: Getting Some Focus on the South African Debate', *Development Southern Africa*, vol. 7, pp. 535–60.

Dasgupta, P. (1982) *The Control of Resources* (Oxford: Basil Blackwell).
Feder, G. and T. Onchan (1987) 'Land Ownership Security and Farm Investment in Thailand', *American Journal of Agricultural Economics*, vol. 69, pp. 311–20.
Hitchcock, R. K. (1980) 'Tradition, Social Justice and Land Reform in Central Botswana', *Journal of African Law*, vol. 24(1), pp. 1–34.
Huntley, B. R. Siegfried and C. Sunter (1989) *South African Environments into the 21st Century* (Cape Town: Human & Rousseau).
Jordan, B. A. (1983) 'Subsistence Farmers or Non-Farmers?', unpublished BSc. (Agric.) thesis, Department of Agricultural Economics, University of Natal, Pietermaritzburg.
LAPC (1993) 'Options for Land Reform and Rural Restructuring in South Africa', revised version of the LAPC paper presented at the Land Redistributions Options Conference, Johannesburg, South Africa, October 1993.
Lawry, S. W., J. C. Riddell and J. W. Bennett (1984) 'Land Tenure Policy in African Livestock Development', in J. R. Simpson and P. Evangelou (eds), *Livestock Development in Sub-Saharan Africa: Constraints, Prospects, Policy* (Boulder: Westview Press), pp. 245–59.
Lenta, G. (1982) 'Land, Labour and Capital in KwaZulu: Some Failures of Coincidence', *Journal of Contemporary African Studies*, 1(2), pp. 307–27.
Low, A. (1986) *Agricultural Development in Southern Africa: Farm-Household Economics and the Food Crisis* (Cape Town: David Philip).
Lyne, M. C. (1989) 'Distortion of Incentives for Farm Households in KwaZulu', unpublished PhD thesis in Department of Agricultural Economics, University of Natal, Pietermaritzburg.
Lyne, M. C. and M. Roth (1994) 'Land Rental Markets in Sub-Saharan Africa: Efficiency, Equity and Institutional Change', unpublished paper, University of Wisconsin–Madison.
McKenzie, C. C. and G. K. Coetzee (1988) 'Estimation of Demand for Farmer Support Services', in Proceedings of the Annual Conference of the Agricultural Economics Association of Southern Africa, Stellenbosch, South Africa (26–27 September).
McKenzie, C. C., D. Weinerand and N. Vink (1989) 'Land Use, Agricultural Productivity and Farming Systems in Southern Africa', unpublished report, Development Bank of Southern Africa, Johannesburg.
Moor, G. M. and W. L. Nieuwoudt (1995) 'The Interaction between Land Tenure Security and Agricultural Productivity in Zimbabwe', *Agrekon*, vol. 34(4), pp. 288–98.
Nieuwoudt, W. L. (1990) 'Efficiency of Land Use', paper presented at the AEASE Conference, Durban (16–18 September).
Olson, M. (1971) *The Logic of Collective Action* (Cambridge, MA: Harvard University Press).
Place, F. and P. Hazell (1993) 'Productivity Effects of Indigenous Land Tenure Systems in Sub-Saharan Africa', *American Journal of Agricultural Economics*, vol. 57(1), pp. 10–19.
Place, F., M. Roth and P. Hazell (1994) 'Land Tenure Security and Agricultural Performance in Africa: Overview of Research Methodology in *Searching for Land Tenure Security in Africa*, ed. J. W. Bruce and S. E. Migot-Adholla (Iowa: Kendall Hunt).

Runge, C. F. (1981) 'Common Property Externalities: Isolation, Assurance, and Resource Depletion in a Traditional Grazing Context', *American Journal of Agricultural Economics*, vol. 63, pp. 595–606.

Runge, C. F. (1984) 'Strategic Interdependence Models of Property Rights', *American Journal of Agricultural Economics*, vol. 66, pp. 807–813.

Stewart, D. A. (1990) (Managing Director, LIMA Rural Development Foundation, Umzumbe), personal communication.

Thomson, D. N. and M. C. Lyne (1995) 'Is Tenure Secure in Communal Areas? Some Empirical Evidence from KwaZulu-Natal, *Agrekon*, vol. 34(4), pp. 178–81.

10 Agriculture in Transition: Land Reform in Former Socialist Countries

Zvi Lerman
THE HEBREW UNIVERSITY OF JERUSALEM, ISRAEL

Traditional socialist agriculture was characterized by dual structure: commercial production concentrated in large-scale collective and state farms cultivating thousands of hectares with hundreds of employees (Medvedev, 1987; Cochrane, 1989), and subsistence-oriented individual farming in small household plots of less than half a hectare based on part-time family labour (Waedekin, 1973, 1990). In most of the region, including the republics of the former Soviet Union and Albania, all agricultural land was owned by the state. In the rest of East-Central Europe (ECE) however, cooperative or collective land ownership emerged in addition to state property as individual land-owners began joining cooperative farms, and private land continued to exist in various forms. Yet even land that was formally registered as individually owned was managed and cultivated by large-scale collectives and cooperatives. Transition to individual land ownership and restructuring of the large-scale 'socialized' farm enterprises is therefore one of the main characteristics of agricultural transformation in the ECE countries and the former Soviet Union (FSU). The present chapter describes the ongoing changes in land tenure relations and farm organization in the former socialist countries as of early 1996.

1 PRIVATE OWNERSHIP OF LAND

Transition from state and collective ownership of land to private ownership is a standard component of economic reforms in former socialist countries. This trend is part of the emphasis on individual property rights, which has been assimilated into the general policies of transition to a market-based economy. The majority of policy-makers in the region have come to the conclusion that former socialist patterns of land ownership are incompatible with market orientation, and that a radical change is needed as a step toward transformation of the economic system.

In ECE, where land has never been completely nationalized (except in Albania), privatization of land mainly involves transfer of collective lands to individual owners. The achievements through 1995 are mixed: in some countries more than half the land has been transferred from the collective to private sector, while others still lag behind (Figure 10.1). In the former Soviet republics, on the other hand, where land was nationalized by decree within days of the October 1917 revolution, the state must first relinquish its ownership of land. In the first stage, land is transferred primarily from state to collective ownership, without necessarily designating the ultimate individual owner. In Russia, for example, 85 per cent of all agricultural land has been 'privatized' to date by this mechanism (Brooks *et al.*, 1996), and a separate procedure now must be implemented to transfer the 'privatized' land of the collectives to new individual owners. The land reform legislation specifies this procedure, but does not initiate its implementation at the farm level. As local initiative slowly shifts land from collective to individual tenure, the land ownership structure in the former Soviet republics begins to resemble the mixed ownership structure that has prevailed in ECE since 1945. In Russia and Ukraine, private land ownership

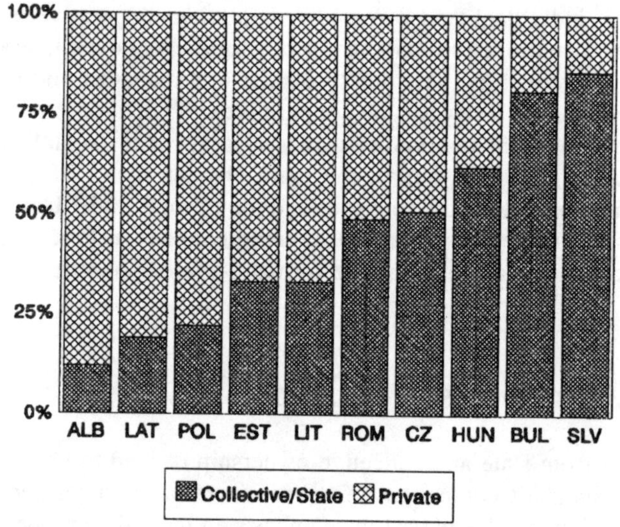

Source: European Commission (1995).

Figure 10.1 Agricultural land in collective and private sector in ECE countries, 1995

has exceeded 10 per cent in 1995, up from less than 2 per cent prior to 1991 (Brooks *et al.*, 1996; Lerman *et al.*, 1995). These numbers are also representative of other former Soviet republics, with the exception of Georgia and Armenia, where more than a third of the agricultural land and most of the arable land has been transferred to the private sector (CIS, 1994).

The principle of private ownership of land and other assets is now established in the legislation of most former socialist countries. Legislation regarding private land ownership was passed in Romania, Bulgaria, Hungary, Czechoslovakia and Albania in 1990–2. In the USSR, 1991 Union-level legislation recognized the right of private individuals to own land, and this right was subsequently incorporated in the land codes of many of the former Soviet republics.

While private ownership of land is almost universally accepted in ECE, it is a subject of continuing debate in some of the former Soviet republics (Table 10.1). In Belarus, the June 1993 land code allows private ownership of land in household plots, but land for commercial agricultural

Table 10.1 Land ownership and land transactions in the former Soviet Union

	Private ownership	*Transactions*
Russia	Yes: all land (no in 10 ethnic republics)	Buy and sell, mortgage (moratorium lifted by 1994 presidential decree)
Ukraine	Yes: all land	Moratorium on buy and sell; no mortgage
Moldova	Yes: all land	Moratorium until 2001
Belarus	Yes: household plots (June 93)	Buy and sell allowed for household plots Use rights non-transferable
Georgia	Yes: all land	Buy and sell allowed only by February 1996 law
Armenia	Yes: all land	Buy and sell, mortgage (law of 1991)
Kazakhstan	Yes: only household plots (decree)	Buy and sell, mortgage Use rights: permanent and tradeable
Turkmenistan	Yes: potentially all farm land (constitution)	Prohibited to sell, exchange, give as a gift; leasing allowed Use rights non-transferable
Kyrgyzstan	No	Use rights secure to 99 years and tradeable
Uzbekistan	No: lifetime inheritable possession	Prohibited to sell, exchange, give as a gift, mortgage
Tadjikistan	No	
Azerbaidjan	No	

production remains state-owned and must be leased by producers (both individual and collective) from the state. A similar situation prevails in Kazakhstan, where the December 1995 presidential decree recognized the principle of private ownership of land, but retained all land outside the subsidiary household plots in state ownership. Azerbaidjan and three of the four Central Asian republics (with the exception of Turkmenistan) still do not recognize private land ownership. In the Russian Federation, 10 ethnic member republics have retained all land in state ownership by exercising the constitutional prerogative that allows local land legislation at variance with the general practice in the country. These are Tatarstan, Bashkiriya, Dagestan, Komi, Mariel, Kabardino–Balkariya, North Osetiya, Tuva, Yakutiya–Sakha and Koryakiya (Brooks and Lerman, 1994). Russian politicians and the general public are engaged in an intense ongoing debate concerning private ownership of land, existing legislation notwithstanding. Echoes of this debate are found in the controversial draft Land Code, which has been tabled before the Russian Parliament on several occasions since 1995 by the conservative agrarian faction. If passed in its present form, the draft Land Code would eliminate most of the (admittedly limited) progress toward private ownership of land that has been achieved in Russia since 1991.

Despite basic recognition of private land ownership, the current laws in all former socialist countries circumscribe owners' rights in the important areas of land transfer, land use, and size of holdings. Sale of privately-owned farmland is often prohibited outright (Table 10.1). Albania, Romania, Moldova, and Ukraine do not allow buying and selling of land registered as privately owned. While the constitution of Turkmenistan recognizes private ownership of land (uniquely among the constitutions of the Central Asian republics), the land code (including the draft currently in preparation) states that land cannot be sold, exchanged, or given as a gift. In Georgia, with more than a third of agricultural land in private ownership, selling and buying of land has been prohibited until very recently. The Georgian land law passed in February 1996 now allows land sales, but requires administrative permission for each transaction. Use of agricultural land is universally restricted to farming, and failure to farm the land for a specified period of time (usually a year or two) bears in all countries the penalty of expropriation. The size of private farms (contrary to cooperatives and other shareholder forms) is limited to a maximum of 20–30 ha in Bulgaria, 50 ha in Latvia, 50–100 ha in Russia, Ukraine, Moldova, Turkmenistan, and many other former Soviet republics, and 100 ha in Romania. At the two extremes of the spectrum we find Belarus and Kazakhstan, where private ownership is limited to household plots of

1 ha, and Hungary, where the new land law allows private holdings of up to 300 ha.

Restrictions on the rights of owners are intended to create owner-operators of farmland and prevent absentee ownership. They are also intended to prevent windfall profits and blatant speculation in an environment where new private owners receive a potentially valuable asset without any payment. Despite laudable social motives, the restrictions on property rights reflect fundamental ambiguity regarding private property in land, even where private ownership is legally recognized. Thus, instead of attempting to legislate against absentee ownership by threatening expropriation when land is not actively farmed, it would be more in line with the desired market orientation of the economy to leave the control to market mechanisms, such as differential taxation on land used for agricultural production and land that is kept idle for possible speculative motives.

The restrictions on ownership rights are being relaxed gradually as the reform progresses. Thus, in Russia, the 10-year moratorium on buying and selling of privately owned land imposed by the 1991–92 land reform legislation was eliminated by a presidential decree of October 1993. While the factious political situation in the Russian parliament has so far prevented the passage of a new land code consistent with the principles of market-based property rights in land, a March 1996 presidential decree allowed virtually unrestricted buying and selling of land shares (certificates of entitlement) and eliminated much of the restrictions on farm size. In the Kyrgyz Republic, where all farmland remains state-owned, a presidential decree of February 1994 made user rights fully marketable and secure for 49 years, and another decree of November 1995 extended the lease term to 99 years. A referendum is planned in the Kyrgyz Republic to vote on a number of constitutional amendments relating to land, among them a decision to allow private land ownership. In Kazakhstan, the December 1995 presidential decree, while still restricting private ownership to land in small household plots, now allows virtually unlimited transactions in land use rights. However, despite the gradual relaxation of restrictions, many obstacles remain to the development of land markets, whether formal or informal, and the frequency of land transactions throughout the region is still negligible (Euroconsult, 1994).

While land sales are still restricted in all countries, leasing is gaining in importance as the mechanism of choice for adjustment of the size of land holdings. Land is leased mainly from the state, and less frequently from other individuals, with the purpose of augmenting the initial allotment of privately-owned land. Thus, in Georgia and Armenia, where plots of privately-owned land average 1 ha or even less, recent surveys indicate that many farmers cultivate more than 10 ha of leased land. Although official legislation sanctions medium- and long-term leasing (usually 5 years and longer), many lease contracts are made on a 1-year basis, probably as a reflection to the prevailing political uncertainty.

Land ownership is an emotionally charged issue throughout the region. Yet despite the ongoing political debate and lack of legal clarity, the former socialist countries appear to be moving toward a radical change in land relations. Much has been accomplished, but much still remains to be done. Although private ownership of land is not legally recognized in some countries, all countries are gradually moving toward more liberal policies of land tenure that will ultimately lead to relatively free transactions in land and development of land markets. Land transactions will provide the channel for transfer of land and assets from less efficient to more efficient producers, and for establishment of farms of optimal size.

2 RESTITUTION VERSUS DISTRIBUTION

The land reform process in the former socialist world is evolving in two alternative modalities, which can be characterized as *restitution to former owners* versus *distribution to individual users* (Table 10.2). Restitution, or reprivatization, normally means that former owners get a physical plot of land and a registered title, although in some countries (notably Hungary and the former East Germany) financial compensation to former owners is chosen when physical restitution of old plots is infeasible. Distribution, on the other hand, most often transfers land rights to people who work the land, but may never have owned it. The process starts with division of the available land into 'conditional' shares, or paper certificates of entitlement, that are distributed to the eligible individuals. Further procedures

Table 10.2 Entitlement basis for privatization of land

ECE	**Restitution to former owners + distribution to workers**
Albania	Workers
Hungary	Former owners + workers
Romania	Former owners + workers
Czech and Slovak Republics	Former owners
Bulgaria	Former owners
FSU	**Predominantly distribution to workers**
Baltics	Restitution to former owners
Russia and other republics	Distribution to workers

are then needed, first, to identify the physical allotment represented by the paper share and, second, to register it and issue title documents. Both restitution and distribution are linked to restructuring of existing farm enterprises, because they are the main source of land in the former socialist countries and because it is meaningless to distribute land to new owners while leaving other agricultural assets untouched.

Claims of former owners and restitution are relevant mainly for the countries where private land ownership existed until after the Second World War and the original land owners or their descendants are identifiable to this day. Land legislation in ECE generally recognizes both the rights of landowners immediately prior to collectivization and the rights of current land users. In Albania, however, only the current land users participate in the distribution of land, and former owners are compensated by a special issue of state bonds. At the other extreme, Bulgaria and the Czech and Slovak republics mandate return of collectivized land to former owners, while workers in collectives may be allotted land for farming, but without any ownership rights.

In countries of the FSU, where land was nationalized many decades ago and the traditions of private ownership were not strong, land rights are distributed to current users, not former owners. The major issues are eligibility and the pattern of distribution, and whether and how land rights should be translated into ownership of physical allotments. Land shares in the FSU are normally distributed without payment to members and workers in collective and state farms (including pensioners) and some other categories of rural residents. Reinstatement of pre-collectivization ownership and compensation of former landowners is practised only in the Baltic states, which initially (in 1989–90) began distributing land to the users, but then switched to strict restitution to former owners. The issue of restitution is publicly debated in Moldova, and to a lesser degree in western Ukraine and Belarus, but it is not reflected in the official approach to land reform in these countries. Although the collectivization of agriculture in Moldova was completed only in 1950, roughly at the same time as in the Baltics, the Moldovan land code explicitly rules out restitution of land or compensation of former land owners.

3 RESTRUCTURING OF LARGE-SCALE FARMS

Actual observations of the implementation process across the region indicate that farm restructuring is proceeding along several alternative tracks. The most conservative and easiest procedure is to retain the prior structure under a new name. Land and assets are distributed to individuals in the form of paper shares, but this is not followed by physical allocation of individual entitlements. The recipients keep their shares of land and assets in the old collective, continuing the tradition of collective production. The collective may change its name to a joint-stock society, or a similar organizational structure, but it continues functioning as before. Another variation on this theme is the separation of a multi-village farm enterprise into several village-based enterprises, each continuing to manage the land and assets of its members collectively. In principle, even in a 'stay as is' situation, the shareholders can be expected to adopt a profit orientation in order to maximize dividends on their shares, yet distribution of dividends in still without much practical significance, and the shares are not tradeable. Without appropriate incentives to shareholders through tangible returns on their investment, no true sense of ownership is created, and the shareholders continue working as salaried employees under the direction of their previous collective manager. These 'new–old' structures retain all the weaknesses and inefficiencies of collectives, although they are often expected to be more efficient because of their modern-sounding names and new charters.

At the opposite extreme are farms that completely dismantle the old structure and physically distribute all land and assets to individuals. The large-scale farm is broken up into small family units, each with its allotment of land and assets (the latter possibly in cash equivalent form). A few hundred private farms are thus created in place of one large collective farm.

A number of farm structures intermediate between the old collective and the new family farm have appeared. In some cases, individual private farmers have combined to form an association of agricultural producers. In some associations, each farm retains its identity, but all farms cooperate in provision of services, where economies of size and the effect of pooling of resources are most pronounced. Cooperative support may include use of transport, input supply, product marketing, purchase and joint use of agricultural machinery, mechanical maintenance, credit, transportation, and even professional services, such as accounting, management consulting and extension. In other associations, private farmers may pool their small plots into larger allotments and form a partnership for production. Several partnerships or associations in the same region may in turn join to form service cooperatives.

A similar associative structure evolves in an opposite direction when the old collective, instead of totally dismantling into hundreds of private farms, reorganizes internally into a system of relatively small autonomous profit centres. The land and asset base of each such unit is the sum total of the land and asset shares of its members or 'active investors.' Because of the relative smallness of such units, which are organized as partnerships or small corporations, the active workers maintain the sense of private ownership of production assets. The old management structures of the collective in turn may reorganize to provide the necessary services and support to these autonomous units. Agricultural production is thus concentrated in units that are small enough to maintain a good sense of personal involvement and accountability, while farm support services and the interface with the environment are provided by a relatively large and professionally experienced cooperative structure.

Initially, the professional cooperative structure representing former management may play a strong guiding role in the new organization. Gradually, as the autonomous units gain experience and confidence, the roles will be reversed, and the producers will assume the leading role in the associative organization, while the management 'umbrella' will begin to function as a true service cooperative supporting the producers. The key difference between this form and the association of private farmers is that the individual may not have converted his or her collectively owned land and assets into individual ownership.

The various restructuring modes of collective and state farms observed in the region are summarized in Table 10.3. Experience in the region indicates that in most cases the process of reform does not lead to a fully fragmented farming structure, contrary to initial expectations. The dismantling approach has been implemented only in Albania, Romania and Armenia. In these three countries, all collective farms were rapidly disbanded and divided into very small private farms during 1991. In other countries dismantling is a rare phenomenon. In Russia, among 21 000 farm enterprises that reorganized by January 1993, only 268 broke up completely into private farms (Brooks and Lerman, 1994).

Table 10.3 Restructuring modes for collective and state farms

- Reconstitution of a collective structure based on individual ownership of land and asset shares
- Transformation of the collective structure into a joint-stock corporation based on individual shares
- Division of the collective structure into autonomous profit-oriented entities based on individual investment of land and asset shares and operating within an association or a service cooperative
- Separation of independent entities from the collective structure (family farms, partnerships, or production cooperatives)
- Cooperation of independent entities

The new land owners are not particularly willing to leave the supportive umbrella of the collective structure and risk everything in independent farming. The overwhelming majority of farm workers surveyed in Russia and Ukraine prefer to leave their land and asset shares in the collective (Lerman *et al.*, 1995). Surveys in the Czech and Slovak republics consistently reveal lack of enthusiasm toward private farming. In Romania, where land was rapidly distributed to individuals, fully 48 per cent of land has been reconsolidated in various farmers' associations (Gavrilescu, 1993). Half the recipients of land through restitution in Bulgaria and a significant proportion in Hungary have also chosen to leave their land in a collective or join a new agricultural production cooperative (Trendafilov and Ivanova-Gidikova, 1993).

Farms tend to reorganize as relatively large units, although with some downsizing. The 'stay as is' approach is popular in Russia and other former Soviet republics, where it is referred to as 'changing the sign on the door' (Table 10.4). Fully 35 per cent of the reorganized farm enterprises in Russia as of January 1993 decided to keep their old form, without even changing the sign on the door, 12 per cent registered as joint-stock societies, and another 40 per cent reorganized as limited liability partnerships (Brooks and Lerman, 1995). In Ukraine, 83 per cent of the reorganized collective and state farms registered as collective enterprises or partnership, and 3 per cent as joint-stock societies (Lerman *et al.*, 1995). An extreme example of 'changing the sign' approach is seen in Turkmenistan

Table 10.4 Restructuring of farm enterprises in Russia and Ukraine (per cent of all farms)

	Russia	*Ukraine*
Not reorganized	**22**	**28**
Reorganized	**78**	**72**
Keeping old form with new charter	27	9
Collective enterprises and limited-liability partnerships	32	55
Joint-stock societies	9	2
Agricultural production cooperatives	6	2
Associations of peasant farms	3	2
Other forms	1	2

Note:
Data for Russia as of January 1993; data for Ukraine as of January 1994.

Source: Brooks and Lerman (1994); Lerman *et al.* (1994).

where all large-scale farms were summarily 'reorganized' by a presidential decree of June 1995, which changed their name from 'kolkhoz' (collective farm) to 'peasant association'. Further presidential decrees appear to encourage internal restructuring of the large-scale farm through 'intrafarm leasing' of land and assets by groups of workers, with support and control services provided by the former management group.

The results of restructuring in the ECE countries and the Baltics also indicate that large-scale farming still plays an important role at this stage of the reform (see Fig. 10.1). Yet here the restructuring has progressed beyond a mere 'changing of the sign on the door'. Many large-scale farms actually reorganized into several smaller functionally specialized units, built around the land and asset shares of their member-owners. The shareholders underwent fairly radical voluntary regrouping in the process of downsizing of the original farms. A degree of separation between ownership and management has been achieved in these new structures, which no longer guarantee employment to their shareholders. The emerging structures are similar to the associative organization described above. The new large farms in the ECE countries appear to be moving away from the traditional syndrome of the 'labour-managed firm' that in the past plagued the socialist economies.

The statistical data about the actual process of farm restructuring and the evolution of the new organizational forms are unfortunately highly incomplete in all countries. It seems, however, that the traditional dual structure of socialist agriculture, where production was concentrated in very large collective and state farms, on the one hand, and in very small household plots, on the other, is becoming less sharp. Data for ECE point to a definite decrease in the average size of large-scale farms and an increase in the size of private farms (Table 10.5). Survey data for Russia also show a definite increase in the proportion of farm enterprises in the lower tail of the size distribution between 1990 and 1993 (Figure 10.2), although the smallest farm enterprises are still very large compared to typical farms in market economies. Household plots in all former Soviet republics practically doubled in size to about 1 ha since 1991 through government programmes that distributed land to the rural population, and a new category of private farms with sizes of 10–40 ha has emerged in the distribution between the two extreme modes.

The continued dominance of large-scale farming structures may be attributed to various reasons. Families apparently feel that a large-scale farm provides a greater measure of safety than individual farming in the rapidly changing environment. The large farms will be unable to provide the same range of social services to their members as in the past in the

Table 10.5 Average size of collective and private farms in ECE and the Baltics, 1990–5

Country	*Collective farms (ha)*		*Private farms (ha)*	
	pre-1990	*1995*	*pre-1990*	*1995*
Bulgaria	13 000	1 100	0.4	0.6
Czech Republic	2 600	1 400	4.0	16.0
Slovak Republic	2 700	1 700	0.3	1.0
Hungary	4 200	1 700	0.3	1.9
Romania	2 400	170	1.5	1.8
Estonia	3 700	600	0.5	2.1
Latvia	3 900	700	0.5	5.8
Lithuania	3 000	600	0.5	3.1

Note: Pre-1990 data for collective farms in the Baltics based on national statistical abstracts.

Source: European Commission (1995).

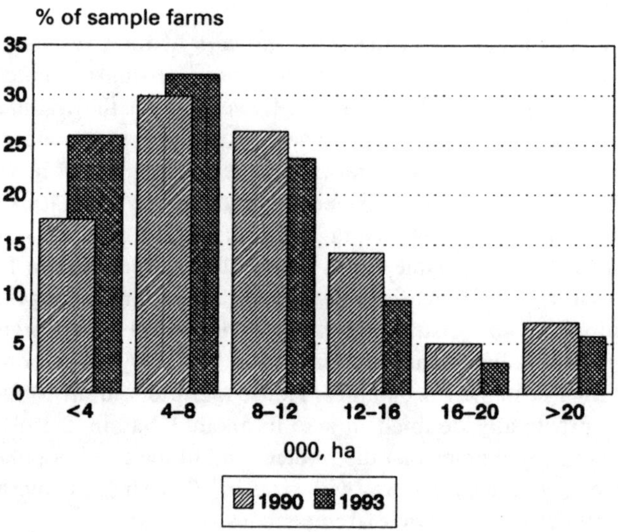

Source: Brooks *et al.* (1996).

Figure 10.2 Size distribution of farm enterprises in Russia, 1990–3

new economic environment, and yet rural residents seem to believe in the safety of numbers, at least at the present stage. Also large-scale farms, with the benefit of accumulated experience of their professional managers, may be better equipped to operate in an environment without fully functioning market services than small individual operations. In a sense, they may provide a natural transition to the service cooperatives of the future. Another factor that must not be ignored is the traditional power of the manager as a representative of the authorities in old collective farms. In many instances, the manager exercises influence to prevent deep restructuring and preserve the large-scale organization in order to keep his former power. All these factors contribute to the observed inertia and the slow transition to new farming structures despite availability of enabling legislation.

Because the economic environment is still changing and the development of market infrastructure still has a long way to go in much of ECE and the FSU, options for restructuring should remain open. Thus, recipients of land rights who at this stage choose to remain in collective-type enterprises should retain the right to exit with land and assets at a point in the future. Whether the exit right is protected, or property rights devolve to the enterprise when a shareholding firm is created depends on how the relevant laws are written and how the by-laws of the enterprise treat the issue of withdrawal. A number of Russian laws and decrees, including the highly conservative land law that was passed by the opposition forces in the Duma in May 1996, but has since been blocked by President Yeltsin and the relatively more reform-minded Federation Council, present severe obstacles to exit from shareholding enterprises with land and assets. When barriers to exit are high, the likelihood is great that the farm structure will be frozen in the form of corporatized large farms created in the first stages of restructuring. These are not likely to be the forms of farm organization that will allow agriculture in the region to become competitive in relatively open market economies. Flexible exit mechanisms, on the other hand, will allow the development of a multiplicity of farm structures and enable the mechanism of evolutionary selection to take its course.

4 EMERGENCE OF PRIVATE FARMING

The most tangible result of the agrarian transformation in former socialist countries has been the appearance of independent peasant farms. While the changes in traditional large-scale farms have been slow and generally superficial, and private land ownership is still hotly debated by politicians and the public in many countries, the number of independent private farmers is rapidly growing both in ECE and in the FSU. On the whole, however – apart from those countries where all or most large farms have been summarily dissolved (Albania and in part Romania) – only a small proportion (10–20 per cent) of cooperative members so far have chosen the path of independent farming. The results in the FSU (with the exception of Armenia) are still modest despite the spectacular growth in the number of private farms (Table 10.6). The independent private farms account for only a small part (2–3 per cent) of agricultural land and their share in total agricultural production is still insignificant. Yet in reality the private, or individual, sector in agriculture is much broader than that. The household plots have been substantially augmented since 1991 through distribution of state land and together with the independent private farms the individual sector now accounts for 10–15 per cent of all land and 30–50 per cent of agricultural production, and in some of the republics (e.g., Georgia and Armenia) this proportion is much higher (CIS, 1994).

In ECE, the overwhelming majority of private farmers are former cooperative members or employees of state farms who have left the large unit with some land (Euroconsult, 1994). The private farms in the ECE countries are in fact enlarged subsidiary household plots that have cut loose from the collectivist framework. In the FSU, a similar situation is observed in Armenia and Georgia, where land formerly cultivated by collective and state farms was distributed in small-sized plots to most of the

Table 10.6 Private farms in the FSU

	Number of private farms			*Average size (ha, 1994)*	*Per cent of agricultural land in private farms (1994)*
	1992	*1993*	*1994*		
Armenia	165 200	238 300	298 100	1.3	30
Russia	49 000	182 800	270 000	42	5
Kyrgyzstan	4 100	8 600	18 300	83	10
Kazakhstan	3 300	9 300	16 300	410	3
Ukraine	2 100	14 700	27 700	20	1.5
Moldova	300	500	3 100	2.2	0.5
Belarus	750	2 400	2 700	21	0.5
Uzbekistan	1 900	5 900	7 500	10	0.5

Source: CIS (1994).

rural population, and the borderline between household plots and private farms is fuzzy. In Russia and Ukraine, on the other hand, private farmers generally apply to receive land from specially created state reserves, and well over one-third of the new farmers are former urban residents who have decided to take up farming (Brooks and Lerman, 1994; Lerman *et al.*, 1994). The average private farm in many of the former Soviet republics is much larger than in ECE (compare Tables 10.5 and 10.6). In all countries, while land sales are restricted, private farmers are beginning to take advantage of leasing opportunities in order to increase their holdings.

The rate at which private farms are spreading in the region lags far behind the original expectations (both local and international) and behind the opportunities provided by the legal framework. Politicians and experts offer different explanations of this fact, based on theoretical consideration and speculation. World Bank surveys in the region actually elicited the opinion of the rural population on the subject (Euroconsult, 1994; Brooks and Lerman, 1994; Lerman *et al.*, 1994). The surveys indicate that the main reason for the reluctance to become a private farmer is that appropriate supportive conditions for private farming still do not exist. Thus, peasants hesitate to start an independent farm mainly because of insufficient capital, difficulty of obtaining machinery and farm inputs, and legal uncertainty (Lerman *et al.*, 1995). The cautious behaviour is an expression of sober and realistic judgement of the situation by the peasantry.

It is sometimes argued that the present generation of peasants in the ECE countries, and certainly in the FSU, has only a small part or none of the skills that are needed for successful operation of a private family farm. But this is not the main restraining factor: the main obstacle is that private farming in the region today is too risky and promises a relatively modest income compared to the risks involved. At this stage, peasants prefer to keep their land and assets in the relative safety of the familiar collective organization (old or newly reconstituted). The continuing development of functioning market services, including product marketing, input supply, and credit channels, will probably create conditions that encourage further transformation of the farming structure.

5 CONCLUSION

The accomplishments of agricultural reform in former socialist countries in Europe have been fairly modest. The main reasons are political and legal uncertainty, including controversy over the general reform programme and frequent changes of legislation; lack of a supportive environment that functioning markets usually provide; and unclear mechanisms for restructuring of traditional farm enterprises and for exit of individual members. The experience since 1990 seems to indicate that the future agricultural landscape in the region will not be based on small family farms. Rather, different forms of farming will coexist, ranging from individual farms through multi-family partnerships to larger corporate farms and production cooperatives. It is expected that the underlying features of all these diverse forms, contrary to traditional collectives, will be private ownership of production assets, personal accountability, and an incentive system that rewards individual effort and motivates performance. The inadequate market infrastructure of the current environment will probably encourage the development of service cooperatives, whose function will be to assist producers, regardless of organizational form, with purchase of inputs, marketing of products, acquisition and operation of expensive machinery, provision of credit, and even supply of managerial services, such as accounting, computers, management consulting, and extension. These service cooperatives, based on voluntary membership of producers, will probably operate alongside large private corporations (some of them owned by foreign investors or organized as joint ventures) that will enter some areas of agricultural marketing and supply despite the high risks.

The remarkable changes in land ownership and farm organization that have taken place throughout ECE and the FSU since 1991 have not yet brought the productivity gains that many adherents of privatization expected. In part this is because the early stages of decollectivization have taken place against a backdrop of general economic disruption, which has led to a decline in use of productivity-enhancing inputs, fall in demand for livestock products, and reduction in returns to agricultural production. In part the gains from decollectivization are not yet evident because the process is long and complex, much more so than originally envisaged. To enable agriculture to reap the benefits of private ownership and individual initiative, governments must provide a stable legislative environment with clearly defined and easily transferable property rights, speed up demonopolization of support services, and encourage the development of functioning markets in land, assets, and commodities. This is not an easy agenda, especially as it must come in combination with effective macroeconomic stabilization programmes, but without it formal privatization of land and assets will not achieve the anticipated goal.

References

Brooks, K. and Z. Lerman (1994) 'Land Reform and Farm Restructuring in Russia', *World Bank Discussion Paper*, vol. 233 (Washington, DC: World Bank).

Brooks, K. and Z. Lerman (1995) 'Restructuring of Traditional Farms and New Land Relations in Russia', *Agricultural Economics*, vol. 13, pp. 11–25.

Brooks, K., E. Krylatykh, Z. Lerman, A. Petrikov and V. Uzun (1996), 'Agricultural Reform in Russia: A View from the Farm Level', *World Bank Discussion Paper*, 327 (Washington, DC: World Bank).

CIS (1994) *Strany-Chleny SNG v 1993 g. Statisticheskii Yezhegodnik* (Member-Countries of the CIS in 1993. Statistical Yearbook), Statistical Committee of the CIS, Moscow.

Cochrane, N. J. (1989) 'Agricultural Statistics of Eastern Europe and the Soviet Union, 1965–85', *Statistical Bulletin*, 778, USDA Economic Research Service, Washington, DC.

Euroconsult (1994) 'Farm Restructuring and Land Tenure in Reforming Socialist Economies: A Comparative Analysis of Eastern and Central Europe', *World Bank Discussion Paper*, vol. 268 (Washington, DC: World Bank).

European Commission (1995) *Agricultural Situation and Prospects in the Central and Eastern European Countries*, Summary Report and Country Reports, Directorate-General for Agriculture (July).

Gavrilescu, D. (1993) 'Romania Facing the European Agrifood Integration: The Shock of Transition', VII EAAE Congress, Stresa, Italy, Contributed Papers, vol. F, *Agricultural Development and Transition*, pp. 15–28.

Lerman, Z., K. Brooks and C. Csaki (1994) 'Land Reform and Farm Restructuring in Ukraine', *World Bank Discussion Paper*, vol. 270 (Washington, DC: World Bank).

Lerman, Z., K. Brooks and C. Csaki (1995) 'Restructuring of Traditional Farms and New Land Relations in Ukraine', *Agricultural Economics*, vol. 13, pp. 27–37.

Medvedev, Zh. A. (1987) *Soviet Agriculture* (New York: Norton).

Trendafilov, R. and V. Ivanova-Gidikova (1993). 'Reform and Market Adjustment of the Bulgarian Agricultural Sector', VII EAAE Congress, Stresa, Italy, Contributed Papers, vol. F, *Agricultural Development and Transition*, pp. 1–14.

Waedekin, K.-E. (1973) *The Private Sector in Soviet Agriculture* (Berkeley, CA: University of California Press).

Waedekin, K.-E. (1990) 'Private Agriculture in Socialist Countries: Implications for the USSR', in K. R. Gray (ed.), *Soviet Agriculture: Comparative Perspectives* (Ames, IA: Iowa State University Press).

Part IV

Policy Aspects of Public Goods

11 Infrastructure: The Contribution of Benchmarking and Economic Analysis to the Reform of the Energy, Water and Transport Sectors

Peter L. Swan
UNIVERSITY OF SYDNEY, AUSTRALIA

Denis Lawrence
BUREAU OF INDUSTRY ECONOMICS, CANBERRA, AUSTRALIA

and

John Zeitsch
SWAN CONSULTANTS, CANBERRA, AUSTRALIA

1 INTRODUCTION

The World Bank (1994, p. 4) points out that despite rapid growth in infrastructure provisions, especially in telephones and power, performance has been disappointing. Resources have been mis-allocated with too much to new investment, particularly those with low priority, and too little to maintenance, especially in terms of road and power station maintenance. There has been massive waste and inefficiency with most power systems operating at between 18 per cent and 44 per cent of best-practice stations in terms of fuel per kilowatt hour with transmission and distribution losses two to four times as great (p. 5).

The main reason for these failures (p. 6) is seen to be the fact that:

> [T]he delivery of infrastructure services usually takes place in a market structure with one dominating characteristic: the absence of competition. Most infrastructure services in the developing world are provided by centrally managed monopolistic public enterprises or government departments. Almost all irrigation, water supply, sanitation, and transport infrastructure is provided in this manner. Until a few years ago, telephone services in most countries were the responsibility of a state-owned post, telephone, and telegraph enterprise. The bulk of power has also been provided by a public monopoly. As a result, the pressure that competition can exert on all parties to perform at maximum efficiency has been lacking.

2 SIGNIFICANCE OF INFRASTRUCTURE

Table 11.1 shows that infrastructure's share of GDP ranges from nearly 7 per cent for low-income countries to over 11 per cent for high-income countries including Australia. It would seem to be a superior good if looked at in terms of consumption. However, it is more revealing to regard infrastructure as an input into most other services and activities. The most important component of infrastructure in most countries is road freight. For example, in Australia it makes up 2.9 per cent of GDP or 25 per cent of all infrastructure. Infrastructure is also typically very capital-intensive. For example, in Australia it makes up 46 per cent of all public sector investment, 7 per cent of all private sector investment and 25 per cent of

Table 11.1 Significance of infrastructure by country group and for Australia

Sector	*Low-income countries % GDP*	*Middle-income countries % GDP*	*High-income countries % GDP*	*Australia % GDP*
Transport, storage and communications	5.34	6.78	9.46	8.3
Gas, electricity and water	1.29	2.24	1.87	3.3
Total infrastructure	6.63	9.02	11.33	11.6

Source: World Bank (1994, p. 13); Lawrence (1995) based on Australia Bureau of Statistics data.

total investment. At the same time, it makes up about 6.4 per cent of the Australian workforce.

3 THE INDUSTRY STRUCTURE APPROPRIATE FOR EACH TYPE OF INFRASTRUCTURE

Infrastructure is by no means homogeneous. Goods and services can be categorized into three basic types: private goods, public goods and club goods. Private goods are rivalrous in consumption with one individual's consumption denying someone else the right to consume the same good. They are also price-excludable, with an ability to deny non-payers consumption rights. For example, a McDonald's hamburger is a private good. Pure public goods are non-rivalrous in consumption and it is difficult if not impossible to exclude non-payers. The archetypal example here is national defence. One person's consumption does not deny another access but denial of access requires deportation and exile of the non-payer. Hence property rights in such goods are very poorly defined. Another way of making the same point is to say that externalities associated with such goods are high. If purely private provision for such goods were attempted there would most likely be underprovision. Unfavourable externalities such as pollution can also be associated with goods and services. These either require proper pricing of such externalities or regulations which achieve the same effect via 'shadow pricing'. Club goods are intermediate in the sense that they are non-rivalrous but are price-excludable. Because property rights in the good can be defined, club goods can be provided either as a sharing club-style arrangement such as a regular golf club with members with common ownership rights sharing the greens or as a purely market-based commercial undertaking such as a private toll road (see Hillman and Swan, 1983). In Figure 11.1 the World Bank (1994, p. 25) has characterized a variety of infrastructure activities into their different attributes.

Pure private goods are shown in the top left-hand corner and pure public goods in the bottom right-hand corner. As externalities increase with movement from left to right it becomes harder to exclude non-payers so that infrastructure has more common property attributes. For example, in the absence of electronic road pricing or similar innovations in pricing it would be difficult for urban roads, located in the top right-hand corner, to be privately provided. By contrast, toll roads, located in the bottom left-hand corner can be privately provided. While tolls are normally based on relatively crude cost recovery, they could be used to improve the

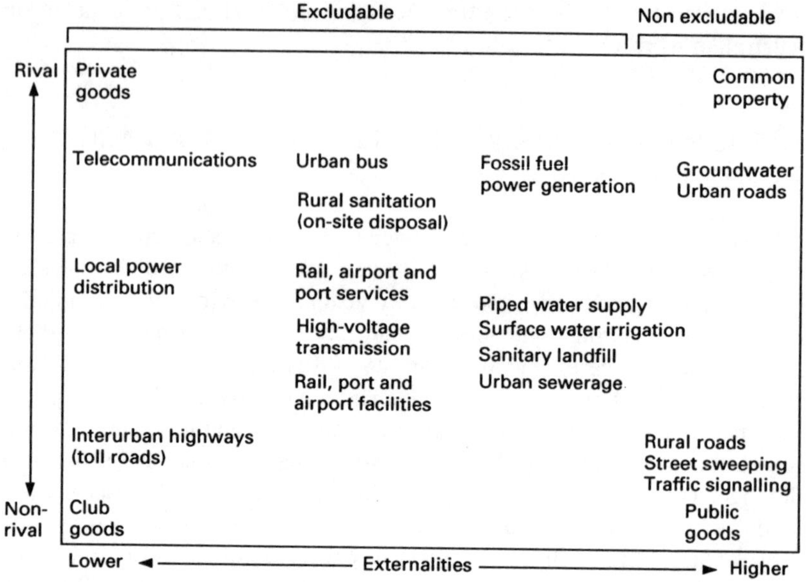

Note: Excludable means that a user can be prevented from consuming the good or service. 'Rival' means that consumption by one user reduces the supply available to other users.

Source: World Bank (1994).

Figure 11.1 Infrastructure services differ substantially in their economic characteristics across sectors, within sectors, and between technologies

efficiency with which the facility is used. For example, peak load pricing could be adopted with relatively high tolls at peak times. Typically, the more excludable is a service, the easier it will be to ensure efficient private provision. With non-rivalrous services it is generally going to be more difficult to ensure that there is adequate competition. Hence with privatization of such activities there is more likely to be some form of regulatory oversight either via a special commission or by the courts.

A problem with examining just broad classes of infrastructure in terms of its suitability for privatization is that there can be considerable variation in the classification of the components of each sector. For example, generation of electricity can be provided under competitive market conditions whereas scale economies associated with long-distance transmission suggest that this component is more like a club good. By unbundling infrastructure into different components and classifying each component as to

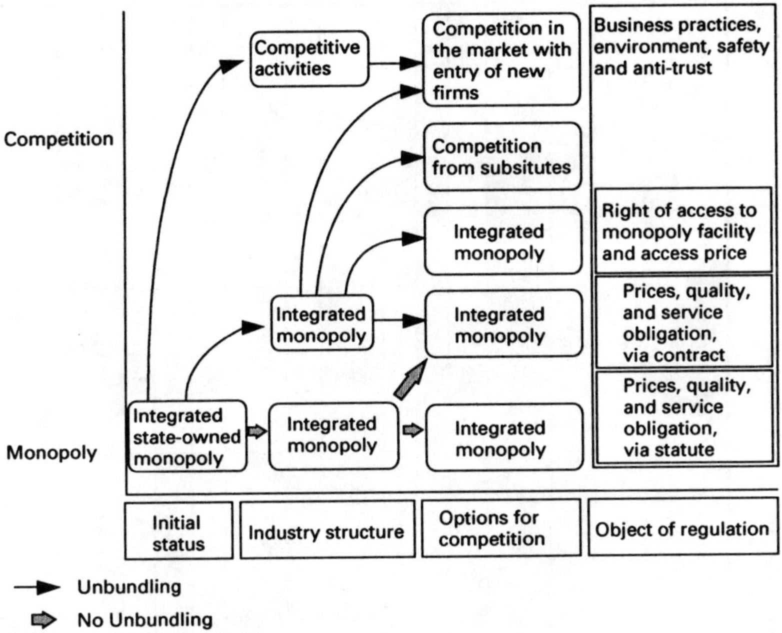

Source: World Bank (1994).

Figure 11.2 Unbundling activities increases the options for competition and private sector involvement

the extent to which competition is possible, a suitable regulatory framework can be arrived at. This process is shown schematically in Figure 11.2, which is based on World Bank (1994, 56).

The World Bank (1994, p. 115) has classified the components of each major type of infrastructure as to its type and the extent to which market competition is possible. This classification is presented in Table 11.2.

4 APPROACHES TO REFORM

4.1 US Model

Most of what we would regard today as 'infrastructure' was produced by private firms without regulatory oversight until at least the 1870s. For example, railroads, electricity suppliers and the telegraph/phone system were in private hands and not subject to what today would be regarded as

Table 11.2 Feasibility of private sector delivery varies by infrastructure components

		Potential for competition[a]	*Characteristics of good or service*	*Potential for cost recovery from user charges*	*Public service obligations (equity concerns)*	*Environmental externalities*	*Marketability index*[b]
Telecom	Local services	Medium	Private	High	Medium	Low	2.6
	Long distance and value-added	High	Private	High	Few	Low	3.0
Power/gas	Thermal generation	High	Private	High	Few	High	2.6
	Transmission	Low	Club	High	Few	Low	2.4
	Distribution	Medium	Private	High	Many	Low	2.4
	Gas production, transmission	High	Private	High	Few	Low	3.0
Transport	Railbed and stations	Low	Club	High	Medium	Medium	2.0
	Rail freight and passenger services	High	Private	High	Medium	Medium	2.6
	Urban bus	High	Private	High	Many	Medium	2.4
	Urban rail	High	Private	Medium	Medium	Medium	2.4
	Rural roads	Low	Public	Low	Many	High	1.0
	Primary and secondary roads	Medium	Club	Medium	Few	Low	2.4

Table 11.2 Feasibility of private sector delivery varies by infrastructure components (*continued*)

		Potential for competition[a]	*Characteristics of good or service*	*Potential for cost recovery from user charges*	*Public service obligations (equity concerns)*	*Environmental externalities*	*Market-ability index*[b]
	Port and airport facilities	Low	Club	High	Few	High	2.0
	Port and airport services[c]	High	Private	High	Few	High	2.6
Water	Urban piped network	Medium	Private	High	Many	High	2.0
	Non-piped systems	High	Private	High	Medium	High	2.4
Sanitation	Piped sewerage and treatment	Low	Club	Medium	Few	High	1.8
	Condominial sewerage	Medium	Club	High	Medium	High	2.0
	On-site disposal	High	Private	High	Medium	High	2.4
Waste	Collection	High	Private	Medium	Few	Low	2.8
	Sanitary disposal	Medium	Common property	Medium	Few	High	2.0

Table 11.2 Feasibility of private sector delivery varies by infrastructure components (*continued*)

		Potential for competition[a]	*Characteristics of good or service*	*Potential for cost recovery from user charges*	*Public service obligations (equity concerns)*	*Environmental externalities*	*Market-ability index*[b]
Irrigation	Primary and secondary networks	Low	**Club**	Low	**Medium**	High	1.4

Key to marketability rating:

☐ = 1.0 (least marketable) ▒ = 2.0 ▓ = 3.0 (Most marketable)

Notes:

[a] Due to either absence of scale economies or sunk costs, or existence of service substitutes.
[b] Marketability index is average of ratings across each row.
[c] Including cargo handling, shipping, and airlines.

Table 11.3 Effect of deregulation of motor carrier rates on carrier rates for different activities

Motor carrier rate	*Fruits and vegetable rates*[a] (%)	*Poultry rates*[a] (%)	*General truckload rates*[b] (%)	*Less-than-truckload rates*[b] (%)
Decline in rate due to deregulation	19	33	25	11

Notes:
[a] ICC exemption in mid 1950s.
[b] Evidence from shippers following Motor Carrier Act 1980

Source: Viscusi, Vernon and Harrington (1992, p. 517).

economic regulation. Viscusi, Vernon and Harrington (1992, pp. 299–302) provide a history of the regulatory process which began with attempts to control monopolies and ended up regulating industries which were largely competitive. For example, Table 11.3 summarizes the effect of deregulation of motor carrier rates. There were similar price reductions and social gains with airline deregulation. See, for example, Bailey, Graham and Kaplan (1985). Inherently, there are little in the way of natural monopoly aspects to either trucking (motor carriers) or to airlines.

More controversial than deregulation of either of these two important infrastructure activities has been deregulation of electricity utilities in generation, transmission and distribution. Jarrell (1978) provides an explanation as to why the utilities may have wanted to be subject to such state-based regulation in the first place. In the United States, state regulation of privately-owned utilities was based on the principle that state commissions set prices such that utilities could cover the costs of providing the service inclusive of a fair rate of return on investment (Joskow and Schmalansee, 1983, p. 13). This fair rate of return would cover the cost of capital investment after properly adjusting for risk.

A problem with this approach to regulation is the padding of the regulatory rate base (Averch and Johnson, 1962). Suppose that the regulated maximum rate of return is above the true competitively determined cost of capital which may not be directly observable. The idea underlying base rate padding is that by substituting a more capital-intensive process using relatively more capital with less labour and other inputs, the regulated firm is able to increase its profits although the chosen technique no longer minimizes cost for a given level of output. Base rate padding has been examined empirically by a number of authors including Courville (1974), Peterson (1975), and Pescatrice and Trapani (1980). Courville (1974) found evidence of a rise in costs due to regulation of 12 per cent while Pescatrice and Trapani found that municipal publicly-owned utilities had costs which were between 23.5 per cent and 23.9 per cent below privately-owned and regulated utilities. While discrepancies of this magnitude could be due to differences in the task of municipal and private utilities reflecting a poor basis of comparison, it could also be due to rate of return regulation. On reviewing the evidence, Joskow and Noll (1981) are sceptical that there is any strong empirical support for the cost-padding hypothesis. Zimmer (1978) also finds that the hypothesis is not definitely established empirically.

While superficially rate of return regulation would appear to be ideal if the maximum allowed rate of return is set equal to the competitive cost of capital, such equality raises very severe concerns. Effectively, there is an 100 per cent tax or expropriation of returns in excess of the competitive level. The regulated firm now becomes indifferent to the level of costs incurred. With less severe rate of return regulation there is at least some incentive to minimize cost even though there are distortions. Given that there are always likely to be some managerial and workforce advantages to incurring higher 'costs' with higher salaries and wages as well as perks for managers and employees, the consequent cost blowout is likely to be worse even than the distortions due to rate- base-padding. Such indifference to excess costs can, of course, be tempered by competition if it is permitted and disallowance of imprudently incurred expenses if such expenses can be detected. Moreover, if there are a number of reasonably comparable utilities operating in different areas then so-called 'yardstick' competition can be used to draw attention to firms whose costs appear to have got out of control. Methods of carrying out yardstick competition and 'benchmarking' are reviewed and illustrated in Sections 6 and 7.

The regulated infrastructure industries in the United States were typically highly vertically integrated and also produced multiple products such as, for example, local and long-distance phone services. While doubtless these structural characteristics were due in part to managerial efficiencies in overseeing and coordinating the different vertical activities and to economies of scope, the regulatory regime played an important role by defining individual markets, constraining entry and facilitating vertical integration (Berg, 1995, p.3). To the extent that the regulatory structure has encouraged vertical integration, we would expect that relaxation of controls on entry would encourage greater diversity and less vertical integration. A schematic casual structure for the regulatory process and its recent evolution which emphasises feedbacks, due to Berg (1995), is set out in Figure 11.3.

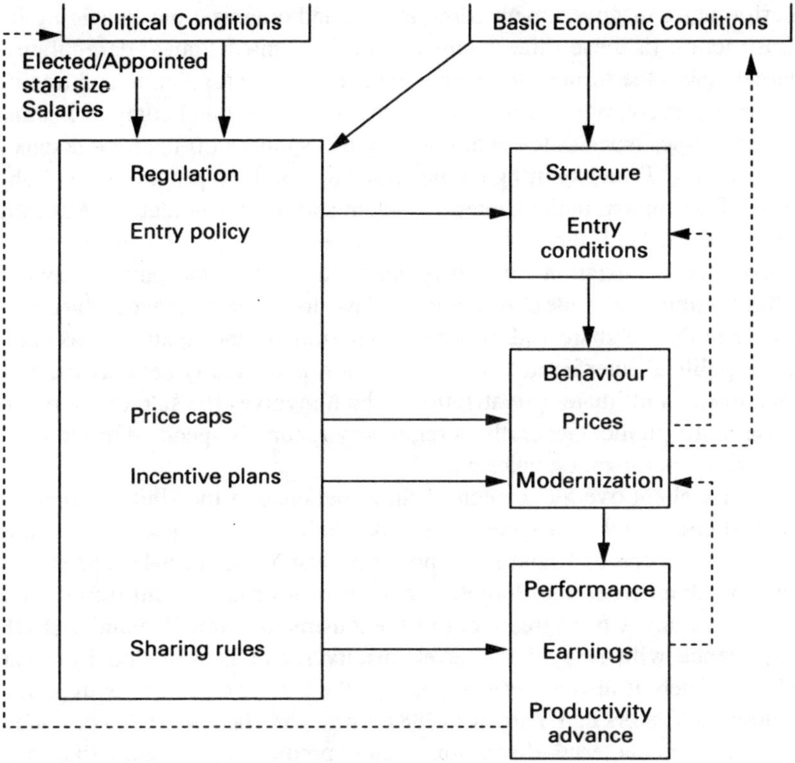

Source: Adapted from Berg (1995).

Note: (1) Performance = *f* (Regulation, Economic Conditions, Structure, Behaviour)
(2) Behaviour = *g* (Regulation, Economic Conditions, Structure)
(3) Regulation = *h* (Performance, Economic Conditions, Political Conditions)

Figure 11.3 Chains of causation: regulation, behaviour and performance

4.2 Australian–New Zealand–UK Model

Unlike the United States, which was unique with most infrastructure privately rather than publicly owned, infrastructure in Australia, New Zealand and the United Kingdom was almost entirely publicly provided. Since, until very recently at least, government-owned organizations were exempt from most regulatory bodies such as the Trade Practices Commission in Australia, there was very little, if any public scrutiny of the performance of government commissions and organizations providing infrastructure in these three countries. In the United States, deregulation largely takes the form of relaxing rate of return type regulation and freeing up prices, encouraging instead of discouraging entry and competition and in some cases (such as telecommunications), splitting off the long-distance carrier, AT&T, and splitting up the regional local-loop providers, the Baby Bells. By contrast, in the United Kingdom and its two emulators, Australia and New Zealand, the first step in the deregulatory process generally involves 'corporatization', which is designed to place the publicly-owned utility within the context of company law, to set performance objectives closer to that of shareholder-owned organizations and to attempt to minimize political interference. Corporatization is generally seen as the first step towards ultimate 'privatization' which involves the sale of the enterprise to the public. Generally, a regulatory regime is specified at the same time as corporatization takes place.

An excellent overall account of the experience of the United Kingdom in particular, and to a lesser extent Australia, with corporatization and privatization can be found in Bishop, Kay and Mayer (1994). The survey in it by Domberger and Piggott (1994) provides some useful information on Australia.[1] A brief treatment of the Australian, New Zealand and UK experience with respect to the electricity sector is provided by Swan (1989). There is also a useful account of the UK's experience with privatization in Vickers and Yarrow (1988). Swan and Garvey (1993) provide a model of managerial discretion which predicts that managerial performance is likely to be better with privatized infrastructure providers, rather than government-owned utilities, because the threat of financial distress such as bankruptcy, which is costly to managers, is only credible for privately-owned organizations.

Apart from considerable inefficiency and in particular overmanning, the state-owned electricity sector in Australia has been prone to cross-subsidize very large consumers such as aluminium smelters which are mobile across state boundaries at the expense of customers with more inelastic demands such as smaller commercial users. For example, in Victoria the Portland aluminium smelter receives bulk electricity from the Loy Yang power station at well below the cost of production (see Swan, 1983). The contract ultimately took the form of a 'risk-sharing' arrangement with the price of power dependent on the price of aluminium (Victorian Government, 1984). Under these arrangements the Victorian taxpayer would directly subsidise any shortfall in return for the construction of the smelter at a distance of about 600 km from the power station. Transmission costs and losses would ensure that even if power from the station was not heavily subsidized, the state would still incur heavy losses. Given a contract which relied heavily on high and rising prices for aluminium in order for the Victorian government to have any chance of breaking even, it is not surprising that the Victorian government has had to directly subsidize the smelter by many hundreds of millions of dollars in present value terms.

Apart from interstate competition to attract mobile industries such as smelters, state governments were also very reluctant to raise electricity prices during periods of high inflation when other energy prices were escalating rapidly due to rising oil prices associated with OPEC. As a consequence real rates of return fell, often to negative levels (Swan, 1990a). When prices were eventually raised to more realistic levels, the high rates of growth due to underpricing continued to be incorporated into planning for new and very large power stations which required very long lead times. This problem was particularly severe in New South Wales and as a consequence capacity utilization is only about 50 per cent. While the NSW Electricity Commission believed that there would be large economies of scale associated with the new power stations, economies in fact are largely obtained by high levels of utilization of baseload stations rather than by the size of units above a relatively low minimum (Swan and Bateson, 1989).

4.3 Transition to Free Enterprise

Not wishing to introduce the rigidities inherent in rate of return regulation, generally some form of 'price-capping' regime has been instituted in both the United Kingdom and Australia when there has been concern over so-called 'natural monopoly' issues. Price-capping involves specifying future prices levels based on *CPI* – *X* where *CPI* represents the increase in the Consumer Price Index and *X* represents an estimate of the price reduction required. The price reduction can be expected either because of technological advances or because international benchmarking studies have indicated that there is scope to reduce prices and costs over time to levels which are consistent with world best practice using like-with-like comparisons.

Price-capping has had considerable application in the United Kingdom (see Rees and Vickers, 1995; Cowan, 1994; Price, 1994, Yarrow, 1994) and also in Australia. Telstra (formerly Australian Telecom), Australia Post, a number of State electricity utilities and the NSW privately-owned gas utility, AGL, are all subject to price-cap regulation. By contrast, in New Zealand the philosophy has been to avoid explicit forms of regulation and to rely much more on the courts.

The basic idea underlying price-capping is that infrastructure providers who can improve their prices and productivity by more than the cap are entitled to keep the difference in the form of higher profits. This should provide incentives for cost minimization. In this respect price-capping has similar effects to rate of return regulation with regulatory lag. That is, suppliers who are able to reduce their costs when prices are set for a period based on the previous rate of return are able to keep the savings as higher profits until such time as maximum prices are once again lowered to restore the allowed rate of return. Of course, if product or service quality is hard to monitor price-cap arrangements could be avoided by lowering quality so long as demand is not too sensitive to quality.

The efficacy of price-capping is not just dependent on setting the *X* component at achievable levels. If the *X* factor is set too low and high profits are made then the regulator is likely to respond by raising *X*. Anticipating this, the utility is likely to respond by allowing cost to blow out. This result is similar to rate of return regulation (see BIE, 1995a, p. 72). Moreover, if *X* appears to be set too high and low returns appear to be earned, *X* is likely to be lowered in response. Once again, the outcome is similar to rate of return regulation.

A less intrusive form of price-capping is known as price surveillance. The surveillance authority can publicly comment on the appropriateness of price increases and may conduct hearings into costs, efficiency and cross-subsidies without having any statutory power to lower prices. While public pressure may prevent utilities from disregarding the surveillance authority, once again it can very readily degenerate into a distorting form of rate of return regulation. At a slightly lower level of intrusiveness, price monitoring, in which the authority does not comment on the appropriateness of prices, can also be used in place of prices surveillance. Once again, price monitoring relies on public pressure to be effective.

In Australia, the former Trade Practices Commission has been renamed the Competition and Consumer Commission with an expanded role to monitor the prices and access charges of various infrastructure providers (BIE, 1995a, p. 81). These infrastructure providers are largely state government controlled and as such have escaped Trade Practices and Price Surveillance Authority and other forms of Commonwealth Government scrutiny in the past.

In addition to regulatory reform, contracting out (for example, Domberger, Meadowcroft and Thompson, 1994, and Domberger, 1995), can be used to improve efficiency in the public sector. Contracting out can also be used in the context of regulation so as to improve transparency. For example, when the New Zealand Electricity Commission was corporatized all transmission functions were placed in the hands of a separate company so that the costs of transmission could be more closely monitored.

Whatever form of regulation and oversight is used, regulatory capture and the private interest theory of regulation is potentially a serious problem (Stigler, 1975, particularly Chapter 8). Even if there is no explicit capture or regulation to limit competition to the benefit of those regulated, the essential monopoly that the utility has on information places the regulator at a severe disadvantage. If only selective or biased information is passed on to the regulator, effectively hidden monopoly rents can be earned. At the same time, considerable waste and inefficiency can occur. One of the few weapons that the regulator has at its disposal under conditions of asymmetric information are international benchmark comparisons as a means of detecting unnecessarily high costs. Another involves the regulator offering the firm a 'menu' of options from which it could choose, thus revealing some of its own assessment of its prospects.

4.4 Price-capping in the United Kingdom and United States

The principle underlying the regulation of the now privatized electricity generation and distribution system in the United Kingdom is that *RPI-X* price-cap regulation is used in both the transmission and distribution sectors of the industry which are regarded as natural monopolies to prevent monopoly pricing with regulation designed to encourage competition in generation and supply (Yarrow, 1994, p. 70). The National Grid Company (NGC) controls all distribution. The NGC is jointly owned by the 12 Regional Electric Companies (RECs) which are the distributors but operates at arm's-length from them. Each REC must make available its own distribution system to others on the same terms that its own distributors are paid. Customers with peak demands of less than 10 MW must have their demands met at published regulated tariffs based on a formula of the $RPI - X + Y$ type, where Y represents the pass-through of certain costs such as wholesale electricity charges. Gradually, all customers of whatever size will be free to seek competitive supplies from outside their local RECs.

The gas industry under the control of British Gas was privatized in 1986 with its monopoly essentially intact in the transport and supply of gas (see, for example, Price, 1994). Smaller customers are price-capped but there was no such protection for larger customers because it was believed that there would be sufficient competition from other forms of energy. Price-capping is based on $RPI - X + Y$, where Y represents the pass-through of so-called exogenous cost such as purchased gas. 'Pass-through' has the problem that it may not provide sufficient incentives to minimize costs or negotiate better prices of purchased inputs. Subsequently, after review by the Monopolies and Merger Commission, gas-to-gas competition was promoted.

In the United States, the price of newly discovered gas was deregulated in 1978. In 1985 pipelines were required to provide equal access to all-comers on a non-discriminatory basis. Full unbundling was required in 1993 to provide equal access to pipelines by all third-party suppliers.

In the US electricity sector Cost of Service Incentive (COSI) regulation has begun to give way to more progressive and less damaging forms. COSI regulation is based on accounting rules, allowed rates of return and cost allocation rules designed to achieve 'fairness' and prevent 'excess' profits This kind of regulation based on principles of command and control usually promotes poor performance (Berg, 1995). In the 1990s co-generation and independent power producers (IPPs) are providing competition to the traditional vertically integrated power utilities. The Energy Act of 1992 created Exempt Wholesale Generators (EWGs) owned by holding companies with regulated subsidiaries. The EWGs are able to enter new markets with guaranteed access to transmission networks. The Act also required utilities to offer 'wheeling' to third parties for a fee. 'Wheeling' is the use of one transmission network to provide trade in wholesale power between utilities. This will enable relatively large customers to negotiate access to more competitive sources of power (Berg, 1995). Hyman (1993) provides an overview of the development of the industry.

5 BENCHMARK COMPARISONS AND THE SETTING OF *X*

From this survey so far it can be seen that 'yardstick' competition and $CPI - X$ price-capping is playing an important role in being able to relax the old style of rate of return regulation, privatize areas formerly regarded as the preserve of the state and throw open to competition highly regulated apparent natural monopolies. How then should the X be set when price-capping is brought in? At the same time the introduction of reforms and new forms of regulation requires close monitoring of performance. How should this be done? The answer to both these questions is to be found in domestic and international benchmarking comparisons to establish both domestic and international world best-practice benchmarks against which performance can be assessed. The benchmark provides a target for monitoring purposes and as a foundation for setting the *X* factor.

There are three related approaches to performance monitoring and target setting. The first is based on partial productivity comparisons (PPC), the second on total factor productivity (TFP) comparisons and the third is based on data envelopment analysis (DEA).

6 PARTIAL PRODUCTIVITY MEASUREMENT

6.1 Introduction

This section summarizes the major findings of a world-wide benchmarking project carried out by the Bureau of Industry Economics (BIE) in Australia using a variety of partial productivity measures. It focuses on infrastructure performance gaps on an industry-by-industry basis. While this study takes Australia as the point of comparison, the same approach can be used by any country to improve its infrastructure performance. A number of earlier related studies by the BIE have also been published (Bureau of Industry Economics, 1992a–1992d; 1993a–1993b; 1994a–1994e, 1995a–1995f). There is also a partial factor productivity study of international telecoms (Swan, 1990b).

6.2 Infrastructure Performance – Key Results

Table 11.4 summarizes the major findings of the benchmarking project. We present key performance indicators relating to price, quality, reliability and timeliness of service, labour productivity and capital productivity. Four key performance levels are identified. These are best observed international practice, best observed Australian practice, worst observed Australian practice and worst observed international practice. The BIE's principal task is to search for best practice and hence the worst observed international practice is the worst that the BIE found in its search for the best rather than the worst overall.

In Sections 6.3–6.4 and Figures 11.4–11.6 we analyze infrastructure services performance gaps for each of the four main indicator categories using the latest available information. Australian best practice is set equal to 100 and all performance gaps are expressed as a percentage of it. The performance gap between Australian best practice and best observed practice is represented by the bar appearing above the horizontal line

Table 11.4 Australian, worst and best observed practice infrastructure performance

	Indicator	*Worse practice utility/state*	*Value*	*Worst Australian utility/state*	*Value*	*Best Australian utility/state*	*Value*	*Best practice utility/state*	*Value*
Price									
Electricity	C/k Wh, (kW) = 10 000, load 80%, 1994	Con Edison (US)	13.08	SECWA	7.21	ESV (VIC)	4.89	Transalta (CAN)	3.79
Telecommunications	Composite business basket, 1994	Japan	158.70	–	–	AUST	95.10	Finland	53.52
Rail freight	Ave revenue cents/ntkm, 1994	NZR[a]	9.00	WestRail	4.91	AN	3.08	BN (US)	2.00
Waterfront (containers)	Waterfront charges ($A/TEU), 1995	Oakland (US)	385	Melbourne	292	Adelaide	278	Johor (Mal)	98
Waterfront (coal)	Waterfront charges ($A/tonne), 1995	Roberts Bank (CAN)	6.10	Abbot Pt (QLD)	5.80	Hay Pt (QLD)	3.08	Hay Pt (QLD)	3.08
Aviation	Airport landing charges (index), 1993	Berlin	100	Claims	29	Syd, Bris, & Melb	23	Toronto	15
Gas supply	Industrial price ($A per Gj), 1991	QLD	6.37	QLD	6.37	SA	3.25	Oneok (US)[b]	1.99
Coastal shipping	Standard dry bulk vessel op costs, 1994	USA	244.00	–	–	AUST	107.10	Korea	87.40
Road freight	Long haul c/tkm (op cost incl tax), 1992	UK	146.00	–	–	AUST	128.00	US	116.00
Service									
Electricity	Ave outage (min/cust), 1994	SECWA	472	SECWA	472	Ophir	55	Tokyo Electric	3.0
Telecommunications	Faults cleared within 24 hours, 1992	Belgium	58.00	–	–	AUST	78.90	Denmark	95.10
Rail freight	Claims (c/$100 revenue), 1994	SP (US)	65	PTC	27	SRA	2	SRA	2

Table 11.4 Australian, worst and best observed practice infrastructure performance *(continued)*

	Indicator	Worse practice utility/state	Value	Worst Australian utility/state	Value	Best Australian utility/state	Value	Best practice utility/state	Value
Waterfront	Time to move 600 boxes (hrs), 1995	Oakland (US)	44	Fremantle	44	Adelaide	27	Zeebrugge	12
Aviation	On-time departures (%), 1993	Hong Kong	66	Melbourne	78	Cairns	85	Copenhagen	95
Road freight	Late delivery (%), 1992	UK	8.00	–	–	AUST	4.00	US	3.00
Road freight	Loss & damage (%), 1992	US	0.90	–	–	AUST	0.40	AUST, CAN, UK	0.40
Labour prod.									
Electricity	Gwh/employee[c], 1994	ESB (IRE)	1.34	SECWA	2.37	VIC	4.43	Transalta (CAN)	12.95
Telecommunications	Partial labour productivity index, 1992	AUST	1.00	–	–	AUST	1.00	USA	2.38
Rail freight	Ntk/employee (mill), 1994	NZR[a]	0.25	PTC	1.53	AN	3.19	BN (US)	11.36
Waterfront (containers)	TEU per employee, 1994	Wellington	350	Adelaide	605	Sydney	1033	Laem Chabang	1298
Waterfront (coal)	Tonnes (000)/employee, 1994	Port Kembla	65	Port Kembla	65	Newcastle	158	Kaltim Prima	245
Aviation	Aircraft moves/fire & rescue employee, 1993	Bangkok	850	Cairns	1100	Sydney	3460	Toronto	7200
Gas supply	Tj/employee, 1994	Toho Gas	15	Allgas/GCQ	18	SECWA	230	SECWA	230
Coastal shipping	Manning small dry bulk vessel, 1994	USA	28	–	–	AUST	18	Norway	15
Capital prod.									
Electricity	Capacity factor (%), 1994[d]	NEPC (US)	39.75	ETSA	44.50	QEC	63.6	QEC	63.6
	Reserve plant margin, 1994	Pacific Power	48.20	Pacific Power	48.20	ETSA	19.7	SERC (US)	10.03

Table 11.4 Australian, worst and best observed practice infrastructure performance *(continued)*

	Indicator	*Worse practice utility/state*	*Value*	*Worst Australian utility/state*	*Value*	*Best Australian utility/state*	*Value*	*Best practice utility/state*	*Value*
Telecommunications	Partial capital productivity index, 1992	Germany	0.58	–	–	AUST	1.00	USA	1.76
Rail (wagons)	Mill ntk/wagon, 1994	NZR[a]	0.5	PTC	1.23	AN, SRA	2.24	BN (US)	5.58
Rail (locomotives)	Mill ntk/loco, 1994	CPR	7	SRA	46	AN	77	BN (US)	169
Waterfront (coal)	Throughput/capacity (%), 1994	Abbot Pt (Qld)	43	Abbot Pt (Qld)	43	Newcastle	103	Newcastle	103
Waterfront (containers)	Crane rate – moves per hour, 1994	Sydney	14.7	Sydney	14.7	Fremantle	18.5	HK, Singapore, etc	30
Aviation	Passengers/terminal gate, 1993	Copenhagen	144	Brisbane	265	Cairns	295	Hong Kong	629
Gas supply	Tj/total main (Km), 1994	SaskEnergy	1.4	Allgas/GCQ	3.0	SECWA	13.0	Peoples Energy	29.0
Road freight	Tonne (000)/km/veh/yr, 1992	UK	281	–	–	AUST	1020	US	1283

Notes:

[a] Based on 1990–1 data.

[b] Alaska excluded as an incomparable outlier.

[c] Includes construction personnel.

[d] Victoria based on 1992–3 data.

Source: BIE (1995e).

marked 100. A higher bar above this line indicates that we are further behind best observed practice. The total length of the bar below the horizontal line marked 100 represents the gap between worst observed practice and Australian best practice. Where there are two boxes in the bar below the horizontal line marked 100 that closest to the horizontal line represents the gap between Australian worst practice and Australian best practice. The lower box represents the gap between Australian worst practice and worst observed practice.

6.3 Prices

Australia's best observed price performance is in waterfront coal handling. Australia also performs relatively well in respect to charges for road freight, dry bulk vessel coastal shipping and electricity. More significant price performance gaps are observed in waterfront container handling, telecommunications, rail freight, aviation (airport charges) and gas supply (Figure 11.4).

The world's lowest observed electricity charges (cents per kWh with demand set at 10 000 KW and a load factor of 80 per cent) in 1995, those of

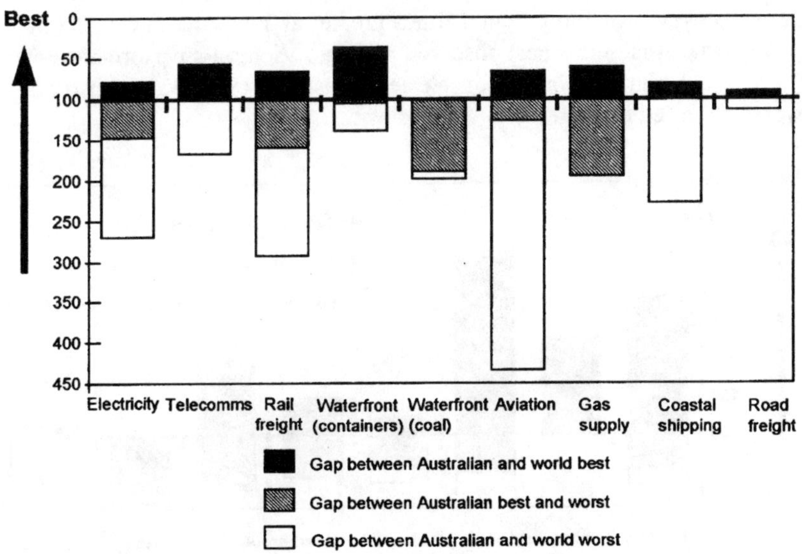

Note: A larger bar above the 100 line indicates a larger gap relative to international best practice.

Figure 11.4 Price performance gaps, Australian, best and worst observed (index relative to Australian best = 100)

Transalta in Canada, were 22 per cent lower than Australia's lowest charges, those for Victoria (ESV). Western Australia (SECWA) had the highest observed charges in Australia, 48 per cent higher than those of Victoria.

6.4 Operational Efficiency

Operational efficiency performance gaps relating to labour and capital productivity are summarized in Figures 11.5 and 11.6.

Labour Productivity

Australia's best labour productivity performance occurred in the gas supply industry, in which SECWA (Western Australia) was the world best observed practice in terms of throughput per employee in 1994.

Australia also performs relatively well in terms of coastal shipping labour productivity, measured as the manning level for a small dry bulk vessel in 1994. At 18 Australia's manning level performance was only 3, or 17 per cent, below the world best observed practice, that of Norway.

The greatest labour productivity performance gaps are in electricity and rail freight. Labour productivity in electricity, measured as gigawatt hours per employee, was more than 4 times greater at Transalta in Canada than in Victoria, Australia's best observed practice. Victoria's performance was 65 per cent higher than that of Western Australia (SECWA), Australia's worst observed practice.

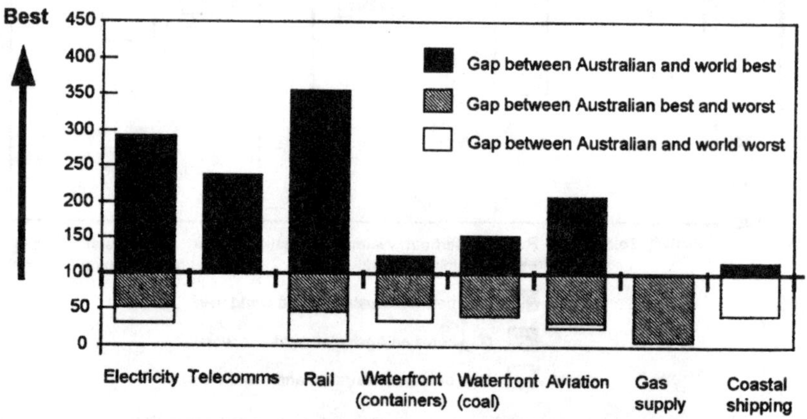

Note: A larger bar above the 100 line indicates a larger gap relative to international best practice.

Figure 11.5 Labour productivity performance gaps, Australian, best and worst observed (index relative to Australian best = 100)

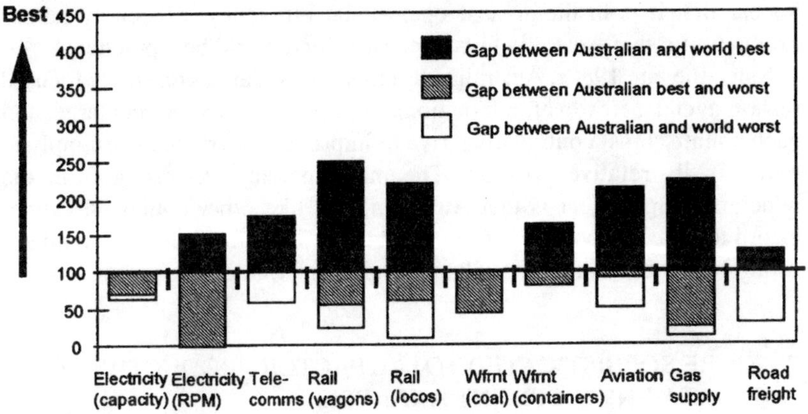

Note: A larger bar above the 100 line indicates a larger gap relative to international best practice.

Figure 11.6 Capital productivity performance gaps, Australian, best and worst observed (index relative to Australian best = 100)

Capital Productivity

Based on unadjusted costs, the greatest capital productivity performance gap occurs in the use of rail rolling stock (Figure 11.6). In terms of millions of net tonne kilometres per locomotive in 1994, world best-practice performance, that of Burlington Northern in the United States, was double that of Australia's best observed practice, AN. The capital productivity performance of SRA (New South Wales) was 45 per cent lower than that of AN.

6.5 Infrastructure Performance – is Australia Closing the Gap?

Analysis of the performance gaps suggests that there is a marked difference in performance between the various categories of indicators. The largest price performance gap between Australia's best and best observed practice is 65 per cent for waterfront container handling. Labour and capital productivity gaps are both larger and more varied. The largest capital productivity performance gap between Australia's best and best observed practice is 150 per cent for wagon utilization in rail freight. The largest labour productivity performance gap is also found in rail freight at more than 250 per cent. Four industries (rail freight, electricity, telecommunications and aviation) have labour productivity gaps in excess of 100 per cent while three industries (rail freight, gas supply and aviation) have capital productivity gaps in excess of 100 per cent. So, it would appear that it is in the area of operational efficiency, especially labour productivity, that Australia falls furthest behind world best practice.

Since the late 1980s, Australia has embarked on an increasingly focused reform agenda. However, international best practice is a moving target and each country must continually strive to improve its performance simply to maintain its relative position. The main message emerging from the benchmarking project is that Australia, just like other countries, cannot afford to relax the pace of reform or let the process falter as this would see it fall further back into the trailing group of international also-rans.

7 MORE SOPHISTICATED TOTAL FACTOR PRODUCTIVITY AND DATA ENVELOPMENT ANALYSIS

7.1 Measuring the Economic Efficiency of an Enterprise

While partial indicators such as labour and capital productivity provide useful information, they can provide a misleading picture of overall performance if viewed in isolation. For example, it may be possible to improve labour productivity dramatically by substituting large amounts of capital for labour. This would have the effect of worsening capital productivity at the same time that labour productivity was being improved. To find out whether overall performance has improved as a result of changes, a wholistic productivity measure is required which takes account of all outputs produced and all inputs used. Total factor productivity (TFP) and data envelopment analysis (DEA) are two such measures.

7.2 Total Factor Productivity: An Application to the Electricity Sector in Australia and the United States

TFP is measured by taking the ratio of total outputs produced to total inputs used by an enterprise. Outputs and inputs are combined into measures of aggregate output and aggregate input, respectively, by the use of various indexing formulae. All enterprises use a range of inputs including labour, capital, fuel, and materials and services. If the enterprise is not using its inputs as efficiently as possible, then there is scope to lower costs and increase profitability through productivity improvements. This may come about through the use of better quality inputs including a better trained workforce, adoption of technological advances, removal of restrictive work practices and other forms of waste, and better management through a more efficient organizational and institutional structure.

TFP plays a central role in benchmarking studies by providing a comprehensive summary measure of overall economic performance. The multilateral TFP technique, developed by Caves, Christensen, and Diewert (1982) and first applied to the Electricity industry in Australia by Lawrence, Swan and Zeitsch (1991a, 1991b), is a particularly useful benchmarking tool because it allows productivity levels as well as growth rates to be compared between organizations.

Figure 11.7 presents an application of this approach to the various state electricity commissions in Australia (based on Lawrence, Swan and Zeitsch, 1991a). It compared the Australian Electricity Supply Industry's TFP with that of US investor-owned utilities in aggregate for the period 1975–6 to 1989–90 (Swan Consultants (Canberra), 1991). The study included one output (gigawatt hours of electricity supplied) and four inputs: fuel, labour, capital and other inputs. Fuel and labour were measured in physical units (terajoules and persons employed, respectively) while capital and other inputs were measured in terms of Australian dollars using purchasing power parities.

The study found that in 1975–6 the Australian Electricity Supply Industry was only slightly more than half as productive as the US investor-owned utilities on average. However, by 1989–90 the Australian industry had closed this gap considerably and was achieving TFP levels around 70 per cent those of the average US investor-owned utility. This narrowing

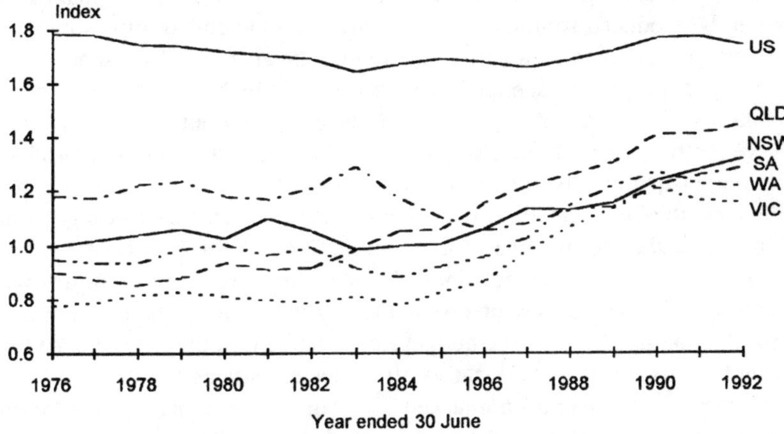

Source: BIE update of Lawrence *et al.* (1991a) and Swan Consultants (Canberra) (1991).

Figure 11.7 Electricity multilateral TFP – Australian states and United States, 1976–92

of the productivity gap occurred mainly as the result of reforms introduced in Australia during the 1980s with the TFP level of the US investor-owned utilities actually falling slightly over the period partly as the result of tougher environmental regulation in the United States. This result also reflects the fact that those lagging behind international best practice have greater opportunity to make 'catch-up' improvements whereas the technological leaders have less opportunity to make large productivity improvements. A more comprehensive comparison of the Queensland Electricity Commission and the best-performing North American utilities is presented in Swan Consultants (Canberra) (1992a).

7.3 Data Envelopment Analysis (DEA)

Both TFP and DEA provide information on a utility's cost efficiency but only DEA can decompose cost efficiency into its component parts of technical and allocative efficiency. Technical efficiency is achieved when maximum output is produced from the use of a given bundle of inputs. In other words, given current technology there is no wastage of inputs whatsoever in producing the given quantity of output. Allocative efficiency, on the other hand, requires that inputs be used in the proportions or combination which would minimize costs given prevailing input prices. These two measures are combined in the concept of 'cost efficiency', which requires that a given level of output be produced at minimum cost. This requires that maximum output be produced from the resources used and the cost of inputs must be the lowest-cost combination that can produce the given level of output.

These concepts are depicted in Figure 11.8, which plots different combinations of two inputs required to produce a given output quantity. The curve plotting the minimum amounts of the two inputs required to produce the output quantity is known as an isoquant. If a firm is producing at a point on the isoquant then it is technically efficient. The straight line denoted as the budget line plots combinations of the two inputs which have the same cost. Budget lines closer to the origin represent a lower total cost. Thus, the cost of producing a given output quantity is minimized at the point where the budget line is tangent to the isoquant. At this point both technical and allocative efficiency are attained.

The point of operation marked *A* would be technically inefficient because more inputs are used than is needed to produce a given level of output. Point *B* is technically efficient but not cost efficient because the same level of output could be produced at less cost at point *C*. Thus if a firm moved from point *A* to point *C* its cost efficiency, or productivity, would increase by $(OA–OA'')/OA$. This would consist of an improvement

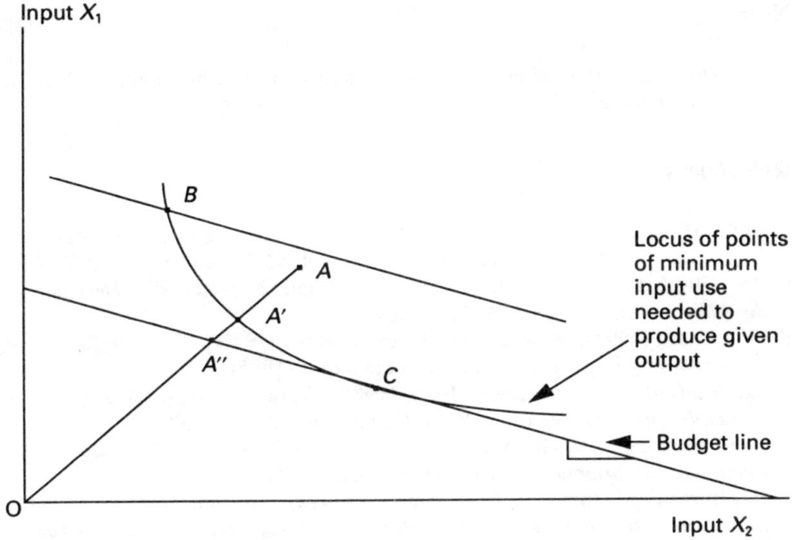

Source: Zeitsch and Lawrence (1993, p. 2).

Figure 11.8 Illustration of cost efficiency in contrast to technical efficiency

in technical efficiency measured by the distance (*OA–OA′*)/*OA* and an 'allocative' efficiency improvement measured by the distance (*OA′OA″*)/*OA*. DEA provides a method of calculating these ratios by means of linear programming.

8 CONCLUSIONS

International benchmarking is proving a useful tool in terms of monitoring performance or a variety of infrastructure providers and in setting targets. Both partial productivity measures and their more sophisticated cousins, total factor productivity (TFP) and data envelopment analysis (DEA) which rely more extensively on economic analysis, have a major role to play in extending and consolidating the major gains that have been made. Without the well crafted use of these techniques in setting the *X* component realistically in price-capping of infrastructure which has some natural monopoly characteristics, society is not likely to reap the full benefits of corporatization and privatization taking place in the electricity, gas, transportation and water industries globally, but especially in Australia, the United Kingdom and the United States.

Note

1. Although it is now getting a little dated as it was first published in *The Economic Record* (1986).

References

Averch, H. and L. Johnson (1962) 'Behavior of the Firm under Regulatory Constraint', *The American Economic Review*, vol. 52 (December), pp. 1053–69.

Bailey, Elizabeth, E., R. Graham David and P. Daniel Kaplan (1985) *Deregulating the Airlines* (Cambridge, MA: MIT Press).

Berg, Sanford (1995) 'What Can We Learn from the US Experience in Regulating Monopolies?', in Bureau of Industry Economics (1995f).

Berg, Sanford and Tschirhart, John (1988) *Natural Monopoly Regulation: Principles and Practice* (New York: Cambridge University Press).

Bishop, Matthew, Kay, John and Mayer, Colin (eds) (1994), *Privatisation and Economic Performance* (Oxford: Oxford University Press).

BIE (Bureau of Industry Economics) (1992a) *International Performance Indicators: Electricity*, Research Report, vol. 40 (Canberra: AGPS) (February).

BIE (1992b) *International Performance Indicators: Rail Freight*, Research Report, vol. 41 (Canberra: AGPS) (April)

BIE (1992c) *International Performance Indicators: Road Freight*, Research Report, vol. 46 (Canberra: AGPS) (December)

BIE (1992d) *International Performance Indicators: Telecommunications*, Research Report, vol. 48 (Canberra: AGPS) (December)

BIE (1993a) *International Performance Indicators: Waterfront*, Research Report, vol. 47 (Canberra: AGPS) (March).

BIE (1993b) *International Performance Indicators: Rail Freight Update 1993*, Research Report, vol. 52 (Canberra: AGPS) (November).

BIE (1994a) *International Performance Indicators: Overview*, Research Report, vol. 53 (Canberra: AGPS) (February).

BIE (1994b) *International Performance Indicators: Electricity Update 1994*, Research Report, vol. 54 (Canberra: AGPS) (March).

BIE (1994c) *International Performance Indicators: Coastal Shipping*, Research Report, vol. 55 (Canberra: AGPS) (March).

BIE (1994d) *International Performance Indicators: Aviation*, Research Report, vol. 59 (Canberra: AGPS) (August).

BIE (1994e) *International Performance Indicators: Gas Supply*, Research Report, vol. 62 (Canberra: AGPS) (December).

BIE (1995a) *International Performance Indicators: Telecommunications 1995*, Research Report, vol. 65 (Canberra: AGPS) (March).

BIE (1995b) *International Performance Indicators: Coastal Shipping 1995*, Research Report, vol. 68 (Canberra: AGPS) (July).

BIE (1995c) *Issues in Infrastructure Pricing*, Research Report, vol. 69 (Canberra: AGPS) (August).

BIE (1995d) *International Benchmarking: Waterfront 1995*, Report, 95/16 (Canberra: AGPS) (August).

BIE (1995e) *International Benchmarking: Overview 1995*, Report, 95/20 (Canberra: AGPS), (November).

BIE (1995f) Infrastructure Pricing Forum Canberra (15 August).

Caves, D. W., L. R. Christensen and W. E. Diewert (1982) 'Multilateral Comparisons of Output, Input, and Productivity Using Superlative Index Numbers', *The Economic Journal*, vol. 92, pp. 73–86.

Charnes, A. and W. W. Cooper (1985) 'Preface to Topics in Data Envelopment Analysis', *Annals of Operations Research*, vol. 2, pp. 59–94.

Courville, L. (1974) 'Regulation of Efficiency in the Electric Utility Industry', *Bell Journal of Economics and Management Sciences*, vol. 5 (Spring), pp. 53–74.

Cowan, Simon (1994) 'Privatisation and Regulation of the Water Industry in England and Wales', in Bishop *et al.*, pp. 112–36.

Diewert, W. E. (1993a) 'International Benchmarking: What is Best Practice?', in Swan Consultants (Canberra), *Measuring the Economic Performance of Government Enterprises, Proceedings of a Conference held at the Sheraton International Airport Hotel*, 12 February.

Diewert, W. E. (1993b) 'Data Envelopment Analysis: A Practical Alternative?', in Swan Consultants (Canberra), *Measuring the Economic Performance of Government Enterprises, Proceedings of a Conference held at the Sheraton International Airport Hotel*, (12 February).

Domberger, Simon (1995) *The Contracting Casebook* (Canberra, AGPS).

Domberger, Simon and Piggott, John (1994) 'Privatisation Policies and Public Enterprises', in Bishop *et al.*, pp. 32–61

Domberger, S., S. A. Meadowcroft and D. J. Thompson (1994) 'Competitive Tendering and Efficiency: The Case of Refuse Collection, in Bishop *et al.*, pp. 188–207.

Farrell, M. J. (1957) 'The Measurement of Production Efficiency', *Journal of the Royal Statistical Society*, Series A, 120, pp. 253–78.

Hillman, A. L. and P. L. Swan (1983) 'Participation rules for Pareto-optimal Clubs', *Journal of Public Economics*, 20, pp. 55–76.

Hyman, Leonard S. (1993) *America's Electric Utilities: Past, Present and Future* (Arlington, VA: Public Utilities Reports), 4th edn.

Industry Commission (1990) 'Measuring the Performance of Selected Government Business Enterprises', *Information Paper* (August).

Jarrell, Gregg A. (1978), 'The Demand for State Regulation of the Electric Utility Industry', *Journal of Law and Economics*, vol. 21(2), pp. 269–95.

Joskow, Paul L. and Noll, Roger G. (1981) 'Regulation in Theory and Practice: An Overview', in G. Fromm (ed.), *Studies in Public Regulation* (Cambridge MA: MIT Press).

Joskow, Paul L. and Schmalensee, Richard (1983) *Markets for Power: An Analysis of Electrical Utility Deregulation* (Cambridge, MA: MIT Press).

Lawrence, Denis (1995), 'Analysing the Role of Benchmarking in the Globalisation of the Australian Public Sector', *Benchmarking for Best Practice in the Public Sector*, AIC Conferences, Sydney (April).

Lawrence, D., P. Swan and J. Zeitsch (1991a), 'The Comparative Efficiency of State Electricity Authorities', in M. R. Johnson, Peter Kriesler and Anthony D. Owen (eds), *Contemporary Issues in Australian Economics* (Melbourne: Macmillan).

Lawrence, D., P. Swan and J. Zeitsch (1991b) 'The Productivity Performance of Australian State Electricity Systems: 1975/76–1989/90', mimeo.

Pescatrice, D. R. and J. M. Trapani (1980) 'The Performance and Objectives of Public and Private Utilities Operating in the United States, *Journal of Public Economics*, vol. 13, pp. 259–76.

Peterson, H. C. (1975) 'An Empirical Test of Regulatory Effects', *Bell Journal of Economics*, vol. 6 (Spring), pp. 111–26.

Price, Catherine (1994) 'Gas Regulation and Competition: Substitutes or Complements?', in Bishop *et al.*, pp. 137–61.

Rees, R. and J. Vickers (1995) 'RPI-X Price-cap Regulation', in M. Bishop, J. Kay and C. Mayer (eds) *The Regulatory Challenge* (Oxford: Oxford University Press).

Stigler, George, J. (1975) *The Citizen and the State: Essays on Regulation* (Chicago: University of Chicago Press).

Swan Consultants (Canberra) (1991) 'An International Benchmark for Australia's Electricity Supply Industry', report prepared for Business Council of Australia.

Swan Consultants (Canberra) (1992a) 'International Benchmarks for the Queensland Electricity Supply Industry', report prepared for Queensland Electricity Commission.

Swan Consultants (Canberra) (1992b) 'Performance Measures for Australia Post: 1975–76 to 1990–91', in Steering Committee on National Performance Monitoring of Government Trading Enterprises, *Measuring the Total Factor Productivity of Government Trading Enterprises* (Canberra: AGPS).

Swan, Peter L. (1983) 'The Marginal Cost of Base-Load Power: An Application to Alcoa's Portland Smelter', *The Economic Record*, vol. 59 (December), pp. 332–44.

Swan, Peter L. (1989), 'Corporatisation, Privatisation and the Regulatory Framework for the Electricity Sector', *Economic Papers*, vol. 8 (3) (September), pp. 55–69.

Swan, Peter L. (1990a), 'Real Rates of Return in Electricity Supply: New South Wales, Tasmania and Victoria', *The Economic Record*, vol. 66 (193) (June), pp. 93–109.

Swan, Peter L. (1990b), Measuring Carrier Efficiency – The Facts', *Australian Communications* (October), pp. 21–5.

Swan, Peter L. and Bateson, Jeff (1989) 'Economies of Scale and Utilisation: An Analysis of the Multi-Plant Generation Costs of the Electricity Commission of New South Wales, 1970/71–1984/85', *The Economic Record*, vol. 65 (191) (December), pp. 329–44.

Swan, Peter L and Garvey, Gerald (1993), 'Linking Rewards to Performance', in Swan Consultants (Canberra), *Measuring the Economic Performance of Government Enterprises, Proceedings of a Conference held at the Sheraton International Airport Hotel* (12 February).

Vickers, John and Yarrow, George (1988) *Privatisation: an Economic Analysis* (Cambridge MA: MIT Press).

Victorian Government (1984) *The Portland Aluminium Smelter: Victorian Government Statement*, Economic Strategy for Victoria Statement, 3.

Viscusi, Kip W., Vernon, John M. and Harrington, Joseph E. (1992) *Economic Regulation and Antitrust* (Lexington MA: D. C. Heath).

World Bank (1994) *World Development Report 1994: Infrastructure for Development*, (Oxford: Oxford University Press).

Yarrow, George (1994) 'Privatisation, Restructuring, and Regulatory Reform in Electricity Supply', in Bishop *et al.*, pp. 62–88.

Zimmer, M. A. (1978), 'Empirical Tests of the Averch–Johnson Hypothesis: A Critical Appraisal,' in G. S. Maddala, W. S. Chern and G. S. Gill (eds), *Econometric Studies in Energy Demand and Supply* (New York: Praeger), pp. 152–71.

12 Economic Regulation and Political Influence[1]

Israel Finkelshtain and Yoav Kislev
THE HEBREW UNIVERSITY OF JERUSALEM, ISRAEL

1 INTRODUCTION

The purpose of this chapter is to discuss the effect of political pressure on economic regulation. In particular, we compare indirect regulation by prices to direct, administrative control of quantities. This is Martin Weitzman's (1974) comparison. However, while Weitzman contrasts controls where information is incomplete, we analyze the consequences of political influence. As a concrete example, we consider an industry employing a factor with external effects – negative or positive. (Drawing water from a shared source may create negative externalities and using reclaimed sewage for irrigation may have positive effects.) The government is attempting to regulate utilization of the factor and the producers react, trying to modify the implemented policy. The ensuing political equilibrium varies with the nature of the externalities and means of control.

The regulation regime may be either an administrative regime with quantity controls (enforcement is costless), or a price regime. Under the latter, taxes are imposed when the externalities are negative and subsidies are used, to encourage utilization of the regulated factor, when the effects are positive. By assumption, the regulation regime is determined 'constitutionally' and is not subject to the political debate (a similar assumption is made explicitly by Rodrik, 1986, in an analysis which resembles ours in several ways). The major question posed is: given political influence, when is regulation by prices the preferred regime and when is direct, quantity control more adequate? In this chapter we describe the problem and survey the findings. A rigorous mathematical analysis is presented elsewhere (Finkelshtain and Kislev, 1995).

2 THE SETTING

An industry with N homogeneous producers is employing a single variable factor with external effects on the rest of the economy. The producers maximize profits and disregard the externalities they create. A planner, taking into account both the value of production in the industry and its effect on others, can determine socially optimal utilization of the externalities-inducing factor.

The role of the social planner is undertaken by the government, with one modification: politicians are sensitive to political pressure, to rent-seeking efforts. We model the pressure as contributions or rewards paid by the producers to the politicians. In this framework, rent-seeking lowers social welfare but creates a political surplus which is shared by the politicians and the producers. The magnitude of the political contributions determines the division of the surplus: the higher the rewards, the larger the share of the politicians and the smaller the share of the producers. The rewards may take many forms: monetary campaign contributions, outright bribes, demonstrations, strikes, letter-writing, and personal services. The political rewards may enhance welfare, the welfare of the politicians or even public welfare as when a constructor builds a school in return for a lucrative permit. Concentrating on political influence, we disregard the particular nature of the rewards and their wider implications.

One assumed characteristic of the producers–government polity which has significant implications for the analysis is linearity: the political rewards are in money or money-like contributions, they are of constant cost and effect. We do not consider the possibility that the cost of collecting political contributions is rising or that their effect may show diminishing returns.

The policy regimes – taxes, subsidies or quotas – have different and opposing income and budgetary effects. Concentrating on allocation, we put the alternative regimes on the same footing by introducing a lump-sum compensation payment which, by assumption, is introduced with the imposition of a regime. For example, the implementation of a tax regime is accompanied by a compensation equal to the computed equilibrium value of the tax and distributed to the producers as a side-payment; when the control shifts to a subsidy regime, the producers are asked to pay the lump-sum. Being a lump-sum payment, the compensation does not affect allocation – either the magnitude of the political rewards or employment of the variable factor. Such payments, which are here introduced as an analytical device, are observed in practice. For example, the government of Israel is now considering a reform in the country's water economy. Prices will rise to replace administrative allocation, farmers will be compensated. The compensation will be a function of the water quota a farmer has held, independent of future water utilization.

By construction, taxes and subsidies are uniform while quotas may be individually tailored. Consequently, free-riding can be expected in a price regime. Accordingly, we assume that only K of the N producers participate in the industry's lobby if prices are the instrument of control. The number K is taken as exogenous; that is, the size of the lobby is accepted in the analysis as given. Under an administrative control, on the other hand, the government may assign each firm its social optimum employment of the regulated factor, producers can then be expected to lobby individually to modify personal quotas. Moreover, as firms are identical, if it pays one firm to invest in political activity, it is worthwhile for every other firm. Therefore, in a quota regime, full participation of all N producers is part of the definition of a political equilibrium (to be further characterized below); is not an assumption of the analysis. Still, to emphasize the possibility of individual political activity, we keep the firm index i in the presentation.

Formally, let net product, or profits – before taxes or subsidies – in the production activity of the ith producer be written as

$$\pi^i(q^i) = \rho f^i(q^i) - pq^i \qquad (1)$$

In (1), q marks the regulated factor; q^i is the ith producer's utilization level of this factor; ρ is the price of the industry's product; $f^i(q^i)$ is the production function with q the only variable input; and p is the private market price of the variable factor. By assumption, ρ and p are constant and so also prices of other, non-variable inputs are constant. It is also assumed that the function $\pi^i(q^i)$ is concave in q^i

Maximizing profits, the producers maximize y in

$$y^i = \pi^i(q^i) - c^i - tq^i + R^i \qquad (2)$$

The variable t marks the tax; for a subsidy $t < 0$ and when the control is a quota, $t = 0$. The variable c indicates political contributions. The compensation payment is R, equal to the equilibrium magnitude of $-tq$. With N producers in the industry, total income, factor utilization and political rewards are given, respectively, by

$$Y = \sum_{i=1}^{N} y^i,\ Q = \sum_{i=1}^{N} q^i,\ \text{and } C = \sum_{i=1}^{N} c^i \qquad (3)$$

If, under a price regime, $K < N$, c^i may be zero for some values of i.

The second sector, the government, is viewed as maximizing the weighted sum

$$W = V(\mathbf{q}) + \alpha C \tag{4}$$

where $V(\mathbf{q})$ is social welfare defined over the vector $\mathbf{q} = q^1, \ldots , q^N$. The constant $\alpha > 0$ represents the preference of the government for political bribes relative to public welfare; it can also be seen as standing for the political power of the influence group in the industry. Lobbies in different industries may have different α values.

Welfare is taken to be the sum of net product and external effects. Accordingly, the function V is written as

$$V(\mathbf{q}) = \sum_{i=1}^{N} p^{i}(q^{i}) + \sum_{j=1}^{M} m^{j}(Q) \tag{5}$$

where $\mu^j(Q)$ is the money-metric utility function of the jth consumer who is influenced by the external effects of the regulated factor. The function μ increases with Q for positive externalities and decreases for negative effects. Utility is also defined over the vector of prices of consumption goods; but, assuming a small economy with all goods traded, prices are constant and they are not represented explicitly in the function. It is assumed that μ^j is concave in Q, and hence in each q^i. Similarly, since V is the sum of concave functions (in each q^i), it is a concave function itself. All functions are second-order differentiable and interior solutions are assumed throughout.

Note that c and C enter linearly in (2) and (4). This reflects the linear nature of costs and effects in the political process and will simplify significantly the analysis below.

3 POLITICAL EQUILIBRIUM

As indicated, politicians in the government are willing to accept political contributions in return for economic favours. In our model the politicians are willing to lower taxes, raise subsidies or modify quotas. By the 'political process', we mean the particular interaction between the politicians and the interest groups attempting to influence them. The threat point of both sides to the political give and take is the social allocation with no rewards. This is the situation either side may retreat to if it is not satisfied with the outcome of the political process. The government can, by assumption, force social optimum; the producers may also decide to accept the social allocation and in so doing deprive the politicians of the rewards they desire.

A political process leads to a political equilibrium. The equilibrium in our model is characterized by a set of rewards and controls. Thus, under a price regime, the equilibrium is defined by a pair of values C and t; under quota, the equilibrium is characterized by C and a vector $\mathbf{q}$. The political equilibrium is process-specific. Several models of political processes have been suggested in the literature (example are Zusman, 1976; Rodrik, 1986; Hillman, 1989; Grossman and Helpman, 1994; Scarpa, 1994). We consider below two game theoretic models, a cooperative bargaining and a political auction. The political equilibrium of the bargaining model, for example, will be the Nash (1950) solution to a cooperative game.

Though often differing in many ways, most processes considered in the literature – including the games employed in the chapter – share a rather natural common property: they are politically efficient. Their equilibria lie on the contract curve where the indifference curves of the sides to the political process are at points of tangency. It will be convenient to rely on efficiency in the presentation below.

In principle, equilibrium political contributions and controls are determined simultaneously; but when, as we assume, the contributions are linear in cost and effect – the equilibrium configuration can be calculated recursively: the controls are set regardless of the level of the contributions (provided that no side chooses the threat point). These are identical levels of controls for all processes maintaining linearity and political efficiency; the particular model specifying the political process can then be seen as affecting only the division of the political surplus between the parties, between the producers and the politicians.[2] We therefore separate the presentation and start with the employment of the regulated factor and postpone the specification of the games and the determination of the political payments to Section 6.

4 FACTOR UTILIZATION

Relying on the linearity of the political process and its consequences, the derivation of the conditions specifying levels of controls and factor utilization is based in this section solely on efficiency of the political equilibrium; that is, on the equality of the marginal rate of substitution between the control and the political contribution for the producers with the corresponding rate for the politicians.[3] The equilibrium is indicated by tangency of social and private indifference curves in the q, c plane, depicted in Figure 12.1 for negative externalities. The indifference curves in the figure are for a single producer and society, where for society it is assumed that all other producers are at equilibrium utilization of the factor q.

A private indifference curve is the graph of points of identical income; it is derived from (2) by changing c and q, keeping y constant. Accordingly, the curves are marked y_1 and y_2. As drawn, $y_1 < y_2$ as for each value of q, the political payment on y_1 is higher than on y_2. Similarly, the social indifference curves are constant W graphs (4), marked W_1 and W_2, with $W_1 < W_2$.

Three levels of utilization are marked on the diagram: q^w for social optimum, this is the utilization maximizing $V(\mathbf{q})$ in (5); q^p for political

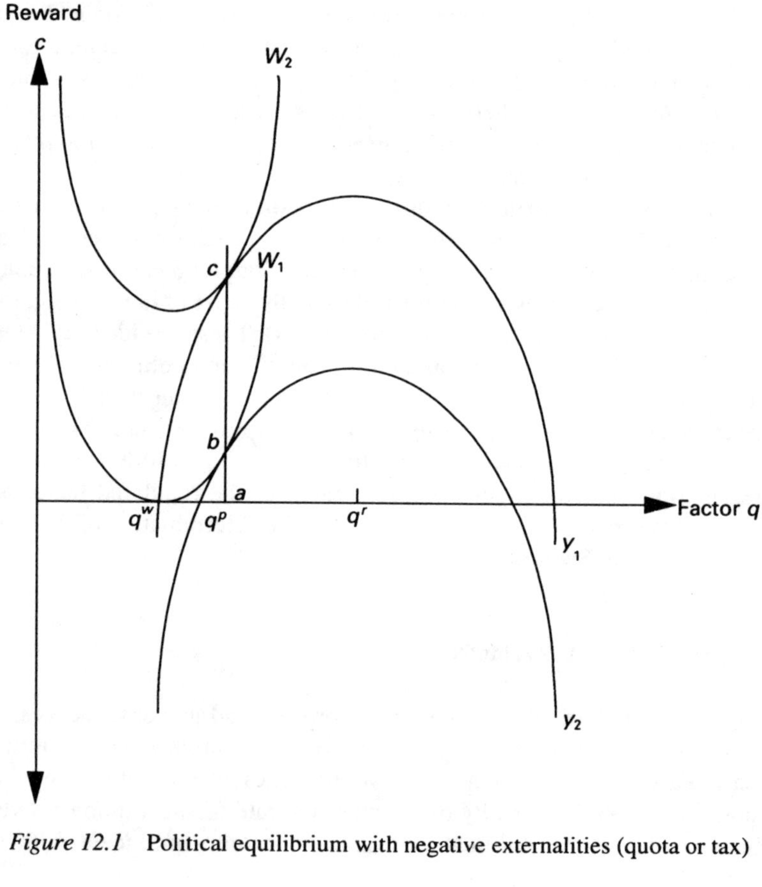

Figure 12.1 Political equilibrium with negative externalities (quota or tax)

equilibrium, and q^r for private, non-intervention, profit-maximizing level. The contract curve is the line extending from q^p; it being vertical reflects the property that the quantity of the regulated factor is the same for any level of the political reward. As Figure 12.1 indicates, when the externalities are negative, the political equilibrium employment of the regulated factor is a compromise between the social optimum and the no-intervention, private profit-maximizing employment of the factor. For negative externalities, the graphical configuration is the same for either a tax regime or a quota control and the political utilization is a compromise for both regimes (not necessarily the same quantity q^p). The situation will be different with positive externalities; but before considering positive effects, it is useful to view the equilibrium reached in terms of marginal magnitudes in panel a of Figure 12.2. In this diagram, π_q marks private marginal profits,[4] while V_q marks marginal social welfare (both termed marginal utility in the diagram). The political equilibrium for negative externalities is again seen to be a compromise in which private marginal profit is positive and social marginal welfare is negative.

The indifference curves Y_1 and W_1 in Figure 12.1 pass through the threat point q^w; the segment *bc* on the contract curve is the core of the political game. The segment *ab* indicates the amount the politicians have to receive to be kept on their reservation utility. It is the minimum political payment for the politicians to participate, to move from the socially optimal allocation to the political equilibrium.

Panels b and c in Figure 12.2 depict political equilibrium for positive externalities. Under a quota regime, equilibrium allocation is a compromise – as it is for negative effects – between the social and the private allocations. Under a price regime, on the other hand, the producers need not be forced to increase production; with subsidies they do it willingly and they further augment the price effect by pressing for even higher subsidies. As a result, the political equilibrium is not a compromise. In Figure 12.2, panel c, q^p is to the right of both q^r and q^w. Consequently, when externalities are positive and the control instrument is a subsidy, the political equilibrium may be socially inferior to the profit-maximizing allocation of a free market without government intervention.

5 PRICES OR QUANTITIES

The central question of this chapter is: when are prices the adequate instrument and when is a quantity control better? A control is preferable if it is relatively more efficient, it will therefore be useful to clarify the different

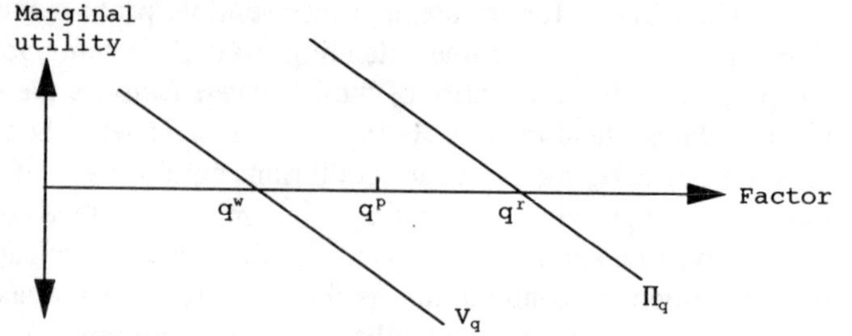

a: Negative externalities (quota or tax)

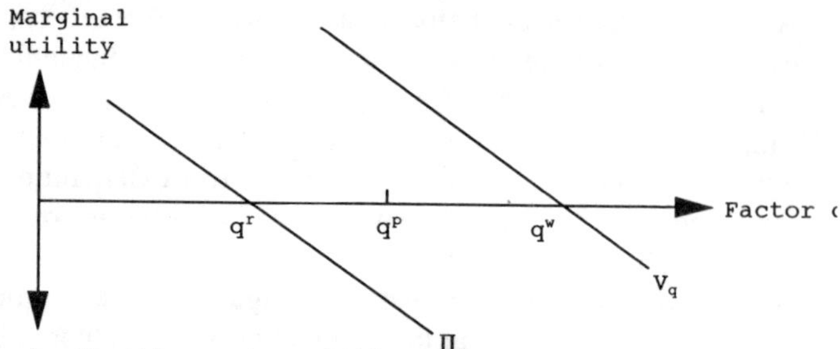

b: Positive externalities, quota

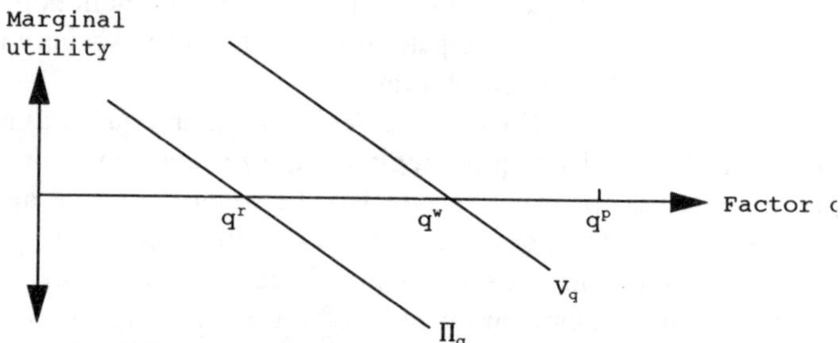

c: Positive externalities, subsidy

Figure 12.2 Marginal welfare and marginal profits

dimensions of efficiency in the analysis. Political efficiency was defined in Section 4 as Pareto-efficiency of the polity: the producers and the politicians are on their contract curve. Allocative efficiency as used below for a political equilibrium is measured by the distance of the employment of the factor q from social optimum utilization. The closer the employment, the more efficient the equilibrium. *S*-efficiency (for rent-*S*eeking) is defined by the size of the political reward: the smaller the reward, the more efficient the political equilibrium.

Since the political equilibrium may be computed recursively in two stages and it is, by construction, politically efficient, the two other dimensions of efficiency – allocative and *S*-efficiency – can also be examined separately. We start with allocative efficiency. Our findings are summarized in Proposition 1, in which the following symbols are used:

$\sigma = \dfrac{Q(K)}{Q(N)}$ the share of production by firms in the lobby under a price regime

η = the elasticity of the demand for the factor q

$s = t/(p+t)$ the ratio of the tax to the producer price of q

Proposition 1

Consider political equilibria calculated for price regimes (either a tax or a subsidy) then,

(i) With negative externalities, a price control yields a more efficient allocation if and only if in equilibrium $|\frac{\sigma}{\eta s}| < 1$. A quantity control is more efficient when the inequality is reversed. The controls are equally efficient when $|\frac{\sigma}{\eta s}| = 1$.

(ii) Under both types of control, the efficiency of prices relative to quotas increases with the elasticity of the demand for the factor and decreases with the share of the producers organised in the industrial lobby.

(iii) Efficiency of both controls decreases with the political power of the producers, α.

(iv) With positive externalities, a price control yields higher utilization of the factor q than a quota regime. Efficiency comparison is inconclusive.

As indicated, a formal proof is given in Finkelshtain and Kislev (1995). We limit the present discussion to a few clarifying remarks and some interpretations and elaborations.

5.1 Remarks

The comparative advantage of a regime can be clearly identified only for negative externalities. When the external effects are positive, the equilibrium utilisations for the alternative regimes – quota and subsidy – are always 'far apart', one being a compromise and the other located to the right of the no-intervention profit-maximizing quantity (Figure 12.2). It is therefore impossible to find analytically conditions under which the regimes are equally efficient and conditions which characterize comparative efficiency of either of the controls. Given the necessary data for any particular situation, one can, of course, calculate the political equilibrium utilization for both regimes and compare their welfare implications.

Item (iii) in Proposition 1 could be expected intuitively: the more powerful the producers, the more they succeed in moving the political equilibrium closer to profit-maximizing allocation and further away from the social optimum.

Item (iv) is again a reflection of the differences in Panels b and c in Figure 12.2.

5.2 Demand Elasticity

The intuition behind the role played by the elasticity of the demand for the regulated factor in comparing allocative efficiency of the regimes in part (i) of Proposition 1 can be explained conveniently for the special case where $\sigma = 1, p = 0, s = 1$; that is, the industry consists of a single producer or of an all-embracing lobby, the factor can be acquired freely up to the designated amount under a quota regime, and the tax is the entire unit price under a price regime. For this situation, let q_0 in Figure 12.3 be an initial quantity, either determined by a quota or reached by the producers when the tax was set to t_0. Consider the rent-seeking effort that increases the quantity to q_1. Depending on the control, the change may be achieved by either an increase in the quota itself or by reducing the tax to t_1. The corresponding gain to the producers is

Price regime	$A + B$
Quota regime	$B + C$
Difference	$A - C$

With unitary elasticity, $A = C$ and the difference vanishes, the regimes are equivalent at the margin. The returns to marginal political efforts of an equal quantitative effect are identical. Alternatively, if the factor demand is elastic, $A < C$, the returns under a price regime are smaller than under quota. Consequently, under a price regime, and with elastic demand, the political struggle will be relatively less intensive, and the equilibrium will be closer to the social optimum. Similarly, for Part (ii): the more elastic the demand function passing through (q_0, t_0) the smaller the area $A + B$, and the less intensive the political struggle. In Figure 12.1, more elastic demand means smaller slopes of the producer's

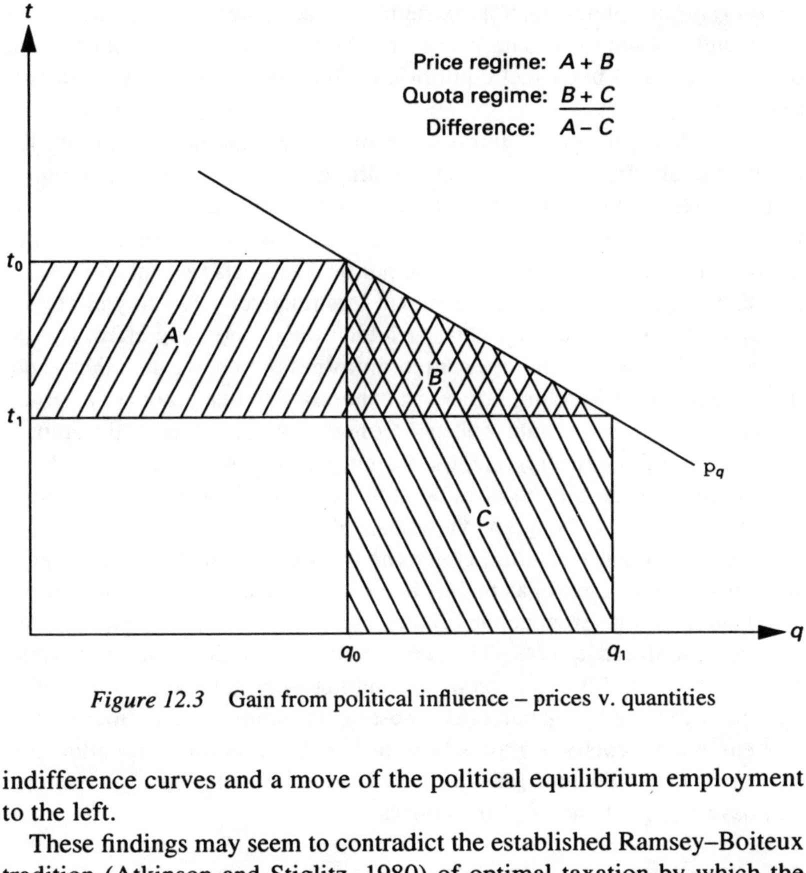

Figure 12.3 Gain from political influence – prices v. quantities

indifference curves and a move of the political equilibrium employment to the left.

These findings may seem to contradict the established Ramsey–Boiteux tradition (Atkinson and Stiglitz, 1980) of optimal taxation by which the more elastic the demand (or supply) the more socially harmful an intervention in prices. The apparent contradiction is resolved by recognizing that when taxes are levied to raise revenue, optimal rates minimize the effect of the tax on resource allocation, while here the sole purpose of taxes is to modify use of resources so as to reduce the harming effects of the negative externalities.

5.3 Organization of Producers

With a single producer, $\sigma = 1$ and the difference between the control regimes is reflected only in the size of the product $s\eta$. It has been explained already that under quota all producers are politically active and the extent of their organization does not enter the analysis of the political equilibrium. Similarly, if in a tax regime all producers are organized in a lobby and operate in unison, $\sigma = 1$ and the number of producers or their organization does not affect equilibrium. But a price regime is conducive to free-riding.

The explanation for the importance of cooperation in determining the political equilibrium of an industry is simple and the situation is familiar to observers of administrative controls. With a quota, every producer is trying to increase his or her utilization of the controlled factor and so does a lobby arguing for its members. The political activists present convincing arguments aplenty. For the government it is relatively easy to yield to the pressure of a particular individual or lobby; the quantitative effect is relatively small. In a price regime with a uniform tax rate, on the other hand, the government is standing firmer – a concession to one producer or group is a concession to the whole industry. Consequently, the greater the amount of free-riding in a price regime, the stronger the comparative social advantage of this control. Similar considerations underlie Rodrik's (1986) analysis of trade regimes, though he views subsidies as firm-specific.

By conventional wisdom, heterogeneity of the production units argues in favour of price control as prices, being uniform, economize on information while, with heterogeneous producers, efficiency calls for unequal, individually-tailored quotas. This argument was qualified by Weitzman (1974), who noted that for iterative planning there is no significant information difference between a price and a quota regime. In a political environment, heterogeneity in production further affects equilibrium allocation as a more heterogeneous industry may tend to be more loosely organized and have a larger number of free-riders.

5.4 A Caveat

The intuitive interpretations, and indeed Proposition 1 and particularly its Part (i), should be accepted with care. The proposition is defined for the conditions of a political equilibrium. The equilibrium ratio s is endogenously determined; the elasticity of the factor demand is also in general an endogenous magnitude. These variables are components of a political equilibrium. The proposition, as indicated, *characterizes* the equilibrium: if in equilibrium for a price regime (with negative externalities) $|\frac{\sigma}{\eta s}| < 1$, price control dominates. It may however happen that even for an elastic demand and a comparatively small lobby, the equilibrium value of s will be so small that $|\frac{\sigma}{\eta s}| > 1$, and then a quota regime will be more efficient. The situation is simpler for an inelastic demand and $\sigma = 1$; it is then assured that $|\frac{1}{\eta s}| > 1$ and a quota control clearly dominates.

6 POLITICAL CONTRIBUTIONS

The derivation of the conditions specifying the allocation parameters – quotas, taxes, or subsidies – was based in the first stage of the calculation of equilibrium solely on the common property of political efficiency. The political contributions, and with them the division of the surplus between the producers and the politicians, depend on the particular characteristics of the political process. We have examined two alternative game formulations: the Harsanyi–Zusman model of cooperative bargaining (Zusman, 1976; Zusman and Amiad, 1977), the equilibrium of which is the Nash (1950) solution to the bargaining game, and Grossman and Helpman's (1994) model which employs the procedure of First Price Menu Auction. As before, the analysis is conducted under the assumption that all producers are members of a single industrial lobby and that in a price regime, some producers may not participate in the political activity. The analysis, for either model, determines the total industrial political contribution; the individual contributions by the producers in the industry are left to the lobby to set.

The two political games differ in the nature of their solution – in the equilibrium level of contributions. By the First Price Menu Auction, with a single lobby, as is the case analyzed here, the industry receives all the political surplus and the politicians are left on their reservation utility. In Figure 12.1, the politicians are given the segment *ab*. A Nash solution divides the surplus and the equilibrium corresponding to that solution will be located on the segment *bc* in Figure 12.1.

As with political allocation, equilibrium political rewards cannot be characterized unambiguously for positive externalities, the conclusions are limited to negative effects. The main findings of the analysis are summarized in Proposition 2 in which the control regimes are compared in terms of *S*-efficiency and a regime is relatively more efficient if it leads to smaller political contributions than the alternative control.

Proposition 2

With negative externalities,

(i) Both for a Nash solution of a cooperative bargaining game and for a First Price Menu Auction: if, in equilibrium under a tax control, $|\frac{\sigma}{\eta s}| < 1$, a quota regime induces a larger political contribution and a price regime is the more efficient control.

(ii) For a Nash solution, if $|\frac{\sigma}{\eta s}| > 1$, and $\sigma < 1$, a quota regime may yield a larger or smaller political contribution. The relative size of the political contribution in a First Price Menu Auction is not affected by the magnitude of α.

The inequality condition in Proposition 2, part (i), is the same condition as for allocative superiority of a price regime in Proposition 1. The explanation being that with comparatively high allocative efficiency, q^p is relatively close to q^w and the compensation needed to keep the politicians on their reservation utility (the segment *ab* in Figure 12.1) is low. Hence the more efficient the allocation in the political equilibrium, the smaller the political contribution if the political process follows the procedure of the First Price Menu Auction. Also, the political surplus to be divided between the politicians and the producers is small when allocative efficiency is high, and so also the absolute contribution to the politicians is relatively small – whatever their share by the Nash solution to the bargaining game.

Part (ii) in Proposition 2 is a consequence of the fact that a small lobby, relative to the size of the industry, will often raise small amounts of political contributions. Hence, even if the sign condition indicates superiority of the quota regime (in terms of *S*-efficiency), it may still happen, in a particular case, that a price regime induces smaller contributions.

7 SUMMARY AND EXTENSIONS

The principal findings of the analysis are:

(a) The comparative advantage of one of the regimes can be characterized only for negative externalities. Then, if $|\frac{\sigma}{\eta s}| < 1$, a price regime induces socially preferred allocation and relatively less intensive rent-seeking efforts.

(b) The political equilibria for negative or positive effects are not symmetric. With negative externalities, the producers struggle to increase quotas under administrative control and they attempt to reduce the tax when regulation relies on prices. The political influence – under both control regimes – results in increased employment of the regulated factor, compared to the social optimum utilization. With positive externalities, on the other hand, depending on the control regime, the producers attempt to reduce quotas or to increase the subsidy. The results are different, higher subsidies increase production.

(c) Consequently, when the effects are positive, subsidization with political influence may reduce welfare compared to a free market no-intervention situation.

(d) Political modification of a uniform price instrument – a tax or a subsidy – is a public good. Therefore, it can be expected that free-riding will erode the political power of the interest group in a price regime.

The conclusions of the analysis are not confined to the simplified framework of the chapter, of external effects associated with the use of a factor of production. They can be extended in several directions. For example, the conclusions apply, with obvious modifications, to external effects caused by a product or a service. Likewise, the analysis is not necessarily limited to externalities, it applies to any case of administrative intervention: of a national government, a municipality, or even the management of a corporation. Political activity is present in any organization in which groups can gather around common interests.

The political rewards are seen here as income transfers from the producers to the politicians. The analysis can be elaborated. Preliminary work we did indicated that the conclusions of the analysis do not change if the formulation of the model covers explicit utilization of real resources in rent seeking. Further, the analysis was made simple by assuming constant costs and effects in the political process. Experiments with increasing costs or decreasing effects yielded similar conclusions. These findings strengthened our confidence in the main lessons of the analysis presented in the chapter.

It is natural to expect political activity to be found only in industries with a specific fixed factor or where entry is limited, as free entry and open access to all factors may erode the achievements of the costly political struggle. We have therefore confined the analysis to an industry with a given number of producers. Still, one sometime observes intense political activity where entry is not successfully limited; several farm industries can be taken as examples. We hope to report in the future on an extension in this direction.

Notes

1. We received useful comments and productive suggestions from Arye Hillman, Yair Mundlak, Martin Paldam, Norbert Wunner and Pinhas Zusman.
2. The rewards, C and c^i, do not appear in the first-order conditions of the Nash solution determining either t or $\mathbf{q}$, while the controls do appear in the equation determining the rewards.
3. The conditions characterizing efficient equilibrium are derived by maximizing W in (4), with respect to the rewards and the controls (either t or $\mathbf{q}$), subject to an arbitrary pre-assigned value of Y, total income in the industry.
4. Remember that $\pi(q^i)$ stands for profits before taxes or subsidies.

References

Atkinson, A. B. and J. E. Stiglitz (1980) *Lectures on Public Economics* (New York: McGraw-Hill).

Coase, R. H. (1960) 'The Problem of Social Cost', *Journal of Law and Economics*, vol. 3, no. 1, pp. 1–44.

Finkelshtain, I. and Y. Kislev (1995) 'Prices vs Quantities: The Political Perspective', *Working Paper*, 9508, The Center for Agricultural Economic Research, Rehovot, Israel.

Grossman, G. M. and E. Helpman (1994) 'Protection for Sale', *American Economic Review*, vol. 84, no. 4, pp. 833–50.

Hillman, A. L. (1989) *The Political Economy of Protection* (Chur: Harwood).

Nash, J., Jr (1950) 'The Bargaining Problem', *Econometrica*, vol. 18, no. 1, pp. 155–62.

Rodrik, D. (1986) 'Tariffs, Subsidies, and Welfare with Endogenous Policy', *Journal of International Economics*, vol. 21, pp. 285–99.

Scarpa, C. (1994) 'Regulation as a Bargaining Process: Negotiation Over Price and Cost Reducing Investments', *Oxford Economic Papers*, vol. 46, no. 3, pp. 357–65.

Weitzman, M. L. (1974) 'Prices vs Quantities', *Review of Economic Studies*, vol. 41, no. 4, pp. 477–91.

Zusman, P. (1976) 'The Incorporation and Measurement of Social Power in Economic Models', *International Economic Review*, vol. 17, no. 2, 447–62.

Zusman, P. and A. Amiad (1977) 'A Quantitative Investigation of a Political Economy – The Israeli Dairy Program', *American Journal of Agricultural Economics*, vol. 59, no. 1, pp. 88–98.